MY WORLD IS AN ISLAND

"*I feel like an elephant carrying teak through the jungle*"

My World Is an Island

BY ELISABETH OGILVIE

Illustrated by Paul Galdone

SECOND EDITION

DOWN EAST BOOKS

Camden, Maine

Cover photograph: Calf Island Meadow, by Morgan Hebard, Jr.

Text copyright © 1950, renewed 1978; 1990 by Elisabeth Ogilvie.
   All rights reserved. Reprinted by arrangement with the author.

Text photos © 1990 by Debby Smith

Front Cover photo © 1990 by Morgan Hebard, Jr.

ISBN 0-89272-288-6
Library of Congress Catalog Card Number: 90-80510

Cover Design by Edith Allard
Printed at McNaughton & Gunn, Saline, Mich.

5   4   3   2

Down East Books
P.O. Box 679
Camden, ME   04843

In memory of Soldi,
who loved to dig clams
and help write books

CONTENTS

PHOTOGRAPHS FOLLOW PAGE 150

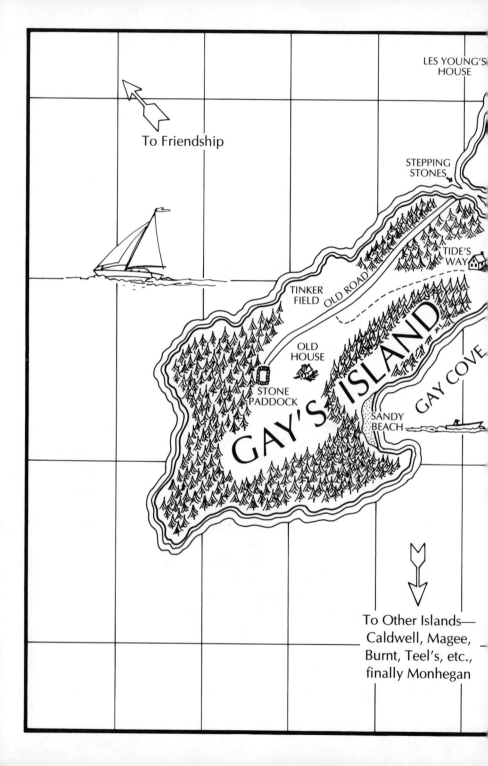

To Friendship

LES YOUNG'S
HOUSE

STEPPING
STONES

TIDE'S
WAY

TINKER
FIELD

OLD ROAD

OLD
HOUSE

GAY'S ISLAND

GAY COVE

STONE
PADDOCK

SANDY
BEACH

To Other Islands—
Caldwell, Magee,
Burnt, Teel's, etc.,
finally Monhegan

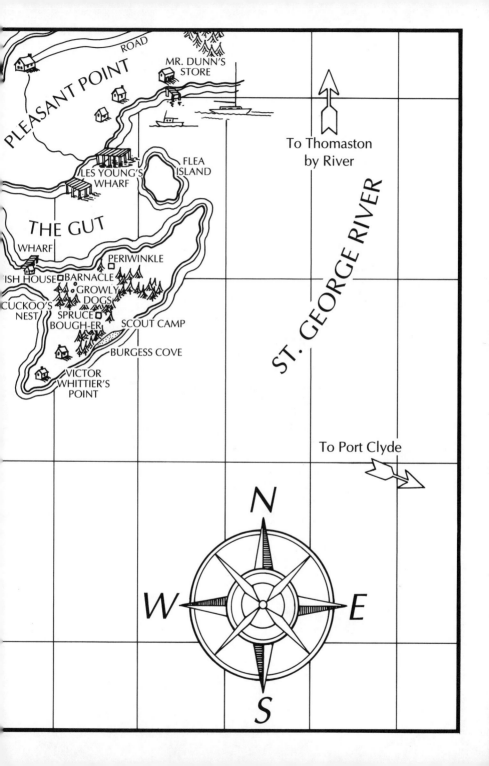

PRELUDE

On a summer day quite a number of years ago a solemn and white-faced little girl of six was lifted from the mailboat to the wharf at Criehaven; and when, on legs staggery from seasickness, she reached the grassy ground, she flung herself down upon it, sobbing, and declaimed passionately, "I wish I hadn't came! I wish I hadn't came!"

That was my mother, on her first introduction to Criehaven. From that time until four years ago she didn't miss very many summers on that faraway island with its red rocks and its constant surf, and, as far as I know, she never again said, "I wish I hadn't came!" Neither did any of her children. Neither did her husband, even though he came from inland farming stock.

When you come to think of it, that was a memorable day for me, even though at six years, quite naturally, little Maude wasn't thinking of little Liz, or of the three boys she would have some day, or of the granddaughters who would collect broken dishes for their playhouses on the shelving, shining rocks beyond Lottie's Cove, with the Atlantic reaching from their feet to Spain.

She was taken there to visit by her grown-up married sister, and from here on the connections grow very involved. . . . Captain Robert Crie, who ruled the island with a kindly but

firm hand, had four sons and a daughter, Charlotte; and Charlotte married Fred Rhodes, from Glen Cove; and Fred Rhodes'
brother, Edgar (who with another brother, Leonard, founded
Rhodes Brothers, Groceries and Provisions, in Boston) married little Maude's grown-up sister May. And so they took
Maude at the age of six, demure in bonnet and bangs, to Criehaven.

There was a time when I was a youngster when we didn't
go to Maine, but I had memories of my summers there from
babyhood until the age of four. Some of them were so vague
as to be nothing at all but a smell, a sound, a sensation, a voice;
but at the same time they were as vivid as the things which I
could reach out and touch—my desk at school, my dog Jock,
my dolls, my roller skates, and the scent of rain falling on a
warm concrete sidewalk. If I had never gone back to Criehaven
I think those fragments of recollections would have stayed with
me always, coming to haunt me at odd unprotected moments.

I would remember spongy black earth under my bare toes
in a marsh, and the clean pale sunshine all around me, scented
with the wild salt smell of ocean; and the world filled with
luminous light so that the horizon glowed; the smell of a long,
dark, covered shed lined with hogsheads, fishy and pungent;
and a red apple given to me by—well, I remember the hand,
and the red apple, but it is only a little picture suspended sharply
and brilliantly in foggy space. In the picture I am sitting by a
gatepost made of pale, rounded field stones embedded in
cement, and I am with a little boy. And someone has given us
apples. The flesh of the apples is very white, with fine red
streaks running through. All my life I have searched for apples
that looked and tasted the same as those.

Until I was fifteen I did not know who that little boy was,
but—possibly because I was Indian-dark—I remembered his
fair hair falling in bangs across his forehead. He came often into
those fragments. He was with me when someone tall put us into

a boat and told us to sit still, and we did, while the boat moved across the water and the vibrations of the engine hummed through our gripping hands.

And there was another boat, that seemed to rush headlong, to fly on curling white wings through the water, while the island looked strange and foreign lying upon the sea. Someone said, "See, there's our house!" And I tried to make it our house, where I went to sleep every night conscious of the dark, ineffable mystery of the big trees on the hill behind us; where the sheep wandered through the wells of shadow, rounded white creatures glimmering through the cold gloom.

But while I was trying to make it seem familiar, spray dashed into my face, icy and salt against my lips, and whenever I remember that, I can hear my piping voice as if it belonged to another child, screaming in something like exultation, "Do it again, Guy! Do it again!"

I remember being lost, and the whole world becoming woods under a sodden dark sky, and a collie shrieking at me from behind windows; I remember standing there in my bare feet, crying helplessly, and then someone found me, a man with a thick dark beard, who carried me home, and I wasn't very far from home after all. It was just across the field.

The man with the beard was Andrew Anderson, Dot's grandfather. The little boy with the bang was Russell, her brother. At that time Guy wasn't her husband, but a few years later he would be.

There was one other thing, vivid and lovely: flowers, brilliant, nodding, sharply fragrant, blooming by a sea wall, and the sea itself beyond. I never forgot the mingled scents of those flowers and the acrid cool breath of the sea.

But I had so little to go on in my own experience, to feed me during those years when we didn't go back. My mother had a great deal to go on, and my brothers had much more to remember than I did. So, in listening to her, I learned about the Criehaven she had known as a child. I knew the names of her friends there, her "gang"—knew them so well that when I met them, and they were grown-up like my mother and had sons and daughters my age and older, I was conscious of keen surprise, almost disappointment, because I had expected John and Agnes and Barney and the rest to be somehow forever seventeen.

Then, because I was back by some miracle in the mystic world of the marsh, the stone gateposts, the spray, the woods, and had found by a second miracle that they were as I had remembered them, I was able to step away from my reticence and become friends with the children of my mother's friends. It seemed meant to be. Events were coming full circle. At last I had my "gang."

Those earliest memories are as much a part of me as the color of my eyes, my white lock that appeared when I was ten, the shape of my fingers, the sound of my voice. They have played almost as big a part in making me the person I am—Myself. It is the same with the later memories. It is a major event for a shy, impressionable, imaginative fifteen-year-old to come to a place which hitherto she has tenanted only in wisps of memories and the stories of another. It is even more of a tremendous thing for her to find that the smells are the same, and the boy with the yellow bang is still there, only older, and most of the names that have grown magic with the years and the stories are still there too; and besides that, the island is full of things which she *hasn't* remembered, which are there for her to discover all over again.

Such a happening in a young life can be in the nature of an upheaval, an explosion. It was for me. I knew, all at once, what was going to become of me. Conveniently, I had two choices; I would either write about the island, or marry a lobster fisherman.

I haven't married a lobster fisherman. I have spent too much time instead trying to get down some small part of the essence of Criehaven. Someone has said that Maine is a state of mind; for me, Criehaven is an island not so much in a geographical sense but in a spiritual sense, for I can carry it with me wherever I go. The Criehaven that became Bennett's Island on paper, and which became when I was two years old an integral part of my existence, will never go away from me.

Little by little the names are changing. Little by little the habits have changed, the customs, the very spirit. But some things are eternal: the damp glistening beach and the skiffs sliding down early in the morning; the rote of the sea, as close and constant as one's own breathing, to put one to sleep; the field between Hillside and the schoolhouse when it was a sparkling, rippling tapestry of red clover, daisies, and buttercups; the sea pigeons around Ten Pound and the black ram watching from the high cliff above the boat; and the heavenly sweetness of wild strawberries ripened in fog and sunshine on treeless slopes above the sea.

Coming back from Matinicus, under the stars, with the wake burning pale green fire behind, the damp, exciting fragrance in the lane leading up to the clubhouse, on dance nights; the sound of the fiddle leaping out to meet you; a lamplit room where you are surrounded by your friends and you ache at the shortness of the summer and the barrenness of the winter away from them.

You all grow up, some miserably, some happily. You meet on the street in Rockland and catch up on the news, and you are older, and so are they, and you're all scattered far and wide, each of you the hub of a whole new universe in which the others have no part. But at the same time, in some secret place, you're all dancing together in the clubhouse, you're romping through the square dances, you're pairing off to walk soulfully home across the marsh in the moonlight, and you're all so blessedly, eternally *young*.

And you're all on Criehaven, which geographically lies twenty miles east of here, and paradoxically doesn't exist. What does exist, what is real, is the Criehaven that was yours in the far-off years and will be yours forever.

I have stopped looking for those very special apples, because I know that the apple in the hand of the four-year-old girl with the gypsy tan and the wriggling bare toes is the best apple of all, and I don't need to look for one if I already possess it. The little boy with the bang is married, but somewhere in Time he plays with the girl beside a tidewater pool and they gather periwinkles, very solemnly, like jewelers matching pearls.

If I should go out to the *geographical* island tomorrow, I should meet a few people I have always known and more people whom I don't know, and there would be some buildings absolutely unfamiliar; but any time I choose I can go back to the *real* island, passing the spot where the other little girl beat the ground with her fists and lamented, unconscious of the new era beginning for her and the effect of that era upon her children. I can go back and sit on the stile by the cemetery, and watch the cuckoos glide between the apple trees; and I can see the Crie house high and secure against the sky, unchanged; I can swing in the hammock at Honeysuckle Cottage and wait for my friends to come up the road. I can do everything I've ever done and loved, and nothing will be changed.

I have not deserted Criehaven. Not my Criehaven. Neither has my mother. Neither has Dot, who in blood and bone is the island's true child. Each of us has taken it with her, and it will be with us for the rest of our lives. No one, or nothing, can take it from us, ever.

But we have found that there is room in our hearts for another island: Gay's Island, in the mouth of the St. George River, where someone long ago built the house we now call "Tide's Way."

CHAPTER ONE

THOUGH THIS BE MADNESS

I am sitting on a flat rock in front of the fishhouse. The tide is going out, rapidly; the tide rushes in and out of Pleasant Point Gut at an astonishing rate, and I'm convinced that the tides here are entirely separate from those of the rest of the coast, operating under their own system. Sometimes they come in an hour ahead of time, and then retreat completely from the mud flats in something under half the required time and stay out all day. At least, that's how it appears to me, when after four years of Gay's Island the tides and I still can't get together, and the accredited tide tables mean very little to me and even less to Pleasant Point Gut.

But on this spring afternoon, since I am not going anywhere, I can enjoy the departure of the water. A narrowing stream the color of delphiniums flows by the wharf and ebbs away from the steep rocky face of the landing. In some places the water is translucently calm and limpid, dimpled only by the mysterious eddies of the current. In other spots it is riffled to the dark, dull beauty of watered satin, like the hair ribbons I used to wear when I was small. And over the mud flats, in the tiny cove just to the left of the wharf, the sun strikes downward through liquid emerald. Where the mussel beds have emerged, glistening purple, the gulls walk and eat and make their scores of sounds, ranging from a simple interrogative "Qwawk?" to a hoarsely ribald type of profanity.

Spring on Gay's Island. . . . Four years ago this spring I had never heard of Gay's Island, or of Pleasant Point. There was only one island in the world for me; it's called "Bennett's Island" in some books I wrote about it. On the charts it is Crie-haven, or Ragged Island. Its rocks are big, bold, and red, and the mainland is twenty-five miles away. Sometimes you can't get off for days at a time, and every resident of the place has his own lurid—and true—yarns of departures and arrivals under the most harrowing conditions. I have a few such stories myself; I've known what is to be terrified to the point of nausea, and yet there is a pride to these things, when you tell them after-ward.

There is always a heavy sea running outside Criehaven, al-ways the vibration and boom of surf in the air and in the ground under your feet, and the island itself has a wild, astounding beauty that can't be equaled. It is hardly the sort of place for training one to appreciate the beauty of water running out over the clam flats.

It was the island of my dreams. For years I had felt my real life was there, even while my family and I lived in Massa-chusetts. I lived in a more or less somnambulistic state through the school year and spent the summers at Criehaven. One day I began to write a book about it because I had to get it down on paper and out of my system, the helpless ache that was the out-break of the island virus in me. No one was more amazed than I was when the book sold. And now, I thought, I can buy a place of my own on Criehaven, own a little stretch of spruce woods, a scrap of meadow, a bit of cove.

I couldn't. There were places going, places I'd always known, but the price wasn't for me, with my one little book. I considered Matinicus, even though this seemed apostasy.

They had rocks and things over at Matinicus, didn't they, just a mile away from Criehaven? There were negotiations begun for a house located on a spectacular place on Harbor Point, with breaking waves dashing fore and aft, and I carried the cash around in my pocket for two weeks, my nerves wracked by an indecision which was nothing to the indecision of the lady who owned the house. She finally decided against it.

In a reckless moment I mentioned islands to Freeman Young, a Young from Matinicus who'd gone to live on the mainland and become a successful real-estate man. Came the day when he met us in Rockland and took us to see Gay's Island. "Us" consisted of myself and Dorothy Simpson. I had known her and her husband Guy all my life; I had lived with them to learn about a lobsterman's life and the island in winter. Dorothy, who has an equally light hand with a guitar, a boat, and an apple pie, passed on to me the history of Criehaven from its earliest days of settlement, as told to her by her Yankee stepfather and Norwegian grandfather; she typed manuscript for me, and listened to my endless laments about my inadequacies as a novelist, and discussed situations that could or could not happen on an island like Criehaven. Guy's father too had been an early settler and Guy also had a good crop of stories. He had been lobstering since he was thirteen or so, knew the treacherous grounds about Criehaven like a gull, and understood engines the way some men understand horses. Loved them that way too. Guy supplied the details about long and short warps, told me how many traps a thirty-foot boat could carry, and saved me from making many a technical blunder when I wrote about the hard side of lobstering. And he knew all the hair-raising things that had happened to lobstermen since before he was born.

Leaving my mother—who had been summering at Criehaven since the age of six—and Guy to keep house out on the island, Dorothy and I had come to Rockland on errands. One saved up

quite a few errands to do at once; twenty-five miles of Penobscot Bay on the *Mary A.* were not to be undertaken lightly,
even in summer. But we had not expected to do such a portentous bit of business, any more than we'd expected Free Young
to meet us on the street and whisk us away from Rockland.
Seventeen miles away, in fact, down narrow spruce-bordered
roads to Pleasant Point, in the town of Cushing.

Decanting us at a small wharf rising from a spectacular sea
of mud flats, he waved his hand across a narrow channel and
said, "There's an island for you!"

We were unimpressed. We had never heard of the place, and
we had the true insular point of view, like the man who kept
talking about "the island, the island," until an irritated listener
said, "For heaven's sake, *what* island?"

The man recoiled in simple amazement and said, "Prince
Edward Island. What other island be they?"

Well, what other island was there—figuratively—besides
Criehaven, Dorothy's by birth, mine and my mother's by adop-
tion? Besides, Gay's was tied to the mainland by mud flats;
worse, at the far end you could *walk* across when the tide was
down. It took two hours and more to get to Criehaven, it was
real pioneer stuff. And there were no mud flats at Criehaven,
where the tide went out cleanly, leaving massive ledges shaggy
with wet rockweed.

But Freeman Young, the David Harum of the real-estate
men, ignored our polite lack of enthusiasm. He is one of the
tall Matinicus Youngs, but where the leisurely island pace has
kept the others from ever hurrying, Free is a sort of dapper
dynamo. His wife is more excited by life than anyone else I
know. Between them, we were swept along on the tide of their
fervor.

"You can trust me," Free told us in his fast, cheerful voice.
"I want to get you something really good. You interested in
this place too?" he asked Dot bluntly. She allowed, faintly,

that she and Guy were interested in making a change . . . if the right thing came along.

"I know Guy," said Free. "This would be a good place for a fisherman. . . . Need a boat, don't we?" He went off, leaving us to contemplate the mud flats, the spruce woods on the opposite shore, and a desolate-appearing yellow house rearing up on a hillside. He came back with a boy and a boat and handed us into it.

Freeman, Jessie, and the boy, whose name was Roland, appeared to be in good spirits. Dot and I had little to say. The sun was very hot and the mud flats had an unattractive odor. When we landed on the other side, we had to climb up over a steep, inhospitable slant of rock. At Criehaven there were clean pebbly beaches.

The stone wharf was unplanked, the fishhouse was a shack; we fought our way through alders and knee-high grass, passed a barn which was a mere shell, and arrived at the desolate house which looked as if seven various civilizations had passed through it and each had merely planted its household furnishings atop the relics of the last, like the seven cities under Troy.

More specifically, the yellow house on the knoll was the classic farmhouse of Maine, with an ell kitchen, an unfinished open chamber over it, and deeply slanting ceilings in the bedrooms. One entered both front and kitchen doors by stepping first on a huge, rough-hewn granite doorstep. Inside, if one could transcend the rubble of the former civilizations, there was a surprising quantity of light and sunshine, there were the corner posts that mark a really old house, and incredibly wide planks in the floors. There was also solid construction, along with a number of fine details in the woodwork and paneling. The old black sink in the pantry was rusty, but there was a big window through which we could watch the birds and the clouds over the mainland while we washed dishes. There was plenty of cupboard space and a long wide dresser.

In the main house, apart from the ell, there were the two big rooms flanking the center hall; one was the front parlor, used now as a catch-all, though we hope to turn it into a charming room this summer. Its two large front windows framed magnificent views of Caldwell and the other islands that went like steppingstones across the sea to Monhegan Island. The opposite room, which we now use as a sitting room, also had its wonderful views, while its side window looked eastward toward the Neck and the woods beyond. Behind both big rooms there were two smaller rooms, suitable for bedrooms.

From the hall, lighted by the strips of small panes on either side of the wide front door, the steep stairs took us up to the other rooms. We were delighted with the one that ran from back to front of the house, with two windows looking westward over the hillside. The other, smaller room had a window that reached almost to the floor and gave a lovely view of the beaches on both sides of the Neck, and of the big cove.

A little windowless room led into the open chamber in the ell.

After a quick look at the house, we went up over the hill. And all the while, back on Criehaven, Guy was tending his traps and my mother was calmly painting pictures, placidly unaware that we were tramping around in the hot July sun on an island in the mouth of the St. George River, deciding their fate for them. And we *did* tramp! Freeman, whose sixty years or so rode very lightly on him, marched us indefatigably through the yellow house and out again, up over the hill and around stone walls until we reached the old Gay house. He must have known how it would affect us, the sight of the old house with its tremendous central chimney, its birch-bark sheathing and wooden pegs and its inescapable sense of history; or perhaps what really finished us was the stone wall, hundreds of years old, upon which he laid his hand and said, "An honest man built this." Or perhaps it was the view across the shining water to Friendship, a white town dreaming among its trees.

Dot maintains that she looked the yellow house over very thoroughly when she was in it, and that she saw possibilities in the land and in the prosperous appearance of the harbor; she was not swayed, she said, by any such impractical ideas as the ghosts of old settlers. Anyway, we weren't going to own the part with the Gay house and the Friendship view. She swears that she was looking for bedbugs while I mooned out of dirty windows.

Be that as it may, we were thinking deeply as we rode back to town; and that night we signed the papers that committed us for better or for worse. We went back to Criehaven with a lightheaded certainty that the *Mary A.* had really made a historic trip this time.

My mother was startled but game. Guy was skeptical. He took a trip to Pleasant Point by himself to talk to the fishermen there and to find out if a new fisherman would be welcome. He came back in love with Gay's—he saw it at high tide for the first time—and warmed by the friendly reception he had received. Guy himself was partly responsible for this greeting; I have yet to meet the person, man, woman, or child, who didn't like Guy at once. . . . We New Englanders are often accused of unfriendliness, but we understand each other's reserve. To move from one place along the coast to another is sometimes a delicate procedure, requiring diplomacy. So we come quietly, without side and minding our manners, and for the most part this is how we are received. But we must continue to mind our manners after we're established; there's always someone to cut us down to size if we get too big for our britches.

And so, we moved. . . . But loving Criehaven is sometimes a little hard on you. It takes hold of you like a boisterous comber, tosses you around and bruises you, but it still won't let you go. It didn't let us go for quite a while, until we'd got more or less used to the mud flats, and had hacked down some alders, and had seen autumn come to Gay's Island and the Point in a pageantry unknown at Criehaven. Not that we regretted the move; we simply had our times of feeling uprooted.

"You'll never be able to stand it!" we were warned. "I know that place, I lived near it once. . . . Mainland!" It was hurled at us with contempt. But if we felt a slight shame at becoming Mainlanders after bragging about the rugged Criehaven life, we didn't show it, but smiled enigmatically.

We broke the news to the boys overseas—one of my brothers and two of Dot's—and they were appalled by our desertion. But we smiled, confidently, as if we hadn't already discovered what sort of job we'd cut out for ourselves before we could begin to enjoy our meadows, our woodlands, our coves, our irrepressible alders, and our rocks. Oh, what an inferiority complex those rocks gave us at first, so gray and undistinguished after the handsome jutting red ones at Criehaven! If we could, we would have covered them when anyone came to call.

That was four years ago, going on five. The house where the migrant tribes had pitched their figurative tents has had many names since then. We called it "Wit's End," feeling that we spoke the truth; we called it "Sixes and Sevens," because that's what we were always at. Others called it, uncharitably, "the Booby Hatch." But after a long period of trying to adjust our comings and goings to those of the erratic Pleasant Point tides, we arrived at a name that stuck. The Gut between us and the mainland flows *behind* the house, the sea reaches in past the islands of Caldwell, Seavey, Teel, and Magee, to wash against the foot of the field *before* the house. So we call the house "Tide's Way." The *Tide* books helped to buy it.

And now, on a spring afternoon, I sit on the warm gray ledge in front of the fishhouse and look around me. To the north and northeast and east, I see the mainland, with the nine houses of Pleasant Point and the harbor with tiny Flea Island in the middle of it; I know who owns each boat now, and each wharf reaching out from the shore, and the Friendship sloops, waiting here for their owners to come and begin a summer's cruising, have the added luster of familiarity. The hill behind Mr. Dunn's house, at the far end of the harbor, is a tapestry of greens, ranging from the dark of the spruces to the tender golden-green of the birches, with here and there the rosy spray of a maple. There's a silvery poplar by the Davis fishhouse, gleaming and twinkling with every breath of wind. The just-painted mast and boom—bright orange—on Harlan Davis's new wharf stands out brilliantly. The biggest wild pear tree I've ever seen is an immense bouquet of white bloom by Leslie Young's wharf, where Freeman took us to see Gay's Island for the first time.

We know all the trees, you see; we know all the boats, and we know all the dogs. And of course, the people. We take a candid pride in Harlan's new wharf, in the improvements Dana Herrick has made on Flea Island, in Jim Seavey's seventieth birthday, in Roland's graduation from Lee Academy. We get a solid satisfaction out of belonging to Pleasant Point and being one of the neighbors. We are affronted when some ignorant soul says (as we did at first), "Never heard of the place!"

To the west, the Gut between us and the Point winds along in a pleasant stream. We've seen it feather-white in a sixty-mile-an-hour westerly, but at the moment it meanders among the mussel beds with the gulls wading around in the shallows as if it were never high, never poured through daily in a broad and lovely current. On either side, the banks are green with spring. We don't miss the big ledges and the surf so much when wild pear and cherry trees foam with blossoms above the rocks whose warm grays and beiges are now ineffably charming to our eyes. On Gay's Island the woods are thick, beginning with yellow-tasseled alders at the bank (try to pick out the yellow warblers among them!), the young rowan trees in their rich

feathery green, the cloudy gilt-green of birches with the sun
shining through, the red maples and tawny oaks, and then the
great spar spruces climbing the slopes to pierce the sky.

We know every nook and cranny along the Gut, having
poked a skiff into them all. We know the best place for
flounders, the best flats for clams. On the seaward side, we have
rowed down to the wide white beach of the cove which Ben
Ames Williams described in the first part of *Come Spring*. We
have rowed beyond, out where you can feel the lift and surge
of the ocean and hear the deep-sea rote.

Once on a shimmering day in October we rowed all around
the island in a nine-foot skiff, and landed on all the little islets,
and picked up driftwood in almost every cove. We know them
all now. We have at last come to accept our acres of woods
as our own, have wandered awe-stricken through long corridors of big spruces we didn't know we owned; we have
named coves and visited them regularly for what the sea has
cast up. We know where to find cranberries in October and
warblers in May.

I have become so attached to the other islands in the Georges
group, lying like steppingstones all the way out to the high
blue bluff of Monhegan, that I can sit absolutely still in contemplation of them; and for me to sit absolutely still is an
achievement. As for the house, it now looks as if only one tribe
had ever dwelt there, erratic as that tribe might be: ourselves.
We have a lawn, where the tall grass and the tin cans used to
be. We have four fruit trees, a birthday gift from my mother;
they aren't much to look at right now, but we have hopes. We
have shrubs and perennials and fences around everything to
keep Blackie the sheep from gnawing them into frayed stubs.

Blackie and the dog, Smokey, came from Criehaven with
us. Tristan, the big yellow cat with the plumy tail, was born
on Pleasant Point the day we moved to Gay's Island.

We have a skiff on each side of the island, and a third one

soaking out at the end of the wharf, and a little dory hauled up on the rocks near me. We are proud of our ability, Dot and I, to get boats and groceries and luggage up over that unfriendly rocky slope. We have four lobster traps—small size—set out by the weir on the seaward side of the island. Dot is building another at the moment. She says that now she is doing things she has wanted to do all her life. A long time ago she promised herself that when her "family" was all grown up she would do the things a person doesn't have time for when she's scrubbing overalls, cooking in large quantities, and trying to help youngsters through the painful processes of growing up.

She has four brothers and four sisters, all younger than herself, and has helped to rear most of them; there has been a younger brother or sister in her house, sometimes three or four at a time, for almost all of her married life. Now they are all settled nicely into their own pattern of existence.

She said a moment ago, "I never had such a wonderful chance to play."

Well, that's what the four years have done to us. We're getting around to doing the things we talked about doing. But, looking back, it seems to me that most of those four years are worth talking about too. Anyway, I know that Gay's Island has possessed us at last, beyond the shadow of a doubt. How do I know it? Because we think the mud flats are beautiful!

CHAPTER TWO

OUR COURSE IS CHOSEN

After the papers had been signed for the property on Gay's Island, and the other mundane details had been arranged, we all sat down to plan the way we would move our things across the twenty-mile stretch of water between Criehaven and Gay's Island.

The most sensible plan, we agreed, would be to clean the house thoroughly before we thought of moving into it. It was inch-deep in dust, hung magnificently with cobwebs, and tinted everywhere a lovely, furry, Oxford-gray tone with soot. The furnishings—kind word for them—left behind by earlier tenants would have to be thrown out before we could put anything in. I had vague and distasteful memories of what I'd seen: mattresses in almost every room, losing their entrails in a disgusting fashion; piles of papers and old clothes one was loath to disturb for what they might conceal; dirty dishes in the sink and on the dresser. . . . And yet there was something else about the house which we remembered, from the one short glimpse of it, with fondness, even with respect. The sturdy self-sufficiency of it, the proportions of ell and house, the plain grace of the front door, the big granite doorsteps. The knowledge that it had been built on the very spot its owner chose, and that the front windows would be filled all day long with

Gay's Island had possessed us at last

a view of the weir, the islands, and, on days when the land loomed, the open sea beyond Monhegan.

Considering all this, and ignoring the Greek chorus of lamentations that arose all around us, we planned to have Guy take us over in his boat and leave us for a week end, armed with brooms, mops, soap powder, and so on. Then the furniture could be moved with tranquillity and dispatch into a sparkling clean house. My mother was going to Nova Scotia with my father, and on their return they would go directly to Gay's Island. We would be there ready to meet them, with callouses from hard work, and the house immaculate.

But life has a way of being as trite as—well, as the saying about the best laid plans of mice and men. No sooner had my father and mother reached Elderbank, Nova Scotia, than two-thirds of the islanders came down with a disorder known variously as distemper, summer complaint, summer grippe, and the epizootic. Of course, the crew who were about to set out for new territory were among the fallen. We were laid low simultaneously on the very morning we'd picked to depart with our pails and soap and mops.

So we lay in our beds all through the lovely summer day, watching the gulls with unhappy envy, and thought of what we could be doing: chasing big fat spiders out of corners, tossing out old beds and dingy bedclothes. But all we could do about it was *think*, while one kind elderly neighbor called to cheer us up.

"You'd better give it up," she advised in a briskly ghoulish voice. "This is the way it's going to be. This means you aren't meant to leave here. Worse things will happen to you over there." She said *there* as if she really meant Gehenna. It was no use to point out that the rest of the island had summer complaint too—even the ones who thought the worst of our going.

Having brightened the day for us considerably, she went away, no doubt mounting her broomstick out by the back door.

"You won't stay," she called cheerfully. "Nobody stays. They always come back." It sounded as if they all came back in their coffins, and I wondered just what she thought awaited us over in the Never-never-land of Gay's Island.

Then, when we were well enough to pack, the weather went bad. Fog and rain, and the sea a vast, heaving plain of uneasy water. But we went on packing up for our week end of house cleaning, and we went on listening to the assorted voices of foreboding, which gathered more eloquence as time went by.

So we were relieved for more reasons than one when Guy came home with the news that Rex Anderson was going to Loud's Island—or more properly, Muscongus Island—next Saturday and would take a load of furniture along and leave it at Gay's Island for us. Of course, this precluded any Utopian idea of moving into a spotless house and getting all settled in a day or two, but we knew the only sensible thing was to accept Rex's offer.

We prayed that the weather would be fine, and for the rest of the week we packed in a frenzy and wheeled and carried things to the wharf where Rex would come in and load. It was a narrow rocky path, twisting downhill from Guy's back door, coming out by the store, and I think we must have worn it deeper in that week than it had been worn in the last twenty years. One of Dot's younger sisters and the youngest brother helped out, but in spite of their assistance the amount of dunnage seemed to have reached stupendous heights. We went to bed at night very cross and frustrated, secretly sure that the ominous neighbors and relatives were telling the truth.

"Goin' to come off and blow by the end of the week," they said happily. "What you want to go off in that gunkhole for?" they asked Guy. "Never anybody made no money over there."

"They looked pretty prosperous to me," Guy said stubbornly. Already his horizons had widened. As proof of his new heresy he added, "This isn't the only place where there's lobsters, you know. Nobody's exactly starving on the rest of the coast."

Operation Frantic went on. The effects of the epizootic (I love that word, it's such a jaunty sound to describe a horrid condition) had left us all weak and inclined to be snappish. Now that the hour for leave-taking had finally come, we were anxious to get it over with; we wanted to put the beloved—Criehaven—behind us as soon as possible. It was like the parting of a man from a mistress whom he loves dearly, but with whom he can have no constructive future.

None of us slept at all the night before. I think the stupendous relief of seeing a lovely pastel dawn break through the silvery fog hit us the final blow, and by the time we had the last box and chair loaded aboard the *Racketash*, we were collapsed and ready to do absolutely nothing for a week. High tide came at noon that day, and we planned to be at Gay's Island by then. The stuff could be easily unloaded, and at least we could get it to the house at our leisure.

Guy had his boat loaded with his trap stuff—bundles of laths and coils of potwarp, and buoys—and fuel oil; Rex's brother Nick went along with him for company. The *Racketash*, thirty-six feet, looked like a giant liner in comparison with Guy's twenty-eight footer, and she was loaded with household gear and with people. She carried everything with ease; she was a gallant sort of boat, built on Criehaven by Leslie Wilson and Peter Mitchell, and since she was wrecked beyond repair in a storm last year all of us who knew her have felt a sense of personal loss.

On that morning, Rex's wife Lois and their little girl Sally were in the cockpit; Nick's wife Hattie and their small son Kenny were there; and sitting in one of our rocking chairs, holding her baby boy Brad in her lap, was Dot's sister, Madelyn Young. Everyone looked very gay—everyone aboard the boats, that is. The handful of folks gathered on the wharf seemed more pitying than cheerful.

But we pretended not to notice that and waved at them with great cheer and a semblance of excitement, even though Dot and I were trembly with exhaustion. Guy's boat left first, and soon the *Racketash* was passing by the familiar gray granite blocks of the breakwater, heading into the west where the far-away mainland was hidden by the silvery mist that lay over the pale blue water. Guy's little boat dipped and rose with the swells, and the *Racketash* took them more sedately.

Dot and I sat up on the bow with her frowsty little black dog, Smokey, and looked back at Criehaven, with its high wooded slopes, its rocky shores, the small harbor that had always been so dear to us; home for Dot, a spiritual home for me. And then, with the tumult and excitement of leaving quieted for a little while, I felt for the first time the strangeness of this action. Criehaven, the island which I had so loved that I had to write about it to keep its beauty from aching in me, was fading slowly astern, the low-hanging mists creeping across the fields and spruces like a veil being drawn across the past. *My* past.

I didn't want to think I had forsaken it, and I told myself then that the departure of the body didn't necessarily mean the departure of the soul. But there was not the smallest part of Criehaven that I could have for my own. People had come— strangers not only to the island but to Maine itself—and had been allowed to buy. But I didn't have the price. Neither did Dot and Guy, and their tiny property, without even a shore privilege, woefully hampered them. They felt continually restricted, tightly bound, in a spot that should have given them a sense of boundless freedom. So in this moment I tried to think that Gay's Island had been lying there in the mouth of the St. George River waiting for three people who needed it almost as much as they needed life itself; and those three people had found it. They didn't have to stop loving Criehaven.

But I could not help the deep loneliness I felt. Dot, too, looked remote and thoughtful. I know she was glad when she couldn't see the roof of Guy's house or glimpse her grandfather's house behind its windbreak of spruces. Guy's father had built his house; Dot's grandfather had built his and made his garden-land out of a swamp. I think that ghosts came down the wooded slopes and stood on the red-brown rocks to watch us sail away.

The *Racketash* surged swiftly on, cutting her way through the long oily waves; and at last Criehaven had disappeared, and there was nothing else for us to see but Guy's boat bobbing easily abreast of us on the gently rolling sea.

CHAPTER THREE

THE ODYSSEY BEGINS

Another brother of Rex's, Harold, had come along on the *Racketash,* and he came up to sit with Dot and me on the bow. After an hour or so he pointed out the foam-washed shores of Green Island, becoming discernible in the fog. He said we were due to pick up the Northern Triangles before long. The name was romantic, but I knew from what I'd heard about them that the Triangles were danger spots on the chart, so I watched for them intently, straining my eyes in the diffused sun-glare and amusing myself with unpleasant little reveries in which the *Racketash* had her bow stove in and sank with all our furniture aboard, not to mention us. I have a fascinating but far from cheering habit of seeing these disasters in the form of headlines, and I always wonder if *this* is the time when we're going to provide something really spectacular for the Rockland *Courier-Gazette*—something that will outdo the murder in the Foss House and the big fire in the Bog.

Guy and Nick had had a narrow escape on the Triangles once, and Harold and Dot refreshed their memories in gruesome detail, while I nursed the conviction that I was the only person aboard who was looking for the shoal. Considering that the Anderson brothers had been making this trip in all sorts of weather for years—their parents lived at Port Clyde—I was taking quite a bit on myself, but this is nothing strange when you consider that at the age of three I could not go to sleep at night without warning the family repeatedly to be sure all the doors were locked. I have always carried the world's burdens conscientiously—and vociferously—on my shoulders.

Harold saw the shoal first, anyway—I was looking in the wrong direction. It is a deceptive shoal; the ocean looked smooth and unperturbed for long moments, and then, far ahead, a little to the starboard hand, a giant wave appeared to rise from nowhere. It rolled up, curled over, and broke in a smother of foam, gleaming strangely against the blue water.

The fog faded out enough to reveal Metinic, a long wooded island inhabited by several fishermen and a flock of sheep. We could see the sheep grazing on the cleared fields, and see the men at work in their boats along the shore of their anchorage, an open rocky beach on the northeast point of the island. Here there was an excellent chance for worry again, but I was cheated out of that, since I didn't know until afterward that Wheeler's Ledge lay off the cove, inviting boats to run ashore on its long submerged ridge. Guy went through the channel first, and we followed close in his wake.

Then Harold told us to watch for the Mosquito Island bell buoy. The fog was lifting all the time, the ocean swells were smooth and glassy, each surge of water reflecting a glaring white sun, and the air from the mainland seemed to sweep out over the sea from an open furnace.

Harold entertained us with stories of his experiences on a freighter that was sunk by a German submarine; he gave us graphic details on how it felt to lie in a lifeboat for days, his flesh torn with shrapnel and machine-gun bullets. We listened with deep but rather queasy interest. On Criehaven we'd often felt the vibrations from depth charges and joked in a macabre vein about spies coming ashore in a rubber boat. It hadn't been a joke, really, and we knew it. But we talked of how it would be if the island should be taken over by a U-boat crew. The Captain of the *Mary A.*, who has never been known to look surprised or dismayed, would go back to Rockland after his regular trip and say in a tone of mild interest, "Store must've changed hands again down at Criehaven. German feller came out on the wharf and got the mail."

But at the moment the war was too close for a joke, and now that I had gotten us past the Triangles and Wheeler's Ledge, I imagined our dramatic consternation should we see a periscope above the shining swells.

When we passed the bell at Mosquito Island, just outside Port Clyde harbor, and could see the Marshall's Point lighthouse, the fog had lifted entirely, and we could see long stretches of wooded mainland on our right. On our left and dead ahead were many islands, some small and treeless, others large and well covered with spruce. Entering Port Clyde harbor we stared at everything as if we were coming into a foreign country; boats hauling traps, other boats at anchor; runabouts with varnished decks and leather seats for the summer people to play in; outboard skip jacks buzzing like insects over the smooth water. A crowd of people were waiting on Fores Hupper's wharf to board the Monhegan boat. The town itself looked cool and snug and busy under its elms. We wondered what everyone thought of this two-boat caravan of gypsies and had no illusions whatever.

We stopped at Mr. Hupper's wharf to let Nick and his wife and little boy go ashore. Harold left the boat, too. Madelyn and I went up to the store to get some food. We were groggy from two hours on the water and from the long week before. Without any great perspicacity we bought a few potatoes, a loaf of bread, some very tough steak, and ice cream cones, which we hurried back to the boat. We forgot canned milk and coffee. A truly tragic mistake.

Soon we were under way again, Guy in the lead. We knew that one of the islands ahead was Gay's Island, but which one? Everything looked alike to us at this point, our muscles ached, our eyes were on fire, and the sun climbed higher and higher with a pale, fierce, unfriendly light. Guy stayed well ahead of us and kept a straight course toward the northern end of a long island that stood fair in our way.

"That's it," said Rex. "Don't you know what your own place looks like?" He was vastly amused, but Dot and I were not in the mood to share the joke. The place looked foreign and inhospitable under the scalding sun, hived up in a river-mouth, surrounded by other islands, anchored to a mainland point. Claustrophobia was beginning to creep up on us already.

All at once we saw the land opening before us and looked down a corridor of water where boats lay at their moorings; on one side rose the settlement of Pleasant Point, neat wharves and white houses built against a background of spruces and hardwood trees. The other side, of course, was the island; Gay's Island, with blue water concealing the mud flats we had seen that fatal day.

It was high noon and high tide. Low-hanging branches of birch trailed in the water; in the shade of the trees the reflections lay on a mirror of jade-green glass. It was incredibly still; there was no movement until Guy's wake and ours sent tiny waves breaking against the pale, shelving rocks, breaking up the illusively cool reflections.

Guy forged ahead, leading a way among the moored boats, and then, halfway down the Gut and apart from the harbor where the boats were, we came to the wharf of Gay's Island. I looked first for the house, and my heart sank. There it sat on its rise, looking even more forlorn in the unkind light of noon than the first time Dot and I had seen it with Freeman and Jessie Young. Perhaps we needed their enthusiasm now, I thought.

There was nothing romantic or cozy about it. I wondered unhappily what Rex and Lois and Madelyn thought.

But there was no time for wondering, with Smokey panting and whining at the end of his leash because he saw land at last, Brad awakening with a howl, and Rex eager to unload us and get out of Pleasant Point Gut while the tide was still safely high. We tied Smokey to a post near the fishhouse and fastened little Brad's harness to a post near Smokey, and then it was all hands on deck to get the stuff off the *Racketash* as fast as we could. It was back-aching toil, moving furniture across the unplanked wharf so the men would have plenty of room for the articles they kept lifting out of the boat. We were forced to step with infinite care from one rock to another, while they rolled maliciously under our feet; and we had to remember to lift our feet high over the logs that were laid at wide intervals across the rocks. The sun burned down on us as it hadn't blazed in many years. There was no breeze at all, no nice cool feathery wind to ruffle the hair on our damp necks; we were hungry and sunburned, and we saw with growing horror that the tide was still rising and would soon flood the wharf.

We found out later that this day was the hottest August fifth in I don't know how many years; and that it was also the day of the monthly flood tide. These facts were all of a piece with the rest of the business. Operation Frantic was the perfect. name for it.

Most of the furniture was mine. I'd bought it from some of the neighbors at Criehaven when I knew that at last I had a house; some of it was my mother's, from the cottage where we'd spent so many summers. The cookstove, a table, some chairs, a couple of bureaus loaded with sheets and good clothing, were Dot's and Guy's. The rest of their household furnishings were left in Guy's house back on Criehaven. Now, as it all sat squatly and malevolently on the wharf with the tide rising about it, it seemed enough furniture to fill ten houses. And now Rex was leaving. With all the trepidation of persecuted souls who have been deliberately marooned on a desert island, we watched the *Racketash* speed triumphantly down the Gut. But the tide was still rising, and in a sort of furious desperation we began to wrestle with boxes and furniture again.

CHAPTER FOUR

THE PIONEER SPIRIT

Madelyn's husband was somewhere at sea aboard an LST. Madelyn is tall and blond, an effervescent Ingrid Bergman type. She is an artist at housekeeping. She performs every rite with such joy that she delights even habitual oh-let-the-dishes-go addicts like us; it is her art, and she takes a deep and abiding pleasure in it, all the while envying people who muddle around with paints and typewriters. We keep trying to convince her that her yeast rolls, her cakes, her sewing, and even her cleaning, reach a high point in creative inspiration.

Naturally, when Madelyn offered to come along and help us move to Gay's Island, we almost fell at her feet with gratitude. So we had counted on her strong right arm, but not on her limitless gusto, her smile, and the way she said, "Oh, I love to *scrub!*" when she saw for the first time the indescribable grime of the pantry at Gay's Island.

When at last we thought we had the most important things out of the tide's reach that day, we took the eighteen-months-old baby, his crib and bedding and food, and went up to the house. We cleaned out a corner and set up the crib. After his lunch, the baby fell immediately asleep. For the rest of us, our stomachs were too quivery and jumpy for food; but we located the well—with great relief, since Dot had remembered after the down payment was made that we hadn't looked for a well —and refreshed our dehydrated systems with good long drinks. Since then we have been told of all the things that have been discovered in that well, but on that day we knew only that the water was cold and sweet and wonderful.

Back to the wharf we trekked, back through the alders, sweat stinging our eyes, branches scratching our cheeks, and found the tide still rising.

"Good God," Guy muttered. "How high does it come, anyway? Well, come on, give a hand here." Cross to the point of tears, we gave a hand. Only Madelyn remained cheerful. As we started back, carrying what we could, she said, "I'm sick of winding in and out of these alders!" She leaned on them until they broke; we giggled like idiots and Guy shouted from the wharf that if we felt *that* happy about it, we could come back and help him move more stuff to higher ground.

Up at the house Dot studied the old stove, which was propped up on bricks, and which would have to be used until we could get the other one up from the shore. We wanted a hot drink; we were sure we would feel a hundred per cent better if we had a hot drink. So she kindled a fire, and instantly smoke poured out from every crack, choking and blinding us. With terrifying visions of the new property being destroyed by fire in one fell swoop—those headlines again—we threw water on the blaze.

When Guy came up with a load, he took down the stovepipe and found it clogged with soot. In a few minutes he cleaned it and built up another fire, and we dug the teakettle out of the box and soon had it steaming over the flame. When I heard the teakettle begin to sing its plaintive little melody, I felt a lot better.

Now we opened the front door and threw everything out. The disemboweled mattresses, the quilts, the broken chairs, the old clothes—they went out with a vindictive vigor on our part. We swept the spiders away from the windows. Spiders are Dot's personal horror, and she went for them first. These must have been part grasshopper because they leaped rather than scurried.

Madelyn attacked the pantry and was positively sunny about it. And so we had a clean place for the food, the floors swept, and the cots set up by the time the teakettle was boiling. But there was still the biggest part of the job to do. Yet, in our present state, we needed rest, and a short escape from the shadowless heat that was so foreign to us. So for an hour we stretched out on the cots in a silence that seemed unbelievable. There was not even the cry of a single gull, not a bird sang, not a whisper of water came from the rocky shore below the house. The baby and the dog slept soundly. But in the strange and incredible stillness there was a quality that gave ease to our heavy bodies and quivering nerves.

A low rumble brought us all up. None of us cares much for thundershowers, and the least hint of one starts an uneasy feeling down Dot's spine. She was the one to discover the dark clouds in the west, piling up in sullen billowy masses that emitted occasional growls like surly dogs.

We hustled down to the shore to get the rest of the bedding. The tide had reached its height and was beginning to recede, so we didn't have to worry about chairs floating off down the Gut when our backs were turned. But with our muscles trembling and our tongues hanging out at least half as far as Smokey's, we got the rest of the bedding to the house, through the clumps of alders that reached out and snagged at our hair and clothing, slapped our faces, sometimes blinding us as a back-snapping twig took someone in the eye. No one spoke, except when Guy wished with fervor for a good drink. We pulled and dragged and grunted, with watchful eyes turning always to those deep-piling black clouds in the west.

We made it to the house. When we shut the door, the rain struck. Then for an hour we sat in the darkened kitchen, too tired to talk, too tense to relax, watching the windows where the rain beat in heavy drops against the panes. The lightning flashed over the unfamiliar mainland to the west; in the sudden flares of blue-white brilliance the line of fields and woods appeared inexplicably hostile to us. The thunder seemed to be the loudest we had ever heard, the raindrops the biggest, the lightning the sharpest. We were too uncomfortably aware of being perched all out to the weather on the top of our rise.

What sort of country had we chosen to live in? Thundershowers were not rare on Criehaven, but they were not like this. Even I was nervous—I who had always loved thundershowers since my little-girl days at Scituate when the noise bounced back and forth like a barrage between Second and Third Cliffs. Brad, pleasantly refreshed by his nap, pursued Smokey around the kitchen, and with purely mechanical gestures we took turns in depriving him of whatever lethal implements he had picked up. He was not bothered by the thunderstorm, and neither was Smokey, who was bothered only by Brad. The rest of us comforted ourselves by saying this storm was surely something out of the ordinary, caused by the unnatural heat of the day and the cool upspringing wind from the west.

But even now, when a thunderstorm rolls out of the sky above Friendship, I feel a certain tingling and tenseness, and it doesn't go away until the lightning is flickering out over Monhegan or up the river toward Thomaston. And on this day, when it had finally rolled away from us, by the river route, we opened the door thankfully to smell the sweet wet fragrance of earth and grass and trees.

Now it was sunset, and the colors that spread over the islands, the still water, the far-reaching woods and fields of the mainland, were like something in a dream. It was a sight we had

never before experienced, the particular luminous peace of
sunset-after-storm among unknown islands, and as we walked
down to the shore we said to each other in awe-struck tones,
"Isn't it beautiful? Did you ever see anything like it? . . . No,
I never did. . . . Look at those boats in the harbor. It's like
a huge painting, the water is so still. It's more like a lake than
a salt-water harbor."

Our previous ideas of salt-water harbors were far different
from this. There was not a whisper of sound on the rocks, not
a ripple. Could this be the coast?

After we had breathed our fill of the cool, color-drenched
evening, we began to work again, like so many pack horses.
Guy had covered the bureaus with a tarpaulin before the storm
struck, so we felt they could stand being left out all night. The
cookstove was full of water, but it couldn't be helped now. It
would have to stand there until Guy could get someone to help
him move it to the house—someone with muscles. Not the rest
of us. We might have been working like Wilma Womarth the
Girl Stevedore all day, but tonight for my money we had
pieces of boiled macaroni for biceps. ,

The varnish on the chairs had turned white, but we didn't
worry about that. As long as we had them to sit on, the varnish
didn't matter, even if it should grow whiskers. Guy's boat
rested peacefully at the end of the wharf. If he'd been at Criehaven, more lines would have been necessary, but in this
motionless water that had no action besides its ebb and flow, he
felt that she was safe.

Now we thirsted—nay, panted—for coffee. Breakfast back
on Criehaven, dropped into quivering stomachs, seemed two
weeks ago. Guy spoke forlornly about something stronger, but
Madelyn and I wanted coffee. Dot is a cocoa addict, and there
was cocoa in one of the boxes but no milk. With all the gallant
resignation of refugees dividing up a shoe sole amongst them—
which isn't too bad a figure of speech, considering the quality

of that so-called steak—we ate a very scant stew which Dot
had somehow concocted over the fiendish old stove. We
managed also to swallow a mixture of cocoa and hot water and
sugar. Madelyn had some canned food for the baby. We envied
little Brad that night. If he wanted to cry, he could. He was
fed, washed, and put to bed, with nothing more to worry about.
And Smokey had his dog food.

Exhausted, grimy, but faintly relieved by the small amount
of food in our stomachs and the feeling that the Worst Was
Over, we sat on the big granite doorstep and felt the cool lilac
dusk sweep around us. The water between us and Caldwell,
the terraced and wooded island across the channel to the south-
east, was the same color as the sky. We tried not to think of
tomorrow, of the rooms as yet untouched, of the furniture
still piled down by the fishhouse.

"My God," murmured Guy wistfully, "I'm thirsty. And
don't anybody mention water to me, either."

"Have some of that milkless cocoa," Dot said unfeelingly.
"And think of the people in concentration camps. At least nobody's holding a gun at our backs. We can stop when we get
tired." This ennobling thought fell on barren ground. I said,
"Gosh, I wish there was a place where we could get some
coffee."

"There's a little store on the other side, down the harbor,"
Guy contributed. "Didn't I tell you?" Madelyn and I at once
straightened up and looked at him the way Smokey gets alert
at the rattle of a candy paper, but Guy at once said, warningly,
"Well, don't think I'm going to row over there *tonight*."

"Do you good to start the day without coffee for once,"
Dot threw in, smugly remembering her cocoa, no doubt. "I
stopped drinking coffee twenty years ago, and look at me."

"Yes, look at you," Madelyn said enthusiastically, if am-
biguously. We became quite hysterical at this, and laughter
took away the remnants of our energy.

There was one other task before we could call it a day. One of the more important things about the place, which Dot had discovered on our first visit, was that it had no plumbing or any substitute for same. So my mother, with a superb flash of inspiration, had ordered a very fancy *Convenience* from Sears Roebuck, and said it would be my birthday present, though not one I could go around bragging about to people I didn't know very well. We had brought the big package along from Criehaven. And now, by lamplight, and with the kitchen door open so we could see the stars trembling in the water of the cove and smell the wet woods, Guy and I set up the contraption while Dot read the directions.

We went on gurgling and chuckling like a lot of irrepressible brooks while we set up the object and bolted it together per diagram. There's a lot to be said for foolish laughter. It relaxed every aching muscle and loosened every taut nerve until they seemed to be dragging around behind us like so many disconnected telephone wires. Finally, with due ceremony, we transported the *Convenience* into the small room at the end of the house that would henceforth be called "the bathroom."

It's a very pleasant little room, too, with a nice view up over the hill. A good room for reading. When I determined to get through Proust I placed the volumes on the ancient sewing machine in the bathroom (one of the things we didn't throw out of the house—it was a real relic) and then everybody in the house, visitors and family, read Proust. There were more confused expressions coming out of that room than you can imagine, but it was a long time before anyone got the initiative to take in a handful of *Reader's Digests*. Finally someone bolder than the rest left *Lydia Bailey* in there, and from then on Proust got short shrift.

It was time for bed, and we were ready. There were no curtains at the windows, and we could lie on our cots and stare out at the starry night before we fell into sleep that was uneasy and heavy at the same time. And the silence still held; a strange silence without undertones, without a murmur, that made you feel as if you were drifting in pure space. In the middle of the night I awoke and for a moment had a sense of disembodiment. I didn't know where I was. The room was filled with a clear white radiance, and I thought it was dawn, until I saw that the moon had risen—a round enormous moon that flooded the whole world with its light. I lay and looked out of the window and watched great fluffy clouds float across this alien sky and saw the water glowing with moonlight, and the dark islands sleeping beyond us, the unknown land all around us.

It was a sort of marriage. For better or for worse, thirty-three acres of Gay's Island were ours, and here I lay, summoning up a spirit of determination and courage which wasn't at all what I'd expected to need. It had been going to be an adventure into foreign lands, through which we'd all breeze with merriment and a pleasant spice of excitement.

I told myself finally it was because I hadn't had a good cup of coffee all day, remembered dismally there wouldn't be any coffee in the morning either, and at last fell asleep again. *But it's lovely here, anyway*, was my last stubborn, conscious thought.

CHAPTER FIVE

IN A FOREIGN LAND

In a day or so Madelyn went from Pleasant Point to her apartment in Rockland, and we went back to Criehaven for the rest of Guy's lobster gear and the livestock. Dot and I hated to part with Madelyn. Her laughter and her uncloying sunniness had really buoyed us up during that age-long day of moving. But, having visited with her mother at Criehaven, she was intending to take little Brad to visit his paternal grandparents at Matinicus, and she promised us she would come back down in the fall and make a *real* visit.

It was a lovely sail back to Criehaven. The air was so crystalline in its brightness that the rocks of Criehaven were visible almost from the time we passed Metinic. The sea was so incredibly blue I still can't understand how the Mediterranean could surpass it. We felt very serene; I didn't even worry about Wheeler's Ledge and the Triangles. Smokey, who had kept pace with every move we had made, composed the whiskers inherited from his wire-haired mother and slept on the bottom of the boat.

Always before when I approached Criehaven I had a sense of homecoming. But now, despite the ordeal of the last few days, the homecoming feeling was gone. *Home* was behind us. I think we were all in agreement about it. Strange as it seems, we must have put down roots in that terrible burning day. In our own fashion, we were pioneering, and I think now that if we had not been obliged to work so hard, if everything had gone smoothly, with no sweat and tears and frustrations, we would not have possessed at once the sense of ownership and of *belonging* that followed us all the way from Gay's Island back to Criehaven.

Not one of us was really at ease now on Criehaven. We were anxious to get started again, even though we knew the rest of the summer would be spent in work. This time the objections and the voices of doom meant no more to us than the sound of gulls—perhaps even less. At night we slept uneasily, almost as if we were visiting Criehaven and really didn't know it very well. But I don't believe any of us was guilty of disloyalty. It was simply that we wanted to plunge ourselves into the new life as quickly as possible.

Rex was returning to Muscongus Island to take his wife's parents home, and he offered to carry a load of lobster traps, which were still wet from Criehaven waters. So we set out again in our two-boat caravan. The chickens, tucked protestingly into some of Guy's new traps, went on the *Racketash*. Guy took Patty, the little Toggenburg doe, and Blackie, the lamb. Patty was a sweet, gentle creature, and Blackie, rather big for a lamb, was a handsome and imposing animal, with eyes like sparkling brown jewels in his long black face, and sensitive ears like soft black felt. If possible, we presented a far more gypsyish appearance when we chugged up Pleasant Point Gut this time than we did the week before. I know the people on the Point must have been both intrigued and appalled. What is there about chickens in lobster traps, and a goat, that will give even the most respectable souls a raffish air? I know I felt far more self-conscious about our ladylike Patty, hanging her head over the side of Guy's boat and flicking expressive ears at the Pleasant Point wharves, than I did about anything else.

We found my mother serenely alone on the island, waiting for us. My father had been obliged to go back to his work in Boston. She looked as if she had been there forever, and she was in love with the place.

"I saw a fox last night," she greeted us. "Imagine!"

We asked her what she thought about the mountain range of junk that surrounded the house, and she told us sublimely that she had simply ignored it. And she had even made the acquaintance of the stove and was not afraid it would blow up if she built a big enough fire to boil water. Intrepid woman. . . .

She and my father had also met the Youngs, who would be our closest neighbors on Pleasant Point, it seemed. Madeline, mother of Roland, had rowed them across the Gut the day before when the taxi brought them down from Thomaston. Mother was one up on us, having established definite contact with the neighborhood. Leslie Young, who owns the big white house at the very end of the road where you turn down toward the shore if you're coming to Gay's Island, his wife Sybil, his daughter Madeline Stimpson, and her son Roland are therefore our oldest neighbors. Now our names are on their mailbox under the big apple tree at the corner, we tie up at Leslie's wharf, and use his telephone.

Leslie is a short, sandy, wiry man who has taken a paternal interest in us from the first. Sometimes I detect a faintly quizzical and humorous gleam in his eyes—as for instance when he asked us awhile ago, "Just what do you plan to do with that great big dory you bought sight unseen?"

This had the effect of reducing both Dot and me to a full realization that we *didn't* know what we were going to do with her; we had always wanted a dory, but we didn't know that this one was going to turn out to be eighteen feet long and as heavy as an LST.

Leslie watched us suffer for a few minutes, twinkling all the while, and then said, "Well, seein' as it's comin' on winter and

you can't launch her till you get the place in the stern fixed—
I'll put her up in the top of my fishhouse till you figure what
you want to do with her."

And there she stayed, safe from the weather and out of the
way, until we swapped her for a saucy little dory that's light
enough for the two of us to haul up our steep rocks without
panting.

It is Leslie, too, who has come over across the Gut in a brisk,
ice-edged wind that brings tears to the eyes, walked into our
kitchen and said, "Come on, come on, you haven't been off the
island for a week—you come over now and have supper with
us, and we'll go to Friendship tonight and see Tony and
Juanita." It is Leslie who, when we left last winter, asked us
anxiously what we had done with our skiffs, and when he
found we had simply hauled them up and turned them over,
he asked for the fishhouse key; he and Roland went over and
put the skiffs into the fishhouse. I could go on and on about
Leslie, who lives every day the meaning of the words "Good
neighbor."

Sybil is quiet, and a homebody, but she's always ready with
a smile and a little bit of news. When we cross the Gut in a rainstorm with our good clothes in a suitcase, bound for a day in
Rockland, we change out of our wet dungarees in the Youngs'
spare room, and sit and yarn with Sybil, perhaps eating some of
her fresh doughnuts, while we wait for George Harvey's taxi
to come from town. Madeline, whose husband Lawrence died
several years ago, is a human dynamo, but no matter how busy
she is she's always offering to do something for us. She's smaller
than either of us, but she has so much git-up-and-go to her
that she shames us. Her boy Roland has grown up since the day
he rowed us across to Gay's Island for the first time, but he
hasn't outgrown his candid, unaffected friendliness.

Sandy, the family dog, part chow, was named after Orphan
Annie's Sandy, but he does *not* answer every remark, like

Annie's annoyingly loquacious dog, with "Arf, arf." He is quiet and very wise. He prefers boats and men to cars and women, but he is charming to us, pays us the compliment of respecting our friends—if they are properly introduced as such—and tolerates Smokey. This last is true proof of Sandy's genuine Good-Neighbor policy. Prejudiced as I am about Smokey, I know how his ubiquitous and extroverted manners must irk Sandy, who has snapped at Smokey only once, and that was when Smokey ruined his mouse-hunt.

So behold my mother, completely settled on Gay's Island after having met the Young family; we knew Roland first, but she was the first to know the others.

We were decanting the goat and the sheep, feeling very grimy and exasperated with their respective goatish-and-sheepishness, when we discovered that we were landlords. Perspiring freely, Guy had got the animals out of the boat and onto the wharf, and Dot and I were struggling to lead a wild-eyed Blackie across the rolling rocks to safe ground (Patty was no trouble, ever), when two ladies of austerely dignified appearance came across the Neck toward the fishhouse. We hadn't yet had a chance to explore the territory on the other side of the narrow, low strip of land that divided the two wide parts of the island; we had seen only woods there and realized that most of our acreage consisted of those tall spruces. But this week end a flag fluttered above a great birch on the shore of the Gut; we were not alone on the island. And here came these two strange women, one very tall, the other much shorter.

They were also immaculate. They looked cool and rested. We were shiny with sweat and smelled like sheep from having leaned on Blackie and embraced him to keep him from jumping off the wharf. We were not good-tempered. On beholding these spotless ladies, strolling toward us like summer residents at a resort, we experienced a common impulse to disappear.

There was no escaping them, and the tall woman said in a

brisk, cool voice, "We'd like to introduce ourselves. This is Mrs. Dornan, and I'm Mrs. Gray."

Guy, never at a loss, was as courtly as if he hadn't just been calling Blackie all the names he'd gathered in his forty-odd years. "I'm Guy Simpson," he said silkily, "and this is Mrs. Simpson. . . ." Dot, intimidated by the obvious loftiness of the newcomers, said "How do you do?" with a ferocious sort of smile. Skulking in the background, wearing a hastily assumed social expression, I too was introduced. At once, the conversation lapsed.

"We're in the first camp, there," Mrs. Gray volunteered, waving at the flag.

"Oh, yes," we said, looking vacuous.

Mrs. Dornan smiled patiently. "I think you are our new landlords. We were wondering what arrangements Mr. Thompson had made. . . ."

"We wouldn't know anything about that," said Guy, and Dot and I made a sort of antiphonal response. "No, we've had hardly any time to look around."

They left after that. We gave them time to get out of earshot and then went into a huddle. "Do we own the camps or the land? . . . Do you suppose they're here most of the time? . . . They're pretty imposing, aren't they? What do you suppose they think about us? . . . We look like Tobacco Road for sure. . . ."

Why hadn't Mr. Thompson, who owned the largest part of the island and who'd sold us our thirty-three acres of it, told Freeman Young about this landlord business? We were discomforted by the thought, having been quite awe-stricken by the unexpected tenants. At least Dot and I were. Guy assumed a masterful air and said he would Find Out Everything.

It turned out that Mrs. Gray owned her camp, the Andrews' of Vermont and Thomaston owned the second camp along the shore, set in a lovely tall grove of spruces; and Miss Hahn of Massachusetts and Thomaston owned the third. They had owned them for a long time; but we owned the land on which the camps stood. Beyond our thick belt of woodland, Jim Seavey of Pleasant Point owned a strip, and the Robinsons and a lady named Leila Clark owned the eastern tip of the island, spending summers in the white house Mr. Robinson had built.

It wasn't until quite a long time later that Mrs. Gray, evidently determined to find some way to break the ice, told Dot that she knew quite a bit about Criehaven. Her father used to go there to paint, and she had always wanted to go with him, but had been too small. And Dot and Guy both remembered Bill Gray, who used to visit Ira Tupper; he was a wartime buddy of Ira's, and Mrs. Gray's husband.

But it wasn't until this year that we confessed how startled and intimidated we had been by that meeting on the wharf, how much in awe of both Charlotte Gray and Lillian Dornan; and then they told us that they'd been afraid of us! I think we've all got splendidly past that moment. I was sure of it on the day when they came up to have tea with us, all decked out in every shawl and kerchief and antiquated jacket the "Barnacle" (the name of Charlotte's camp) possessed, with ancient hats ornamented magnificently with Queen Anne's lace and clover, and white canvas gloves on their hands; we met them at the door dressed suitably to compete with them. We have sat around Ed Dornan's bonfires and sung "The West Virginia Hills" which for Dot and me is as sure a guarantee of friendship as Sandy's wagging tail.

Memorial Day always marks the official opening of the "Barnacle" for the summer, and from then on through October—if the weather holds good—we can look for Mrs. Gray and the Dornans to come down from Thomaston each week end to lie on the rocks and read, to dig clams, fish for flounders, and pack some thirty-six hours of relaxation into their otherwise crowded schedule. Smokey leaves the house as soon as he sees the skiff coming across the Gut on Saturday afternoon, and greets them all affectionately as they come ashore. Tristan, the cat, digs at the door for admittance, and inspects every corner of the "Barnacle" with the inoffensive curiosity of an old friend.

But back there, on the wharf in that hot August sun, we didn't know about these things. We were only bowed down by the new responsibility of being landlords.

My mother wasn't bowed down, but then she wasn't one of the landlords. She was indefatigable. She spent the rest of her summer scrubbing, lugging, sweeping, giving us a hand wherever needed, and found time to plan out a color scheme for the kitchen and donate the paint and linoleum. We thought that the woodwork was dark gray; we knew that the plaster had never been painted in the kitchen but had been used for paint brushes to be cleaned on, while various generations of small boys must have tried out their new jackknives on the window sills.

The space behind the kitchen stove under the back stairs, known as the Lazaret, housed unseen horrors, as far as we were concerned; the back stairs winding to the ell chamber were not passable, and the ell chamber itself was tenanted by spiders who lived a happy and untrammeled life in the unspeakable debris that covered the floor.

With one accord, we ignored the ell chamber. The Lazaret— yes, that would have to be tackled. We had to have a place to put things. But the ell chamber must be left until we felt strong —very strong.

We would be spending a lot of time in the kitchen, and that came first. My mother discovered the woodwork was really apple-green under the dark gray. We cleaned paint until we should have had bursitis in the shoulders. Then she and I, while Dot and Guy did heavier work outdoors carting rubbish away to the shore, Kemtoned the plaster in aqua and began to paint the woodwork white. The change was incredibly cheerful. Dot cleaned out the cookstove that had been left standing on the wharf in the thunderstorm, Guy installed the oil burner, and the malevolent old stove that had made meals a series of nightmares went out of the house and over the bank.

Now, at last, we could begin to *live*. Oh, there were years of work ahead of us yet. We had no illusions about that. We couldn't walk through the yard without turning our ankles on the tin cans that must have been thrown from the doorstep for years. Every room needed painting and papering. There was the ell chamber. The outside of the house needed paint. The well curb was rotten to the point of being dangerous. The fishhouse needed extensive repairs before cold weather came.

But we could do no more than one day's work at a time, and meanwhile we were getting acquainted with the neighbors. Leslie Young and his fishing partner Jim Seavey were showing Guy where to set his traps for the best results. There was no hostility here, and at the lobster car the Pleasant Point men congratulated Guy when his big Criehaven four-headed traps caught lobsters so well. Mr. Dunn, in the big house at the end of the harbor, invited us all to ride along with him to Grange suppers, and Melba Ulmer, his housekeeper—a girl of my age —went out of her way, busy as she was, to make sure we felt welcome at Pleasant Point. The young Sevons found out about Dot's guitar, and asked her to bring it over and play. The Herricks offered to drive my father to the train when he left after Labor Day.

One morning when we were down at the wharf, an elderly man and woman rowing through the Gut in a peapod stopped and introduced themselves. They were Rich and Susie Davis, well into their seventies. Vigorous and gay, they went out to haul together. "This peapod," Mr. Davis told us, "is older than I am." He was very proud of it.

There was no strangeness here. It was true that we were

working harder than we'd ever worked before, and we didn't know when we'd be able to rest. But there was satisfaction in it. Every time Guy went out to haul, on those calm pleasant waters so different from the heavy, swelling seas outside Crie-haven, and every time we rowed across for the mail and then came back to the increasingly familiar landing, we knew that Gay's Island was tightening its grip upon us.

CHAPTER SIX

EXIT, PURSUED BY A BEAR

When our Criehaven friends (and relatives, in the case of Dorothy and Guy) found out we were unmoved by their criticism, they took to slurring our strength of character. Whenever they arrived to visit Gay's Island (usually at dead low water on one of those days when there was an exceptionally low tide and a reek of mud flats in the air) someone was sure to say, "I can see why you left Criehaven. It's pretty rugged out there. You can't be soft and get along at Criehaven." Though why in the name of heaven they thought Gay's Island didn't have its rugged moments, when we were puffing and dragging to get a skiff launched over the mud, or—if the tide happened for once to be high—we had to battle a fast current and a strong wind to get them across, I don't know.

Anyway, except for a few kind words from Dot's stepfather, Fred Wilson, who used to pasture calves on Gay's Island when he lived across the river at Turkey Cove, and some pleasant approval from her uncle, John Anderson, who lived at Port Clyde, everyone else was pretty disapproving, in one way or another.

The idea that we were all getting too effete for the Criehaven life took root. We began to examine our consciences. Personally, I was rather glad to have softened to this extent, when I remembered all the times I'd been scared into a horrible bone-melting state between Matinicus and Criehaven. But at the same time I was writing a trilogy that made the Criehaven exist-ence seem positively idyllic. Was it true, then, that I was at heart a coward?

We had only been there a few weeks and knew little about the island. We hadn't even explored our own part, let alone the vast wooded section that lay far beyond our line. And then, one night when we had all retired to our rooms with our lamps and books, *Something* ran around the house. It sounded like a horse. Smokey barked frantically. After a stunned moment, everyone was calling back and forth, "What was *that?*"

Innocents that we were, fresh from life on that rugged little Corregidor out by Matinicus Rock, we could hardly wait to ask Leslie Young if he had any idea what it was.

"Most likely a moose," he told us calmly, as if to have a moose run around your house was a very ordinary occurrence. We looked at him with new respect. Maybe he'd never lobstered out at Criehaven, but he was accustomed to having moose run around his house, and it didn't faze him a bit. He was amused by our astonishment.

If he could have guessed at the state of our stomachs, he would have been even more amused. A moose was a large ani-mal equipped with a formidable armory. I'd seen them at the Franklin Park Zoo.

"They're dangerous, aren't they?" I asked weakly.

"Only in the matin' season," Leslie reassured me.

"When's that?"

"Fall," said Leslie. It was September now. Supposing one of us had been out of doors last night?

On Criehaven, wild life was restricted to birds and the world's most frivolous and fearless mice. There were not even rats, though I understand the fear of rats once loomed as large in the islanders' minds as the fear of fire; one never knew when some might come ashore off a coastwise schooner which put in at Criehaven for the night. But the days of the schooners departed long ago.

Twenty-five miles out from the mainland, Criehaven and Matinicus have no chance to foster anything else in the way of wild life. There were once rabbits on Criehaven, but they had been brought there originally by people who intended to raise rabbits. When they were allowed to go wild, for a few years dogs and men went rabbiting to their heart's delight. Now there is nothing; the hawks in the woods give the wilderness touch, but I had to come to the mainland, to Gay's Island, to become accustomed to the daily sight of great fish hawks soaring and circling over the water.

As for the four-footed critters in the woods here, the Stepping Stones between us and the mainland explain them, as they explain the game birds and occasional snakes, and our as-yet unrealized expectation of meeting a bear in the moonlight.

After the moose visit, we didn't go out after dark unless in groups, and then we made plenty of noise, so that any moose lurking in the alders, with the intention of tossing somebody on his antlers like a green salad, would know very definitely that there were Plenty of Us. I flashed a light out one night for Smokey and scared myself into an unpleasant tizzy; at a crucial moment the battery began to fail, and I was conscious of the fact that *Something* was standing just beyond the reach of the light. Something was lurking there beyond a doubt. . . . I snatched the dog in, hissing at him fiercely when he took his time about it, locked the door, and went to bed feeling like a native in a Hindu village where a man-eating tiger makes frequent visits.

The next morning, in the dazzling sunshine, I discovered that a deck chair was still lurking on the lawn and baring its teeth at me. Fortunately I had told no one of my adventure—

not wanting to alarm the others—and I could continue to assure myself that it was simply a matter of luck. It might have been a moose out there, after all.

Bit by bit, our sense of superiority began to rise. Meeting Islanders—Criehaven ones—we could throw casual remarks into the conversation. "A moose ran around the house the other night . . . the woods are full of 'em!" A shrug, light laughter. "Heaven knows what comes over the Stepping Stones at low tide!"

We could always repeat Madeline Stimpson's story of being followed home from the post office by a Canada lynx. This is always impressive but has a way of bothering me if I walk down to the shore alone at night, just as the pleasant excitement occasioned by the bear over in Waldoboro, or in the bog at South Thomaston, has a way of coming back at us like a boomerang, if we've been up to Rockland for the day and come home after dark. I see bears behind every alder clump, and if I could possibly get Blackie into the house for the night, I'd have him bedded down behind the kitchen stove.

Along with this new and titillating sense of danger, we realized that those poor souls at Criehaven had been practically living in quarantine all their lives. All they could talk about was the ledges and the heavy seas, but their woods were as safe as a nursery. There wasn't even a chipmunk to chatter at them.

Of course, until we got used to the chipmunks, a stroll through the woods became portentous with unknown hazards. The hair stood up on the back of our necks at the sound of one, and Smokey had hysterics and tried to climb trees. When we mentioned the partridges whirring up from under our feet, or the cock pheasants strolling past the house, the people on the Point answered with the indifference bred of long acquaintance with partridges and cock pheasants.

"Used to be a lot more of 'em," someone said. "But the foxes got 'em."

Game birds . . . foxes . . . woodchucks . . . skunks . . . porcupines . . . rabbits . . . the woods in which we walked, trying to reassure ourselves that they *were* our woods, became a kingdom which could never belong to us. The certainty grew, whenever we strolled, that a whole mysterious way of life held its breath until we went by, and then began again. The crows, to be sure, were loud in their resentment at our presence, but we knew and felt the existence of the others without seeing them. Even if we had stayed out of their orbit, never going past the frontier of the alders, they came to us. Blackie, the sheep, who never went out of sight of the house, was discovered with a noseful of porcupine quills. We took them out; and then Smokey, whose black patent-leather nose is considerably smaller than Blackie's, also made contact with a porcupine. That was a painful time for us.

The kittens were menaced by hawks. My mother was also menaced by a hawk, when she waved her apron at one to drive him away from a kitten; an owl appeared in a horrifying, silent fashion just at sundown one November day and hovered over the same kitten. It was Soldi, whose softly blended three colors should have camouflaged her well. But she was forever in danger, whereas Tristan's red-gold coat and plume didn't attract anyone but the people on the other side, who thought he was a fox.

When Smokey, exuding avuncular affection, tried to herd the kittens off toward the alders to do a little hunting, we rushed to bring them in, since everyone had warned us that foxes stole kittens. But with the cats safely in the kitchen, we were fascinated the first time a fox came close to the house.

It was on a winter day, one of those still, shining days when the snow has shadows of rose and lavender, and the sea is as blue as a summer sea could ever be. There were black ducks and old squaws paddling contentedly in the shimmering water of the little cove just below the house. We were watching them when the fox came out of the dark woods on the side of the hill. His coat was burnished red, his legs were black, and he looked exactly like a fox in a storybook. He was Reddy Fox come to life, about to accost the Little Red Hen; he was Reynard, looking for the crow with the piece of cheese in his beak.

He was interested in the ducks when he came out of the woods, stepping lightly with his black feet over the rocks. He paused frequently to admire the birds so deliciously near, so tantalizingly far. Sometimes he dipped his paw into the water and then drew back. He went all around the cove, and the ducks went on paddling without a glance in his direction. It was an unforgettable picture; the glowing red coat against the white snow, the ducks above their reflections in the clear glassy water; the channel a wide strip of forget-me-not blue stretching to the snowy terraces of Caldwell with its crest of dark spruces. I don't know how long Dot and I watched, hardly breathing, until someone in the house closed a door.

The fox heard it. He seemed to flow over the snow-covered ground, up the slope, and into the woods. We were limp and silent, as if a moment of incredible beauty had come very close to us. Not its terror, not its unknown noises, but its pure, fundamental vitality.

There was a lame old dog fox we watched as he hunted mice in the field; he'd sit with his head cocked, and then he'd pounce, all four feet together, like a cat, or like Sandy the chow. He hunted for a long time, and when he got tired of it he loped up over the hill in a leisurely manner. And then there was the little fox, just at daylight one spring morning. We'd let the cats out and were just starting breakfast, when we heard a strange sound which we'd never before heard on Gay's Island. Looking out, we saw a charming sight. It belongs with all the funny, enchanting moments that are precious forever because of their very brevity.

Tristan and Isolde were on the doorstep, not alarmed, but rather scowly. At the corner of the house stood a small fox, not much bigger than they were. His head tilted, his eyes bright with excitement, he was barking at them, like an impudent and curious little dog.

Oh, yes, they're devils, and they eat partridge eggs, and they kill chickens; but *there* was one I'd have taken to my heart.

There's another fox who is probably still wondering what happened one mild spring day. He came trotting up from the Neck, where the island narrows down and where our wharf and fishhouse are; in all innocence, as businesslike as a family dog loaded with responsibilities, he came up the path by the barn. Blackie, grazing in the field, gave him a cursory glance, flicked his ears forward at him, and turned away. Perhaps he thought it was Sandy, the Youngs' chow. Seeing the fox from the window, we thought he was a dog, too. Foxes weren't supposed to go walking across lawns in broad daylight like pets; they slunk out of the alders after dark.

Tristan sat on the outside window sill and watched his approach. We watched from the inside, too excited to speak. Naturally we expected Tris to have the common sense to stay where he was.

The fox, looking pleasantly intent on whatever he was planning, swung across the lawn, and Tris flew off the window sill in pursuit. In full cry we rushed out, Smokey shrieking in frustration as his toenails skidded going around corners. We boiled out through the doorway, shouting at Tris, who kept on going, his plumy tail out straight behind him. The fox flowed up the slope toward the woods; and Tris had almost caught up to him.

Smokey, told to go get Tris, followed his invariable procedure; he raced off with passionate eagerness in the wrong

direction. In this case he ran for the barn, where he startled
Blackie, who thought he was about to be attacked by his ancient
enemy. (They wage a constant war of nerves in competition
for our affection.) He stamped, reared, pawed the air like a
stallion, and blew through his nose. Smokey made a discreet
circle and came back to us. By this time we were on our way
to the woods, and when I stepped into a rosebush I discovered
I had no shoes on.

Dot found Tris just inside the limits of the woods, wandering around with a scowl on his face. He had lost the fox. She
picked him up and he hung over her arm like a fur scarf, still
scowling. She asked him what in heaven's name he was going
to do with the fox if he caught it, but to this day we have received no answer. But we remember the scowl stayed all afternoon on Tris's ordinarily delightful broad face, with its golden
eyes and turned-up coral nose. (Dot calls him "Old Baseball
Face.")

Smokey started off belatedly in the right direction and returned some half-hour later, with his tongue hanging out so
far that he almost tripped over it when he came across the lawn.

Smokey is a small, black, hairy mongrel, with whiskers and
eyebrows like a Scotty's, and the eager stance of a wire-haired
terrier; he has also the spaniel's infinite capacity for loving, being loved, and being sensitive. With people he is wistful and
wheedling; his bright brown eyes work miracles on those
hardy souls who think it wrong to Feed the Dog Between
Meals, and he is so easily hurt by criticism that a mere cough
drops him in his tracks, and if the cough wasn't directed at him
in the first place, he must be soothed and reassured, which sends
him into a hysterical transport of pantings and sneezings.

That's Smokey with mere human beings. . . . But Smokey
with Gay's Island wild life is something else again. He was six
years old when he moved from Criehaven, where there'd been
nothing more exciting to pursue than cats. One would have

expected a certain amount of mature intelligence from Smokey, at the age of six; but I suppose one must expect something less than discretion from a dog who, after refusing to swim all his life, begins in his middle age to swim daily to the mainland in spite of icy cold water and a current that bothers strong human swimmers. And so at nine years of age, with all his teeth extracted because of a bad jaw infection, Smokey has suddenly turned into a roaring lion who cannot be taken anywhere on a leash because he insults German shepherd dogs and great Danes; swears at them first, slaps his glove in their faces, and has to be carried home ignominiously struggling and cursing. . . .

It wasn't until the teeth extraction that Smokey, no doubt spurred on by some of Sandy's exploits with woodchucks on Gay's Island, became a definite aggressor. There has always been a woodchuck behind the barn, a polite old Thornton Burgess character; he leaves us alone and we leave him alone, and in this case *laissez faire* has worked out very well indeed. One year he ate all the lettuce in our garden, but nothing else, and he hasn't touched the lettuce again either. Perhaps the marked backwardness of our lettuce has something to do with it. It takes all summer to reach transplanting stage, and by that time the leaves are as thick as bark, and no doubt resist even a woodchuck's teeth. . . . But I had never thought of a woodchuck as a hazard.

One day, not a month after Smokey's teeth had come out, when we took him for a carefully chaperoned walk, we stopped to look at some very early white violets in a swampy place, and to speculate for the fiftieth time on the whereabouts of the spring that Susie Davis swears is there, and to pace around solemnly with an alder fork which remained disappointingly dead in our hands. While we stalked over the wet places like necromancers, Smokey escaped us. After we'd decided that what we needed was a real water dowser because neither of us had the power, and had commented on the Oriental effect of silvery, ancient, bare alder boughs against the delicate blue spring sky, we tried to collect Smokey. Dot's piercing whistle ran unanswered through the dark mysterious woods on the crest of the island.

She has a maternal feeling of responsibility for Smokey, but she's not the Mom type.

"To heck with him," she said pleasantly. "He's been trying to run away from me for a month. Let him have his run and come back when he's ready."

It was then that we heard him barking. Far-off, short, jerky, hysterical barks. . . . We knew we'd have to look for him then; it was obvious that he had something cornered.

"I hope to God it isn't a moose," Dot said as we plunged through underbrush, waded through dead brown ferns and dried swamp, all the time getting nearer to Smokey. This happy suggestion gave me pause; to me all moose are of one sex, all bull moose with incredibly wide spreads of antlers. I've heard of cows and calves, but I have the dread certainty that if I ever come face to face with a moose it will be neither cow nor innocuous calf, but bull. *Enraged* bull.

However, Smokey was somewhere on the seaward shore of the island barking his lungs into tatters, and we couldn't turn our backs on him. So we went on, and Dot picked up a heavy stick, though of what use it would be in the event of a moose—bull—I didn't know.

At the edge of the woods, facing a rocky meadow, we knew he was somewhere beyond the outcroppings of granite. Dot told me to stay back, and she went ahead with her stick. Smokey's bark reached a crescendo of lunacy. From out of sight, she called to me, "It's a woodchuck."

"Oh," I said happily, and went forward. Dot was endeavoring to get some sense into her dog.

"Go on," she told him, brandishing her stick. "Go on home

and leave him alone." The woodchuck rocked around on his haunches, defending his castle; Smokey insisted he had work to do, he couldn't go home yet. But Dot prevailed and finally, with drooping head and tail, Smokey turned away toward me. Unfortunately he looked back and saw the woodchuck in pursuit. I think the chase would have ended as soon as the chuck saw that Smokey was really leaving, but Smokey had no way of knowing. He only knew that this impertinent character who was neither dog nor cat nor good red fox had the temerity to chase him. With an embattled roar—and no teeth—he sprang at the woodchuck's throat.

Needless to say, it was the woodchuck who made contact. He caught Smokey by the tongue. Dot's stick, intended for some sort of futile defense against a moose, was eventually used to kill the woodchuck. Smokey, bleeding profusely from the mouth, was hoisted up to be carried home. We took turns carrying him, staggering through the woods on tottery legs—our sinews feeling like snapped violin strings—while Smokey bled down the backs of our jackets and glared victoriously in the direction of the corpse.

If anyone—Sandy, perhaps—had asked him, he would probably have insisted that he'd killed the woodchuck in that glorious moment when he seized him by the throat. Anyway, he spends his days in readiness for another such exhilarating experience, convinced that he has teeth like a dinosaur's. We spend our days being sure the occasion doesn't arise.

CHAPTER SEVEN

THE FOUR-LEGGED FAMILY

"Animals are such agreeable friends," said George Eliot. "They ask no questions, they pass no criticisms." And Walt Whitman observed that he would rather enjoy living with animals, who are so placid and self-contained. I don't know to what species of animals they were referring. In my experience, even cows, supposedly the personification of serenity, are loaded to the horns with temperament. And at the other extreme, anyone who has ever lived in the same house with a cat, be it five weeks or five years old, knows that a four-footed creature covered with fur and sporting a tail can ask questions all day long, make any number of criticisms, and be anything but placid.

Pigs are notoriously easy to spoil; hens have their whims. The dog, traditionally man's best friend, can develop an incredibly long list of peculiarities that have to be crushed at the start—most of them—if you expect to live in any sort of peace with him and keep the upper hand. This, of course, doesn't apply to certain large, peaceful dogs of my acquaintance who seem to have been born desiring responsibility and persist in shouldering it, even though for generations their ancestors have been removed from their natural environment.

It is possible to teach manners to the most happy-go-lucky

mongrel pup. It may take three years and a superhuman amount of patience to teach him what a collie or a Norwegian elkhound knows from birth. But it can be done. Smokey has excellent manners. He has a certain earnest politeness that endears him even to the owners of sleek thoroughbreds. Perhaps it's because he isn't *slightly* homely, but *very* homely, except for his bright and expressive brown eyes which peer out from under eyebrows of the John L. Lewis or Scotch terrier variety. And he obeys. Reluctantly, sometimes, and hoping against hope that you'll forget what you told him to do, if he takes long enough and stops to scratch several times, but he does obey, finally.

The only trouble is that at ten years of age Smokey has discovered psychosomatic illnesses, and he has several of them. He has now realized there are ways and means of getting special privileges and a lot of flattering attention.

We left him with my mother for a week once. She was worried when we came back. "He's a wonderful dog," she said. "He obeys perfectly and stayed right at my feet all the time, but he's got something terribly wrong with his ear. He'd dig at it, and cry and cry. You should take him to the veterinary."

Dot regarded her dog, who promptly shut his eyes. "There's nothing the matter with him. You should have scolded him."

My mother was shocked. "What? When it hurt him so much?"

"Has he cried about his ear since I came home?" asked Dot. He hadn't. Now, if Smokey is alone with my mother—and he begins his act the moment Dot goes out the door—a stern command to stop that foolishness settles him down. Alone with my father, Smokey develops a kidney complaint that has him looking soulfully at the door every half-hour, and whining sadly to himself. He has a number of other troubles, like insomnia and bad dreams, that can be cured only by allowing him to sleep with someone. And a pillow to put his head on is all he needs to make him happy for a long rainy afternoon.

Of course, at his advanced years, he should have some privileges. But if he had them all, there'd be no living with him. The same with Susan, my mother's dachshund. It's been said that if you don't have a firm hand over a dachshund, you're lost.

Yes, it's entirely possible to have a firm hand over a dog. But it is not possible in the case of cats, as anyone knows who has stood at the door in bare feet, with Arctic winds whistling about his ankles, while the cat, who has awakened him with a piteous howl, hauls back from the night in maidenly hesitation and decides it wasn't *out* she wanted, but a snack. Or, as in the case of Tristan, companionship.

One can order a dog to go out and perform and then call him in again. Or one can tell the dog to go back to bed and be quiet. There is no such course of behavior with a cat. To get any peace from the rest of the night, it is necessary to find out what the cat wants and placate it. We all do it, without shame or apology, because there is something so infinitely flattering and soothing in the purr that tells you you have guessed right this time, and now you may go back to bed, and tomorrow you will be repaid for this effort as only a cat knows how to repay.

A pet sheep manages to get along in much the same fashion. Blackie clatters over the doorstep, bawling, secure in his belief that he'll get fed shredded-wheat biscuits out of self-defense on our part, and even then he can always find something else to shout about. (And we once had a hen who steadfastly refused to go to bed at night in her own quarters because she was sure, in her hennishly obdurate little brain, that if she perched on the chopping block outside the back door in a rainstorm, the person who went out with the dog the last thing at night would bring her in and let her roost on the treadle of the sewing machine in the kitchen.)

Blackie came into the Simpson family one summer when Guy went to shear sheep on Ten Pound, the little rocky island between Criehaven and Matinicus where Cliff Young keeps his flock. Instead of taking pay for shearing, Guy brought home a black lamb. It could be killed in the winter and supply some fresh meat.

Dot had expected something babyish and cuddlesome, but Blackie was far too big for that. He was as wild as anything could possibly be, panting with fear if we approached him, running until his tether snapped taut and pulled him head over heels. His eyes flashed with terror. No one could stand the sight of his panic, and finally he was untied to go loose. He made his way to the lonely western end of the island and there he stayed throughout the mild, hazy days and crisp nights of the fall.

Dot let her goats go loose, late in the fall, and even when they were gone all day they always came back at night. One evening when she went out to close up their quarters, Blackie was with the goats.

After that, he stayed. Of all the goats, he adopted Patty as his own. She was a shy little Toggenburg, clean and dainty, and much smaller than Blackie. When he thought he was hiding behind her, actually he loomed over her, staring at us across her oblivious back with panicky eyes. Patty munched tranquilly on her cud, came to the back door for cookies, put her soft warm muzzle affectionately into our hands. Always Blackie was behind her. Eventually he came into the house when Patty did, although he would step no farther than the door, standing with twitching nostrils and ears while she inspected the kitchen, dresser and table, and all the chairs. He was with Patty in their shed when she gave birth to her kid, and like a sort of lumbering but devoted uncle he used to run up and down the yard with the diminutive Dew-drop. The love and trust he had for Patty was touching, and after she died he turned toward us with the same love and trust, expecting us to take Patty's place.

It's quite a responsibility. One feels rather absurd, telling people the huge black beast is far more timid than a kitten (who is a raging lion in comparison), and please don't try to catch and throw him, he's not used to that sort of thing. A pet sheep is far more of a nuisance than a pet goat could ever think of being. A goat has a certain sophistication, a *savoir-faire* that helps him to rise to any occasion. A sheep is nervous and suspicious, but inclined to be lordly toward the persons he doesn't fear.

Blackie is tremendous, with creamy sides and back, thick sturdy black legs, and a magnificent black head. There are times when he is sure he is no bigger than Tristi. And a sheep who thinks he is a wee bit lambie is a disconcerting addition to any household. The thunder of hooves behind you, the sudden stop as you swing around to look at him, the ferocious snorting through the nostrils, the stiff-legged running and bouncing just because the cat is running, with the forward tilt of the ears, the warning shake of the head which means he is going to rear, to paw the air, to twist and leap, and racket off after the dog, is extremely startling, especially to outsiders. They usually come up from the shore walking backward, in lopsided circles, because Blackie's nose so close to the seat of the pants suggests an unavoidable conclusion. We rush out and trill merrily, "Don't mind him, he won't hurt you!"

"Oh, yeah?" is the excusably cynical answer.

"He just wants a cigarette," we explain. This startles them even more. They wonder if they should light it for him, or if he'll be cross if they don't carry his favorite brand.

He'll snap a cigarette down in one swallow, which is what he learned from the goats. The rattle of paper is as intriguing to him as it is to the dog. It means cigarettes, candy, molasses cookies, saltines, shredded wheat. He will eat anything; baked beans, freshly made salad dressing set out to cool, liquid jello, moldy bread, soup. He will pick pencils out of pockets and pull at the corners of a manuscript on my knee. He is jealous of the dogs. Smokey is afraid of him, but Blackie has yet to realize that Susan, the dachshund, is a dog, so he is somewhat in awe of her.

When frightened by any sound he can't understand, or when he recognizes deep in the woods the baying of hounds, he stands on the doorstep making guttural sounds of alarm, deep in his throat, managing to make it clear that he would like to come into the house with the people, please. When, at regular intervals, he is tied to the flagpole, he bawls at the world in general, all the time eating in a methodical manner, so that the bawl comes out in a throaty vibrato around a mouthful of grass.

Like the Elephant's Child, he has a 'satiable curiosity. He likes being tied to the flagpole because he can see everything that goes on at the house. If we are mowing the lawn or weeding, it's all very chummy and sociable. But let one of us go around to the back yard for a moment and he begins surging back and forth like the tide on the end of his rope. As soon as he is let go for the night he gallops to the back yard, muttering indignantly to himself, to see what we did out there *that* time.

Human hands delight and puzzle him. When my father was working around the house and sat down to fix a tool, Blackie stood pressing against his knees and watching his hands. If he is loose when I'm planting or weeding, he has his black nose close to the spot where I'm working.

The little hen who liked to roost on the sewing-machine treadle at night used to follow Blackie all day and sit on his back when he lay down. Now he has two cowbirds for company. Wherever he grazes, they are picking along beside him.

Once, for a little while, he had the company of his own kind —Hezekiah Horne.

Hezzie was Blackie's baby from the time that Guy brought him to Gay's Island. He was a three-month-old lamb then, and Blackie watched and worried over him until he was full-grown. When Hezzie's ropy wool caught in the raspberry bushes, Blackie raced for the house making sharp alarm-noises, got someone out, and raced for the thicket, looking back to be sure he was being followed. When Hezzie was rescued, Blackie inspected him from stem to stern, like any anxious mother.

That was in the fall. But by spring Hezzie was a handful. No one had performed a slight but highly effective operation on Hezzie in his infancy. Hezzie was a ram, and no mistaking it. His horns had a magnificent backward sweep and a forward curl. He used them on Blackie; he used them on the barn and loosened boards. We would hear the rhythmical pounding of those hot and growing horns even when the door was closed. But he was docile when he was tied and still liked cookies.

If you happened to encounter him when he had broken loose from his stake in the field, and your arms were full of empty boxes you were taking to the shore or fishhouse, there was nothing to do but prove to him that everything was empty, and even then he was likely to give you a good clip just to Show You Who He Was.

By summer it was taking two of us to untangle him when the tie-rope got caught around his foot. Still fond of him, we invested in an electric fence and set up a fine, spacious corral, with plenty of shade, for the two sheep. Hezzie came to it willingly. He always remained short, broad, and competently calm of manner, even when he was going to knock the devil out of somebody. Blackie would not lead on a rope. He cavorted. He balked. I coaxed him with Milky Way bars, and finally we had him inside the fence.

He ran to the middle of the yard and stood there, panting suspiciously. Guy switched on the current. Hezzie approached to smell the wire. We could hear the clicking of the controller, and we waited for Hezzie to flinch. He didn't. He leaned his nose against the wire with evident enjoyment.

Guy said something profane to himself while Dot and I stood

around uttering cooing sounds of comfort to Blackie, like a mother and aunt who have just placed their darling in a boarding school and feel like brutes. Blackie gazed back at us bitterly. We could tell he wasn't ever going to speak to us again.

Guy did something to the controller and found out what was wrong. But when Hezzie did get a shock he merely moved his nose a quarter of an inch, as if a fly had lighted on it, and looked perfectly at peace.

"Come on," I said to Dot, cravenly retreating from Blackie.

At nightfall everybody took a walk over to the corral to give the sheep some cigarettes and prove they had not been forgotten, even if they couldn't stand on the front doorstep and intimidate the dogs and people.

They approached the fence wires gingerly and took their cigarettes. "Good boys," we encouraged. "Nice boys!" Well satisfied, we went back to the house.

"Hey, look!" somebody shouted. We looked back and were dismayed. We were being followed by a bounding ram and a gamboling wether.

The fence needed another wire on it, it seemed. But somehow or other it was never added, and the two were tied to stakes again, within handy reach of their cool shed. They had water, they had grass. They had salt. They had company who provided cigarettes. They never had it so good.

But we knew in the fall that Hezzie was more than we could handle. What we needed was a Good Home for him, with Nice People. We couldn't bear to think of anyone being mean to him. That's the trouble with women, they aren't realists. Hezzie went around inviting people to be mean to him. He dared them.

However, I picked a name off a mailbox on the road near Thomaston, where I had often seen sheep around the house. I wrote and asked if they would like a nice ram, for free. Nobody was more surprised than I was to receive a pleasant letter in reply, saying that he—Nicholas Kariganis—would like very much to have Hezzie.

Dana took Hezzie up the road in his trailer, and Mr. Kariganis seemed so pleased to get Hezzie that we all felt very happy about the whole thing. It was really going to be a nice home for our *enfant terrible*. We were sure of it after we dropped in one day, to see how Hezzie was situated. He was doing very well indeed. He was living with a family of high-bred white-faced Herefords, a champion bull named Caesar, and a champion Red Duroc boar bigger than an old-fashioned kitchen range. He had a lot to live up to, Hezzie did, but he looked confident enough. He had a harem of three, and after the first moment of recognition when he came over to us and took a cigarette— which touched us deeply—he left us to drive his women into a corner and stand before them, lifting his fine head and beautiful horns in a proud, defiant gesture.

Hezzie had found his true place in life at last.

There came a time when Dot and I knew it would be up to us to shear Blackie. We hesitated to ask anyone on the Point to come over and shear one solitary sheep. Besides, we knew what an ordeal it would be, for both the shearer and Blackie. He didn't like being held, and even when Guy had sheared him he never stopped struggling in panic.

The weather grew hotter and hotter. Blackie panted and panted under his thick coat and splendid ruff.

So, equipped appropriately with a pair of barber shears and my mother's best sewing shears—the oil in the wool would be good for them, I assured her—we nervously approached Blackie. He was as nervous about receiving us. Something about the glint of the sunshine on the shears made him apprehensive and he retired at once into his shed and stood in the farthest corner, pointing his black-felt ears at us.

But a short rope fore and aft—one around his neck and tied to the wall, and one around a rear leg—kept him still. Touchy as Blackie is, he becomes as docile as an elderly ewe when he feels a rope holding him. Of course, he's pretty ticklish around his legs, and there was a lot of scuffling for a few minutes, but soon he was secure, and the three of us were panting only slightly.

I began on his ruff and Dot began on his rump. The scissors clicking so near his ears kept him diverted from what was going on at the rear. He was remarkably well-behaved. He rolled his eyes toward the shears like a small boy at the barber's, who is afraid to move his head one fraction of an inch lest he lose an ear. Otherwise he didn't move. He stopped panting. Dot and I kept up a low, casual conversation and Blackie, lulled and confident, began to chew his cud, and the wool fell off in thick rolls, creamy, tawny, warm brown.

"You're a lamb, Blackie darling," I told him unnecessarily. He gave me a sidewise don't-be-silly look and went on chewing his cud.

As time went on, a delicate question arose. How to get Blackie on his back, so as to clip the wool off his stomach? We hated to shatter the calm that lay so pleasantly about us. The only time Blackie had been disturbed was when Soldi came in, to see what was happening to her hero, and insisted on walking under his belly and leaning against his ankles. Then she went outside and climbed up the wall of the building. Some boards in the roof were gone, and through this opening she went to explore Blackie's ceiling of glass cloth and loose boards. This seemed to intrigue him no end. It would have been a betrayal to flip such a good-natured creature over on his back, if we could have done it. But since Blackie was bigger than either of us, we entertained no such high-falutin' ideas.

There seemed to be only one way to get the wool clipped off

his stomach, so Dot lay down on the floor, on her back, and reaching up gingerly, began to snip away with her barber shears.

Blackie looked around curiously, his head cocked and his ears pointing at her. "You look mighty silly down there," his expression said. "But if it pleases you, who am I to interfere?"

"I might as well be lost in the forest primeval," Dot said cautiously. "I've never clipped this part of a sheep before. In fact, I've never clipped any part of a sheep." At any moment Blackie's calm might vanish in an explosive leap, and with it his trust in us.

She cut practically one fiber at a time, murmuring, "I wonder how I'll look with hoof-marks stamped all over my face?" It was a pretty tense time for all of us. When the danger areas were done, and she crawled out from under, she was weak, but triumphant.

We were a good two hours shearing Blackie, and he was scalloped in places, but he was cool, and so were we. The time is coming for another shearing, and I'm really looking forward to the luxurious pleasure of cutting through that thick wool. It's so clean and fine. If I ever discovered a sheep tick I would probably squawk once and drop the shears for good, but Blackie has never had any. He gives between eight and nine pounds of wool a year, and we send it to Harmony to be made into yarn, so that Blackie can have more of an excuse for being around than a lot of people realize. After all, if he can provide socks and mittens, if he can keep the tall grass eaten down in the field and provide us with limitless quantities of manure, he is working his keep, and what more can an animal, two-legged or four-legged, do in this world?

Blackie also provides atmosphere. Tremendous with his broad back and thick strong legs, his long black face and huge ruff, when he runs loose he is as intimidating as any Doberman could be. When he stands on the rocks at the landing, his feet

"I might as well be lost in the forest primeval"

braced, his eyes bright with curiosity (inimical to the stranger),
his nostrils flaring, he can make a timid person very nervous.
Our neighbors on Pleasant Point and in Cushing, and friends
from farther away, know that Blackie is interested in the new-
comer only as a source of cigarettes. He will race up behind a
stranger, or around in front of him to bar his way; if the air is
crisp and he's feeling kinky, he will shake his head and mutter
deep in his throat and give one of his elephantine leaps. The
visitor doesn't know whether he's to be bunted off the rocks
or trampled to death.

Sometimes Dot says wistfully, "I wish we had a hundred
like him." I know she's thinking of the overgrown fields, but
I have a vision of a hundred Blackies; possessive, uninhibited,
lordly, all trying at once to stand on the doorstep and beg for
cigarettes and biscuits. She assures me they wouldn't be like
that, but she can't fool me.

With his fine old wire-hair ancestry, Smokey hated cats.
And he was five years old when the kittens came. But *his*
kittens had no connection with the malevolent creatures he had
chased out of the yard at Criehaven. These small critters, especially the fuzzy yellow one, tottered under his tongue when he
washed them, and purred. He had little use for Soldi, but Tris
was a boy, he could go hunting and do all the things boys do.

The kittens were born in Rich Dunn's house, on Pleasant
Point, the day we finally settled in at Gay's Island. So it seemed
meant for us to take them, when they were five weeks old and
not half so long as their fancy names, Tristan and Isolde. Tris
was as yellow as a buttercup, with wide-set blue eyes, a tail like
a question mark, and a manner as ingratiating as a politician the
week before Election Day. Leave him alone on the grass for a
moment, and Smokey was herding him away from the house
toward the woods. We'd all go out and look behind tufts of
grass for a jolly ball of yellow fur with a purr that was bigger
than he was.

Always merry, always social, Tris has stayed the same. He is a great companion, especially when the mousing isn't very good. An indefatigable traveler, he loves to go on long walks and picnics and is the most extroverted cat I've ever seen. The inevitable cries of admiration that come from strangers when Tris first appears to their view, his great tail swaying gently over his back, drop him in his tracks. He falls on his head first, then on the rest of his spine, and rolls ecstatically as long as the song of praise goes on. For family and a very few close friends, like Charlotte Gray and Lillian Dornan, he has his own love songs, and has been known to drape his length across the shoes of the Adored and impede progress until he has been hoisted over someone's shoulder.

Tris loves to go rowing. He stands in the bow of the skiff, rests his front paws on the edge, and watches the water. Sometimes he mistakes rockweed for solid ground, and jumps onto it, to his ensuing astonishment. He does it often; in some ways he is not very bright. When he is not allowed to go, he wails from the shore and waits at the fishhouse like the famous Faithful Dog until we come back. As the skiff approaches the rocks, we rigidly ignore Tris; his ecstatic rollings on the edge of the wharf, or on a jutting shelf of rock overhanging the channel, do enough to our nerves without our encouraging them by loud salutations.

All this sounds as if Tris were merely a fluffy milksop of an animal, a gigolo type among cats. He is bland and good-natured, wide-eyed and affectionate, tawny and beautiful. All this would be enough, I think. This, and the fact that his fur smells deliciously of green grass and wild flowers. . . . But Tristan is a hunter, too. When his special season is on, he goes out in the morning as a bureaucrat to his office. He needs only a felt hat and a brief case to complete the illusion. He kills his prey in the first attack and does not insist on bringing dead things into the house, dancing strange mazurkas around them, and growling horribly at everyone's feet. Admirably, he does not bring his work home but enjoys his leisure time to the utmost. We enjoy it too.

Tris was always charming. But at first Soldi was undersized and unbeautiful, and nobody liked her. While I, secretly, didn't like her very much, I defended her, and gave her warm milk whenever she began nursing on my blouse collar. When she was old enough she went to the veterinary. Thereby her infancy—prolonged six months beyond the ordinary time—came to an end. We were glad about that; her babyhood had been studded with near disasters such as running into the point of the sickle, and getting caught on dead branches and being scared into convulsions.

Of course, it was a hectic time for us when Soldi was worrying about her stitches. She was determined to break them, and we were vastly surprised when she stayed sewed up and re-covered intact. In less than a month after that we realized we had a surprising little cat, on her way to being beautiful, and fey, and willfully determined.

Soldi was a money cat, which means she had three colors—black, yellow, and white. Only females can be three-colored cats—except in the case of about one male in a thousand. Besides her three colors she had lovely black stripes, bracelets, enchanting tufts of smoky hair in her ears, and a fluffy tail.

She began her career by charming everybody in the family who had disliked her. She knew words; it seemed that she had known them all the time, but she shrugged at showing off. Whereas the amiable Tristi, who strolls through life smiling faintly to himself and waving his tail on high, ran from a room full of people, Soldi surveyed the fine assortment of laps, picked out the one that looked best, and climbed aboard. She wound under Smokey's chin; she deliberately wooed my father, who even offered to swap his beloved Alec for her. *Never underestimate the power of a woman.* Soldi was the eternal feminine, with forever-immaculate white gloves and ruffles under her

chin. She walked through a room like a small girl tossing back
her curls and delightfully conscious of her satin sash and the
Hamburg edging on her panties. Also, like the same small girl,
when she wanted to get into a room where the door was closed,
she was *going* to get into that room. Tris gave up gracefully
after a few attempts. Soldi started with a ladylike scratching
and ended—no, she never stopped until the door was opened to
her—by working up to a fine and nerve-shattering series of
onslaughts at the doorknob. When the door was opened she
immediately subdued the fire in her eye, straightened up her
ears, and Made An Entrance.

Nobody ever spanked Soldi. Nobody ever tried to teach
her anything. She gave the impression that she had forgotten
more than any of us had ever known. In the two households
where she spent her time—at Gay's Island from March until
Christmas, and in Quincy, Massachusetts, with my family for
the winter—where Tris and Alec have been punished for rum-
maging in cupboards and eating the centers out of fresh pump-
kin pies, Soldi walked her serene way.

On Gay's Island she sometimes disappeared for three days
at a time. When she came home, she refused to talk. Tris always
came home in a good humor, and never repelled our advances,
but Soldi was a great one for shrugging off caresses. Giving us
a cold glance, she would fling herself down under the stove and
ostentatiously turn her back on us. Getting caught up on her
sleep at last, she was ready for sociability; and when Soldi felt
sociable there was no avoiding it. She adored the clatter of the
typewriters, and when a book was in the making Soldi was always sitting on the table to help, moving from one pile of paper
to another, until she finally went to sleep curled up against one
of the typewriters.

Whoever she chose to receive her affection was inevitably
flattered. Even non-cat-lovers fell under her spell. When she
walked, it was with fastidious grace. When she cuddled with
anyone who lay down to read, she was all purrs and fragrant

fur. Her face stayed always a kitten's face, but she had the learned and regal simplicity of a Marie Antoinette.

Soldi left us one bleak and foggy day, with a suddenness that still shocks us whenever we think about it (which isn't any oftener than we can help). We have never understood what the sudden sickness could have been. We only knew that it came without our knowing it, and was gone—taking Soldi— when we had just realized that she wasn't feeling right.

We spent a wretched spring after that. We tried to harden ourselves against Tristi, feeling that the same thing could happen again and we must be ready for it. But Tris defeated us; overnight, in the seemingly mystic fashion that makes people attribute extraordinary powers to a cat, he adopted little ways which had been particularly Soldi's. We had no armor against him. And besides, he was lonesome too.

Alec was born in the same litter, and because he spends his summers with us, he's a Gay's Islander too. He's a lean, tall, short-haired yellow cat, with a pawky sense of humor and an ingenuous, innocent face. He sits up to beg for doughnuts as if he were a little dog.

The mother of these cats was a small gray cat, and the father, so I'm told, a yellow Persian who went wild. I don't know whether the offspring get their mild, wide-eyed faces and capacity for affection from Mom or Pop, but I do know that they make themselves felt in a household, and manage to stand on equal footing with the family dogs.

Alec is not indiscriminate in his loving, and never purrs at anyone except his family unless they happen to be using the telephone, for which he has a deep passion that perhaps Freud could explain. He has large strong feet, and his canines make him look like a saber-toothed tiger, but rather than fight he will allow himself to be cornered, screeching, in a tree by a tomcat less than half his size. However, he has been known to leap out from behind a door, growling, at the man who reads the meters. Like Patience on a monument, he will sit with closed eyes while Susan, the small red dachshund, chews off his whiskers, and the family is continually explaining to callers that Alec is not a curiosity, that ordinarily his whiskers would be *very* long, only Susan eats them. And to prove it, Susan dashes at Alec, wagging her impudent stern, and has a nourishing snack of whisker.

When Alec arrives at the island, in his special box which my father made for him, he wanders around in a dream for several days, looking at the water, which he loves, and catching mice in a desultory fashion; he brings them to the house to show my mother and then lets them go. He puts on a great act wherein he is utterly terrified by Tris. The mere sight of Tris sets off menacing growls that turn into uncatlike shrieks. Bland and curious, Tris pursues him with the attitude of the amiable little boy who used to chase my brother, "I likes to hear him holler!" After a sufficient display of anguished suspicion Alec drops the pose. He and Tris become reacquainted and get very busy with their summer projects.

Susan is a dachshund, which should explain everything. She is small enough to walk under Smokey's belly with ease and thinks nothing of shouldering him away from his dish, baring her teeth, and finishing his supper in one gulp before Retribution catches up with her. She takes mice from the cats and runs across the lawn eating them while my mother hurls anathema at her, "Pig! Pig!" This used to reduce Susan to a gratifying state of shame, but now she's getting hardened to it, and we'll have to find a new word. She is satin-smooth, sleek as a seal from the tip of her small eager nose to her tail. She is the color of ripe horse chestnuts and as delightful to the touch. She has an abiding suspicion of strange men and wouldn't hesitate to attack an intruder; at such a time I think she would be convinced she was as big as Blackie. She adores being made much of by her friends, and gives an impersonation of a useless lap dog made only to be cuddled; but she can outrun Smokey and her little body is solid with smooth muscle.

Smokey greets Susan each June with mingled pleasure and disgust. She's all right to run with, but she gets so darn much attention. They carry on a quiet but very persistent campaign to keep each other out of the limelight. When Smokey had two visits to the hospital to have his mouth fixed, and everyone babied him and spoon-fed him and worried about him, Susan spent hours huddled under a chair, her face in the corner and her rear turned eloquently toward the room, as indicative of the way she felt about all this foolishness. During the time when he was in the hospital, she blossomed. She sparkled. She was utterly charming. When he came home she bared her teeth at him and retired to her sulking corner.

Mandy joined the colony recently. She came from Pleasant Point Post Office, and no doubt that is why she is so uninhibited about meeting the public. My mother wanted a nice, friendly little female, since Alec was so distant at times. She was not prepared for the rangy gray cat who leaped out of the basket, propelled by the longest hind legs this side of a kangaroo.

"I thought she was going to be *dainty!*" my mother wailed. She'd had a dainty name picked out: Stephanie. One week of the Girl from the Post Office (not yet six months old and as tall as the adult cats) and the name Stephanie was tossed out, and Amanda was in. It's been Mandy ever since.

Many a long-legged, overgrown, and plain-colored girl would envy Mandy's gift for convincing people that she is really still a kitten and a rather sweet one. Aside from her aerial habits—(she never crosses a room by the floor if she can go from chair back to chair back and take a short cut around over the mantel)—and her unladylike proclivities—(she sits in my father's lap and drinks beer from his glass, and raids unemptied ash trays for cigarette butts, which she carries around the house in her mouth, like Carmen)—aside from all this she is perfectly charming. She has no strange moods. There's no Oriental mystery about Mandy. She is always meltingly affectionate, always conversational, always a pest.

Theoretically, since she was adopted into my mother's family, she is Alec's sister, but Alec dislikes her with an admirable consistency. It is Tristan who loves her, who rouses himself sleepily to wash her face for her when she bunts him awake, who makes no objection when she elbows him out of his dish, who condescends to play with her when she chirrups an invitation to jujitsu or Let's Take All the Glass Balls off the Christmas Tree. The relationship between them is rather touching. It almost seems as if Tris remembers Soldi, to whom he was always a kind and loving brother even when she was in her most difficult moods.

To many persons who are not fortunate enough to be acquainted with a cat, the animal represents an unknown quantity, a discomforting presence, or a cold and indifferent character, rather stupid, who cares only for food. And there are the poetical souls who go into long dissertations about the mystery in a cat's eyes, their supernatural history, Egyptian cat worship, and so forth. Those are all pretty thoughts. But confronted by Tristan's honest, unflagging, sturdy affection, and Mandy's Beatrice Lillie clowning, and Alec's unreasoning passion for the telephone, I forget all about mystery. There's nothing mysterious about them. They are as understandable and as capable of love as dogs. They are not stupid, but stubborn, and they are admirably self-contained. (Whitman must have been thinking of cats, I've decided.)

Blackie, Smokey, and Tristi, who live at Gay's Island most of the time, and aren't summer visitors, leaven the occasional spells of loneliness with their comedy, their demands, their moments of unconscious beauty. (Even Smokey has such moments.) The lawns and the fields have known their passage; in the woods they have met foxes and chipmunks and woodchucks; and they have become as much a part of Gay's Island as the very trees themselves.

CHAPTER EIGHT

ROD AND GUN CLUB

It was on Gay's Island and on Pleasant Point that I first saw deer outside of a zoo. Perhaps I'm used to the other animals now, but I'll never take the sight of a deer for granted. To see a doe poised in the ruddy sunset light against a leafy green bank of alders, gazing back at me in one long moment of curiosity and astonishment before she disappears in a flowing leap that leaves only a faint trembling among the branches—this will always stop my breath; or to see a doe and her twin fawns feeding on a hillside in the opalescent mists of an early May morning; to see a buck run across the road, crowned with a kingly spread of antlers and moving in long effortless leaps—I'll never be casual about these things. Neither will Dot. Religiously she renews' her hunting license each year and stocks up on shotgun shells and announces that she's going to have a deer. There's something so rich-sounding about the word "venison." And then she gets as dewy-eyed as I do when she sees one.

Victor Whittier, who in summer lives across the cove from us, had a charming experience when he was clamming in Gay Cove. He was far out on the sand flats when four little fawns appeared at the edge of the sun-dappled spruce woods. He remained perfectly still while they played along the shore, leaping and chasing each other in complete unconsciousness of him.

Toward these infants—seen and unseen—and their parents, we feel a protective responsibility. We think of them with fondness, even though they are deep in Mr. Thompson's woods. For all the year except the deer season, they are safe, since in this region there is no illicit gunning.

When we first lived here, strangers came hunting; they had been coming to Gay's Island for years to hunt. But gradually they stopped coming, now that someone was living in the house. We didn't do anything to stop them. There is a peculiar system of ethics involved. As long as people conduct themselves decently, and show consideration for our privacy, we don't call them trespassers, even if they are strangers. What all of us hate—on Pleasant Point and on Gay's Island—are the picnickers when they depart. They saunter by the house on residents' driveways without a by-your-leave. (And they *will* do it, incredible as it seems.) The same type build fires without mentioning it to the owners of the woods and fields that will go up in flames if the campfire gets out of control, or is left burning by the picnickers when they depart. They saunter by the house on Gay's Island and look in the windows, they pick the raspberries that we've been saving along the path, light on the blueberry patches like a flock of gulls, and plunge their questionable water jars into the well without permission.

These are not the local people. They have no connection with the sardine fishermen who row ashore sometimes and ask for water; or the youthful clamdiggers who come to the house for a drink; or the couple from up on the Cushing road who ask at the door if we mind their crossing the lawn to get to Clam Cove; or the Pleasant Point men who still ask, after five years, if they can ground out their boats on the flat rocks down beyond the Neck, to paint and repair them.

We use their wharves and floats and sometimes are forced to park a guest's car on their properties for an hour or so. Always we ask, always we try to repay the favor with another one. Consideration works both ways, and there is a fine neighborly feeling at Pleasant Point which will be eternally green because it is nourished with good manners.

Our neighbors arrive on Gay's Island, come the first of November, in small regiments; they scatter and deploy, working out a carefully conceived strategy, bound to net them the big buck someone saw on the shore a few days ago . . . and then they go home again, in good-humored frustration.

But young Dana Herrick, who is married to Dot's youngest sister Bette, lived up in the country beyond Camden before his family came to Pleasant Point to become lobstermen. Dana is lean and long-legged and woods-wise. He knows the way of deer as if he were part deer himself.

Dana and Bette went hunting last fall, leaving year-old Loren with us. Bette is a long-stemmed blond, an ex-Wave. She has wide blue eyes that can look attractively amazed, and she looks elegant even in dungarees, boots, and a raincoat. It was raining that November day when they went tramping off into the woods, Dana with his rifle, Bette carrying Dot's small .22. It was strictly for atmosphere, since a single-shot .22 rifle is not the accepted weapon for deer-hunting, and besides, nobody expected Bette to be able to take straight aim.

They were back in a few hours, trembly with excitement. Dana had stationed Bette in a certain spot, told her not to move, and had gone off to see if he could drive out a deer. But Bette was the one who saw a deer, about a hundred yards away on the opposite side of the clearing. Without thinking she raised the little rifle and fired. The one shot brought the deer down, and Dana came out of the woods shouting.

They were a long way into the woods, and by the time the deer had been gutted and they had dragged it as far as the old Gay House, they were worn out. Dana is high-strung—the ulcer type—and he was so excited that he was stammering when they came into the kitchen. They'd have something to eat and then take the wheelbarrow far up on the island to the Gay House.

We had dinner ready, but we were the only ones who ate. Dana was too wrought-up to eat. He was divided between a huge and exhilarating pride in Bette and a determination to get a deer for himself as soon as possible. Bette sat very still, not eating anything. Her eyes were glistening, as if they were ready to brim over. Suddenly her lower lip trembled.

"I wish I hadn't done it," she said. "I'll never forget how it looked at me. . . . The minute I did it, I wished I hadn't. I kept thinking about Bambi and the Yearling."

It was a doe, and we kept assuring her it wouldn't have left any helpless young at this time of year, but I was proud of Bette both for her good aim and for the fact that she admitted regret. I couldn't have fired at all. But Bette, who is the youngest girl in a family of nine, has had to take a lot of the kidding that older brothers and sisters give out with such abundant generosity, and sometimes I think she felt inadequate and childish. Though why anyone with flaxen hair, sea-blue eyes, beautiful teeth and beautiful figure, superlative ankles, and an Honorable Discharge from the Waves, should feel inadequate, I don't know.

But now Bette had done something none of her sisters and brothers had done. She would be able to give them jars of deer mincemeat and serve them venison steaks. Never mind if they all said, "Of course it was just *luck*—just the luckiest shot in the world!" She had done it.

The next day all of Pleasant Point, including some of the disappointed hunters, went over to Flea Island to view the doe. Bette was still suffering acute regret, and the neighbors' praise rubbed salt into the wound. But by the time she gave me a quart of deer mincemeat to give to my parents and calculated the saving in the winter's food bill the canned deermeat would make, she was not quite so sad.

When we first lived on the island, people came here often to hunt, but we had been prepared for that. Roy Vose, of Stone's Point, was one of the regulars, and when he went by on a crisp autumn morning, or on snowshoes through a light, gentle fall of snow, his shotgun under his arm and his well-bred hounds showing remarkable dignity in ignoring Smokey, the sheep, and the cats, we enjoyed the sight of him immensely. We still do. It's like an animated magazine cover; it's like things we read about. And the fox has a fifty-fifty chance.

One warm October day a group of perfectly strange men arrived, five or six of them, with a dog. I say "perfectly strange," and mean it. With their nondescript clothes, knee boots, shotguns, and long haircuts (their hair scraped against the collars of their shirts) they needed only beards to look as if they belonged to the clan of Devil Anse Hatfield. They arrived without warning; they were simply *there*, tramping up over our lawn without a word, taking up positions on the hillside and the shore. No matter what window we looked out of, these characters of the nether world and their hound of hell were sure to be in sight.

We were a houseful of women at the time, except for two very little boys; Guy had gone back out to Criehaven when Dot's brothers came back from the Service and they were bunking together in Guy's house out there, keeping bachelor hall in blissful freedom from women. Bette was staying with us—being courted by Dana; my sister-in-law, Mary Ogilvie, and her small sons Peter and Douglas, aged three and four, were staying with us while my brother Gordon house-hunted in Boston.

When the mysterious Mountain Jims appeared, we kept the animals in the house and the boys close to the door, and wondered if we were the innocent victims of some sort of vendetta. It's on occasions of this sort, or when unidentified fishermen arrive at dusk and stay tied up at our wharf for the evening cozily occupied with a bottle, that we wish Smokey was reinforced by some large type of dog—shepherd, great Dane, or boxer.

When the hunters tramped by the door at the end of their first day's hunting (if that's what they were doing, just standing around like that), we went out and smiled pleasantly at them. After all, they were tramping around on our thirty-three acres, and not Mr. Thompson's unoccupied lands. We were used to greeting and being greeted. Most people who wandered past the house stopped and introduced themselves, by way of being courteous.

"Good evening!" we chimed graciously, and they stared at us suspiciously from under their eyebrows and their hatbrims. Maybe they'd been taught never to speak to strange women; can't tell what sort of scrapes one might get into, that way. But the dog hadn't. He wagged his tail. When one of us, rather timidly, spoke a kind word in his direction, someone called him back in a sort of rusty growl, as if his vocal apparatus weren't used often. Maybe they didn't even talk to each other, we thought, and were relieved when at last they'd rowed across the Gut.

That was the beginning of five days of the same. They stood around, cradling their rifles. They prowled stealthily over the rocks. Each day their stubbly beards were longer. We tried to imagine them living domestic lives, with wives and children, but for some reason were only able to conjure up pictures of caves; our hunters looked uncomfortable in clothes, as if they should have been wearing skins.

They never spoke. They didn't shoot anything, as far as we know. They didn't allow their dog ever to speak to us. Finally they didn't come any more. We asked about them over on the Point. Nobody knew who they were, nobody had ever seen them before. They haven't been seen since. Sometimes I wonder if they were some sort of manifestation. But I think they should be classed as wild life. Definitely.

Now that we're used to sharing Gay's Island with another race, so to speak, we're rather proud of our wild life here. I realize it doesn't sound as wild as it might; no mountain lions. The Canada lynx was an exceptional visitor. The bald eagle that flew past our windows the other day—flying low because of a storm—thrilled us to the marrow, but it was nothing out of the ordinary to the folks on the Point. A great many people are used to deer in the back yard, and moose tramping through, and foxes, and all the rest of it. But it's quite wild enough for us, savage enough to give a spice to life, and lend us a little flare of importance when we talk to city-dwellers. (Or outer-island dwellers who see only seals for wild life!)

Even the little white-bellied field mice that have their complicated housing projects scattered through the fields, and furnish unlimited business for Tristan, add their own atmosphere.

"What a lonely place it must be!" the uninitiated say. But we are never alone.

We don't very often take long walks into the deep unexplored woods at the southern end of the island, where the deer and the fox have their shelter. However, there are times when we are a little ashamed of that fact. When Susan Davis, whose fine strong face has had more than seventy years to add character to it, came onto the island to go berrying, she tramped miles in an afternoon, visiting all the cuttings she knew, and exploring strange ones.

Stopping in for a drink of water, she said heartily, "My lands, I never worry long's I've got Sandy with me." Sandy, staying with her while his family was away, squired her around the island as if his gay chow tail were the plume of a cavalier. But we admired her courage just the same. What would she do if Sandy attacked a moose? we asked her.

Mrs. Davis laughed. "I'm not looking for that to happen right off," she said comfortably. "Anyway, I got me a lot of Highland cranberries. I'm partial to 'em."

She went off down to the shore, Sandy running importantly ahead, climbed into a skiff, and rowed herself home.

"Maybe we're scared of the woods because we've got the wrong idea," I suggested to Dot. "She's not looking for anything to happen right off. . . . And we are. We're always sure we're going to run into something."

With an admirable shift of the subject, Dot saved face by saying casually, "I'm not much on long walks, anyway."

Mrs. Jim Seavey also puts us to shame occasionally. We came across the Neck one gray, blustery day last fall to find her at the fishhouse. "I was just going to borrow a skiff!" she called to us. "I came on by the Stepping Stones at low tide this morning and I've been looking for cranberries ever since!"

Olive Seavey is a small woman, also in the direction of seventy, and she didn't even have Sandy with her. We gawked, I'm afraid.

"Weren't you *nervous?*"

"What for?" She laughed because she had twigs in her hair where she'd pushed through the underbrush.

We rowed her across and left her. We didn't have much to say. On the way back I said gloomily, "I should think after that you'd at least be willing to walk up to the Old House once in a while. It's out in the open, anyway."

Dot gazed at me earnestly, a hard thing to do in an eleven-foot skiff bobbing along in forty-mile-per-hour gusts. "I can't," she said. "I keep thinking something's going to happen. Indians coming out of the woods. . . . It must be inherited memory." She was off again, having a safe subject far removed from uncomfortable fact. "In another incarnation," she went

on with an intense and scientific frown, "I must have been cap-
tured by the Indians, because every time I go near the Old
House I feel very uncomfortable and I want to go right home
again. I can't really explain it. . . ."

"At least," I said with chilly dignity, "what *I'm* afraid of is
a real flesh-and-blood moose, and not some imaginary Indians."

"Then you *admit* you're afraid," she pounced on me. We
have not discussed the subject since.

But even close to the house there are still things to be discovered in the immense and lively world that exists alongside
our humdrum one. Down by the fishhouse one day we saw
a strange little animal run out from under the wharf and over
the rocks. When we'd cornered him where we could look at
him we were charmed by his big eyes and tiny face, his soft
cocoa-brown fur and white stomach, the slimness and length of
him.

"A weasel," someone told us. "Been living around here for
years. Mink on the island, too. Why don't you catch ye some
and start a mink farm?" Vastly amused laughter followed this,
but we were still serious.

"A weasel?" one of us said. "I didn't know they were as
pretty as that."

The answer was a grunt. "Can call 'em pretty if you want to,
I suppose, but they're dangerous little devils if you've got
poultry. In the winter they're ermine."

It was all we needed. The cup was brimming, the picture was
complete. We have ermine on our island. It sounds so rich,
so fantastic, so utterly foreign to all we'd ever known before
we heard of Gay's Island. And yet as I look out at the snow,
and the blue shadows on it almost as blue as the sky, I think of
the cocoa-brown fur turned white for winter, of the swift slim
little beast running almost unseen over the snow. Does Blackie
see it sometimes, and flick his black ears forward in a question?

Has Tristan ever met it while he is on his long walks? He has seen many things of which we can never know.

Yes, we have ermine on our island. We have named it Ermintrude.

CHAPTER NINE

ISLAND EXISTENCE CAN BE COMPLICATED

The food situation when we first came to Gay's Island was impossibly complicated, not only by the war, but by the locality. Not having a car, we realized that our supplies would have to come from Port Clyde, some three miles across the river. We could go over and do our shopping in Guy's boat. And as long as the weather remained fair, we enjoyed the trips to Port Clyde. It was relaxing to get away from the house and watch the shores of Gay's Island turn smoky-blue with distance, and the shores of Port Clyde come clear and sharp. It was food for the soul to get into the boat and feel the rush of the sea along her sides and smell the salty air (somewhat mixed with oil and lobster bait) and to watch the contours of the islands change as we moved over the stretch of sheltered blue water.

After knowing only Criehaven and Matinicus for Maine islands, where the ocean pounds ceaselessly, the tranquillity of the river mouth was at once soothing and enchanting. In Kenneth Roberts's book *Trending Into Maine*, we'd read of the Englishman, Captain Waymouth, who discovered and named the St. George River; we had been touched by the scribe's description of "this goodly and pleasant land." We never crossed to Port Clyde without speculating on how Gay's Island, Pleasant Point, and the riverbanks farther up, had appeared without houses, camps, wharves, and powerboats; with no gaily painted buoys to dance on the water when the wind ruffled it.

We enjoyed the sight of the woodland growing blue and thick on the slopes. We compared the trip with all the times we had gone from Criehaven to Matinicus to buy groceries. Out there, peaceful as the water may be at times, there is always a long lifting swell when you round Ten Pound; and if it's a windy day, the seas off Ten Pound lift the boat up and up, and then let it down so far that all you can see for a moment are the sleek green-glass-sided waves as you pass through their valleys.

This high rocky island of Ten Pound, with the black sheep to watch your progress; Pudd'n Island, a tall crag made barren by the gulls; the Hogshead, a big round ledge dangerous in rough weather; and off in the distance, Matinicus Rock Light and Wooden Ball Island; and miles of clean-cut bare horizon all around . . . that was what you saw when you went from Criehaven to Matinicus for food.

But here we saw instead the Georges Islands strung out for miles toward the open water, with Monhegan's high blue bluff at the outermost reach; we could look up the St. George River toward Stone's Point and Maplejuice Cove, which has been called by that delectable name for hundreds of years; we could see a little stretch of open water if we looked south past Caldwell, and when we came into Port Clyde we could see Hooper's Island and the lighthouse on Marshall's Point. We learned that there were shoals and ledges to watch for, as between Criehaven and Matinicus. But always, during that summer, the trip was an easy and pleasant one.

At Port Clyde we tied up at Fores Hupper's wharf, and tried not to stare too obviously at the people waiting for the Monhegan boat, though some of them were indescribably fascinat-

ing. They found us fascinating too, and stared at us with far
less discretion. We must have been interesting; Guy with his
whiskers, exchanging picturesque and backhanded compli-
ments with acquaintances; Dot, brown and stocky and compact
in her dungarees, her hair windblown; my mother tanned to a
gypsy color and looking like one with a kerchief tied around
her head. I, worn very thin by heat and work, darkly tanned,
and no doubt looking like a caricature of my former self, a
string bean with dark glasses and a long nose, dressed in snug
and faded dungarees and a jersey.

The summer people bound for Monhegan must have been
puzzled as to our various occupations. Guy's boat needed paint
and the rest of us looked as if we needed renovations too; but
we swarmed over the wharf without self-consciousness, not
appearing as "woodsy" as we might have. And when we went
into Hap Wilson's store we ordered with the prodigality of
spendthrifts; cases of everything that was point-free, dozens
of boxes of mixes; fresh fruit and vegetables in huge quantities;
puddings, jellies, cookies, crackers, candy. By mathematics be-
forehand we had figured out from the assembled ration books
how we could do best in cheese, meat of some sort, and mar-
garine. . . . We had decided to get a fifty- or sixty-dollar order
at one time that would take care of us for weeks, with frequent
replenishings of the fresh food whenever one of us got a chance
to ride up to the store in Cushing. Then Hap Wilson, who
always waited on us with the air of a genial host (even in the
thin times that came later, when we were far from lavish),
would load everything into his station wagon and drive it down
to the wharf for us. If the Monhegan crowd hadn't gone yet,
they looked at us with renewed interest, and probably hunger,
while the boxes and cases went down over the side of the wharf
into the boat.

The standard end of the shopping trip, the crowning glory,
was the ice cream. We came away from the wharf in a burst

of speed, every one of us equipped with a double-decker cone, and sailed homeward secure in the knowledge that now we had something to eat for the next month. Of course, there was always the unloading at that unplanked wharf at Gay's Island, and the trips with the wheelbarrow, and the stowing away in the Lazaret and the cold cellar, but there was also the prospect of a fairly interesting supper that night.

We took our milk from Clarence Wales, in Cushing—he left our every-other-day quart at the Youngs'; we found we could get eggs down the harbor, in Mr. Dunn's little store. What with our justly famous Gay's Island clams, we were doing all right. We had found a system, we believed. All was arranged, all was safe.

In the fall Dot's sister Madelyn came back for the promised visit, which turned out to be a continuation of her earlier efforts. She *worked*. Well, we all worked. But Dot and I, after my mother left, had fallen into a jaded state where we were unmoved by the dingily active pattern of the sitting-room wallpaper. (Lamplight on it made it fairly crawl, so one had the impression of sitting in the midst of an anthill.) We could sit in the kitchen in the evenings. At least that was all painted. And we were willing to let the ell chamber go indefinitely. Once we used to make our perilous way up the winding stairs and at least *look* at the sea of junk; now we never opened the door at the foot.

But Madelyn was not jaded. She had been visiting, and her own little apartment didn't contain much in the way of housework. Carried on by the momentum of her personality, we were mesmerized into tackling the ell chamber. It was like digging into a long-forgotten tomb, only not half so fascinating. At one time the tenants had inexplicably lugged their garbage up there. (All but those hundreds of cans that hid in the tall grass.) We uncovered boxes and boxes of other empty cans, and coffee grounds, and indeterminate objects that might have

been banana skins at one time, and things that looked like dried
scalps but probably weren't.

All the magazine articles about fixing over old houses tell
how the authors discovered in the attics priceless things like old
butterfly hinges (we didn't even find an old butterfly, but
hundreds of old spiders and horseflies), Wedgwood soup
tureens, a sugar bowl made by Paul Revere, Sandwich-glass
sauce dishes, Limoges chamber pots, dropleaf tables which re-
vealed rare mahogany and the name of Sheraton under their
scaly white paint. Well, in the open chamber at Tide's Way we
found by way of precious discovery two tubs of trawl, a pair of
dory oars, four life belts (children's size, and they get trotted
out for all the junior visitors, who enjoy wearing "life pre-
savers"). We found a plain white Ironstone platter, which
wasn't much for looks but was undeniably Ironstone, and
which Tristan smashed into bits at three o'clock one morning,
along with two dozen eggs, when he endeavored to stand on
the edge of the platter and open a cupboard door. And we
found a soup tureen, too; cracked and extremely ordinary. We
found innumerable glass jars whose dubious contents had dried
unpleasantly; and more garbage. The hand-hewn beams were
draped thickly in cobwebs, and small things scurried rapidly
over all. We took out the window and hurled everything un-
usable into the grass.

Spiders being what Dot hates most, she made a cowardly
retreat before long, and entertained Brad; Madelyn, her sunny
curls done up in a kerchief, swept away cobwebs and together
we pawed over the less repulsive part of the collection.

Madelyn could even be enthusiastic about the things that
looked like scalps. "Perhaps they *are* scalps," she said solemnly.
"Did you say the Indians used to be around here?"

"Not since this house was built," I told her, and she looked
disappointed. "Nothing I'd like better than a good Indian

fight," she said, which didn't surprise me, since Madelyn can milk a cow and wouldn't dream of being scared.

Dot vindicated herself by scrubbing and painting the back stairs, with white risers and dark red treads to match the dark red linoleum presented to the white and aqua kitchen by my mother. For a long time we kept the door open, since the neat flight of curving steps presented such a satisfying sight after the paper in the sitting room, but then the usual accumulation of paint cans, turpentine bottles, tools, and boxes of nails began to gather, and tempted little Brad too much, while disturbing our artistic sense. So we shut the door. Several times a year, however, we clean the steps and leave the door open for a while. . . . The ell chamber will someday be made into a pleasant bedroom and study—when we can afford it; meanwhile, it's a good place to store winter clothes, jars for canning, tools, and the cats. In summer the cats sleep up there, which prevents them from crawling into bed with the guests or landing with precipitate devotion and B-29 purrs on the chests of their respective owners.

I like to remember that first fall on Gay's Island, when the pressure of work was lifted (because it took money to paper and paint and we were rather broke). Madelyn stayed with us well into November; she is the sort of person whose visits are never long enough. We shared her anxiety about big Brad, over in Europe, shared her happiness whenever a letter came, and we were used to the sight of Madelyn by lamplight at the kitchen table writing her nightly letter to her husband. Guy was gone from the island a great deal of the time, and we three, with young Brad, carried on a slightly giddy existence. We could be as funny as we wanted to be; each one of us appreciated highly the others' jokes. With the baby bathed and in bed, we sat down to suppers of steamed clams and some sort of confection Madelyn had concocted. We spent the evenings talking and talking. The freshness of Madelyn's viewpoint, her often unconscious wit, and her general sunniness, were a revelation to me, who had known her as a shy and prim youngster, often misunderstood and called "stuck-up."

As for little Brad—who appears in print as Jamie in *The Ebbing Tide*—he was our mascot. Not quite two, but with a doggedness quite adult in its concentrated energies, Brad kept us all busy. He began each day by trotting out to the kitchen in his Dr. Dentons, ignoring all greetings; his fair hair standing up in a fluff, his blue eyes narrowed, and his lower lip protruding, he turned the cats' dishes upside down. If diverted from this—and he usually was—he attempted it again at intervals all through the day. His own day was not in any sense a success until he had done it.

What this was a symbol of, I don't know. But his persistence was rather admirable. He wore no expression of malice, but instead he was brooding and stern, like a Calvinist reformer. Having his bath at night before the open oven, his baby skin moist and velvety in the lamplight, he was still the baby. But in the mornings one had a formidable picture of Brad as a man, upsetting idols and smashing slave blocks, and maybe even re-forming politics.

Out on the clam flats he staggered behind me, pulling his booted feet stubbornly out of the clinging mud, his face getting redder and his lower lip getting more eloquent, until at last he burst out in a roar of rage that stopped me in my hitherto-oblivious tracks. Back in the house, he shucked clams, armed with a dull old table knife and a pie plate. He worked on his half-dozen clams until he had them in the pie plate, and could call Soldi to the feast. Soldi was his favorite kitten; he claimed that the less-inhibited Tris bit him frequently, though neither cat ever grew any front teeth of any sort, canines or incisors, after they lost their baby teeth. He loved Soldi when he could give her clams, but there were times when he followed her around looking for a chance to sit on her, wearing all the while the expression of a scientist planning out an atom-smasher.

Brad is going to be a lobster fisherman. His mother found it out on Gay's Island, when her baby boy, who didn't remember his fisherman father, and had been living in a city apartment since he was born, drummed hysterically on the window at the sight of a boat in the cove. He turned almost with a shrug from conventional toys and was happy with a hammer. Harmless, too, when Soldi was removed to a safe place. A can of water, an old paint brush, and some buoys from the fishhouse kept him busy for hours.

He "painted" buoys with uncanny skillfulness, holding them just so and drawing the brush carefully down the sides as he had seen Guy do. To be in the fishhouse was his delight. When he had to stay in the house he rigged himself a dory, a cardboard carton just big enough for him to sit in, with laths for oars. He was looking for "lo'sters."

It was fall, and the Port Clyde trip for groceries was taken for granted. So was the water between us and Port Clyde. When there was a delightful little breeze to make the boat bounce, we welcomed it. It was just enough to relieve the monotony. It would be the same, no doubt, from one year's end to the other, a pleasant sail for all concerned, with Hap Wilson to greet us in his well-stocked store. (Hap is a cousin of Dot's stepfather, Fred Wilson, so he was more or less of a tie with familiar things. But in his own right he is one of the nicest persons I know.) Then when we returned home we would zoom up the harbor to our own wharf, and nonchalantly stroll to the house where we would sit down in the pleasantly warm kitchen, for a cup of coffee to stay our stomachs until suppertime.

A charming arrangement all around. Until Madelyn and I went with Guy one bright blue October day, while Dot stayed home with little Brad. The water was nicely choppy, blue-green flecked with curling white. The islands were brilliantly clear upon the sea and the air pure and cold. Madelyn and I rode up on the bow and enjoyed an occasional flick of spray in our faces.

We were leisurely about assembling the order. The whole thing was more or less a delightful social occasion, a visit with Hap and his father combined agreeably with business. Then Guy met Gene Crouse, whom he'd known when he fished from the Wooden Ball out near Criehaven, and exchanged the time of day with old Fores Hupper. By the time we were ready to start, the wind had smartened up considerably. But after some of the trips we'd made from Matinicus to Criehaven in fishing boats, we weren't worried. When I was a teen-ager I thought no trip was complete if I didn't get soaked with spray and thrown around the cockpit like some unfortunate contender for Joe Louis's title.

It was fine, going out of the harbor and heading toward Caldwell. It was just the way we wanted it to be. It wasn't until we left the lee of high Caldwell and started across to Gay's Island that I began to lose my enthusiasm. It seems—we found out later—that when the tide is running out fast between Caldwell and Gay's Island, and the wind is southwesterly, one runs into a short but exceedingly nasty stretch of sea. It may have been short, but I thought it was going to take us a week to get out of that tide rip.

One after another the seas raced down the channel and smashed against the side of the twenty-eight-foot boat, lifting her up and tilting her until we expected to be thrown out. Guy had always said she was a wet boat. Today she streamed water and so did we. I could have enjoyed a plunging and pitching motion, but I hated this ugly, treacherous rolling motion against which we were helpless. Madelyn stood up beside Guy and watched each sea tear toward us, her eyes widening; I decided

it would do me no good to see my doom coming at me, so I
climbed in under the washboards and hung on.

As they say in stories, after what seemed an eternity we came
into calm water and rounded the point of Gay's Island. Well,
it did seem an eternity. A horrid, wet, cold, rolling, smashing
eternity. Until then I'd been pretty supercilious about the
whitecaps out in the channel, but when I climbed out on the
wharf at Gay's Island my legs were wivery. Even Guy admitted some slight nervousness; it was his first experience with
this particular wind and tide. Madelyn said nothing, but hugged
little Brad extra hard.

Now we knew beyond a doubt that there would be many
days when it would be impractical or impossible to go to Port
Clyde. The autumn here had teeth in it after all; until now,
they'd been well-masked by the brilliant foliage of oaks and
maples among dark spruces, by the islands floating against the
motionless lavender haze of October, by the warmth at noon.

We looked out at the channel with new respect. It had given
us as bad a time as we'd often had between Criehaven and
Matinicus and we didn't look forward to trying it again. And
then, later, we heard that Hap Wilson was selling out. We took
it as a personal tragedy, that he wouldn't be behind the counter
when spring and summer came again; buying groceries would
become a humdrum procedure, entirely devoid of charm,
without Hap.

And thus we came to know the Fales family, whose store
has stood at the junction of the roads to Cushing and Friendship
for generations. We had thought we couldn't shop there because we didn't have a car; we didn't know, at first, that we
could make out a list incorporating everybody's suggestions
from such luxuries as candy and cigarettes down through the
staples to dog food, put it in the mailbox or give it over Leslie
Young's telephone, and have the Fales' truck deliver it at the

wharf the next day. It's so simple that we wonder now why we were ever so stupid at the beginning, going for long stretches on a Cream of Wheat and Spam diet because the weather was too bad for us to get to Port Clyde.

Besides that, the Fales family makes up for missing Hap. They serve the community in the true sense of the word, Irving and Lizzie and their son Richard. Since Guy returned to Crie-haven, and Dot and I are alone on the island for weeks at a time, working hard and getting our groceries the best way we can, we've come to rely on the Faleses more and more. . . . Driving to the store for some ice cream, which is a nice thing to do once in a while on a warm summer evening, you have to slow down when you come around this corner, because Richard Fales' duck family might be promenading across the road for a swim in Broad Cove. And when you slow down, you see the cosset lamb and the white rabbits and the varied dogs, one of whom was a stray who recently turned in at the Fales' drive and was adopted. You will also see a number of cats. Lizzie told me there were five mothers-to-be living in the barn, and she'd have a dozen or so kittens running around before long because none of the men in the family would drown them.

What may appear to be a constant struggle for existence—such as rowing across the Gut for the groceries and rowing them home, and then wheeling them up to the house—is to us a valuable and heartening point of contact with our neighbors. When we go to Leslie's wharf we almost always see Margaret and Roy Seavey who live near the wharf; Roy may be painting his boat or working on his engine, and Margaret might call to us to come and see whatever new thing she's knitted or crocheted, or to ask us to set a date for coming to supper.

If we stop in at the store on the way to Rockland, there's al-most always someone in the store whom we wouldn't have seen otherwise; Stan Ripley asks, "Is it true they've posted the clam flats on Flea Island?" Stan digs clams for a living.

So Dot explains Dana Herrick's experiment in planting seed clams. We hear that Mildred Marshall is sick; that Inez Geyer might go to California this winter to visit her parents; that one of Harry Young's Walker hounds has pups.

Food, with the physical fact of attaining it (outside of earning the money, which is an endless procedure and about which I shall not become lyrical), thus becomes a social medium. It's wonderfully convenient to shop in a supermarket, and if I go into one in Rockland I become intoxicated with the long aisles of brilliant labels and immediately buy all sorts of things I don't really want and nobody else does. The elation dies out at the checking counter, where a polite girl whom I don't know tells me I owe twelve dollars and forty-five cents for assorted juices, canned meats which will all taste the same, various coffee breads, cheeses, chocolate peppermints (Ugh! But I'll save 'em for juvenile guests), a new kind of dog food, and some excruciatingly expensive and *small* chops. Once I'm outside, I think only of the work entailed in getting all this stuff home. Whereas, when we bring an order from Fales' store, or have arrived at Leslie's wharf just as Richard Fales, big, young, and good-natured, arrives in the truck, we've usually gained some scraps of news or the memory of an unpremeditated joke to enjoy all day.

All things being relative, news about the neighbors—like the time the fish warden had to shoot at somebody's tires before he could arrest the somebody for transporting clams across the county line—is very important, and kaleidoscopic in its charm. One can get a different picture every time one turns it over, and the conjectures are endless. It's like wondering what Russia is up to, and not half so depressing.

So this all goes along with food, and while it may not be exactly Gracious Living as described by the magazines, it's at least Living.

CHAPTER TEN

GRACIOUS LIVING

Gracious Living is a phrase coined by a certain set of magazines (the kind one never buys but reads under the dryer at the hairdresser's) to describe an Elysian state or stupor; it is presumably known only to the people pictured in the aforementioned magazines, so that one gets the idea of a one-dimensional and altogether delightful world that exists only on paper. Analyzed, Gracious Living is supposed to be the *sole* way of living. On lesser levels, the process of breathing is merely existence. One is led to believe that to struggle for the necessities of life—the earthy and squalid necessities such as food and fuel—puts one on a par with the beasts of the forest. This Nirvana of Gracious Living means that the house is run without effort, fuel is never mentioned because ample proof of its presence is in the perfectly aired and warmed—or cooled—rooms, and coal dust or range oil never sullies the fingers; food is hailed only as an artistic triumph. . . . And who hasn't dreamed of belonging to that select and blessed group who live on the heavenly paper plane? Who has not desired to eat exotic dishes with French names from delicate old Spode, by candlelight, while wearing a simple but timeless dinner gown and matched pearls?

Who has not—but why go on? Sometimes I make a stab at reaching this enlightened state by resolving to get out of my dungarees and into a dress by suppertime, but it doesn't work, because there'll always be something to do after supper that requires my getting back into dungarees again. However, I can plainly see that the way we live now is *definitely* gracious living as compared with the first year or so.

Food, fuel, and communications are the three adjuncts to living—no, to life itself—which one finds extremely easy to take as a matter of course, especially one who has never been obliged to give much thought to them. (This does not apply to mothers and fathers.) It applies to me. Oh, I had a thrifty enough way with a dollar and I could plan meals. But food had always been handy—until we came to Gay's Island. As for fuel, at home in Wollaston, Massachusetts, one called up the oil company and the coal company, and presently a truck came; the fuel was put in the cellar with no effort on the purchaser's part beyond opening the cellar door and paying the bill. Communications came from the telephone, or the mailman, and as long as the telephone company was paid, and the dog didn't bite the mailman, *that* was taken care of.

For Dot and Guy, too, the situation was different. It began to appear to us that living on Criehaven, commonly regarded as a rugged enterprise fit only for the stalwart, was really a pretty comfortable affair, insulated nicely from the facts of life . . . at least as far as the three essentials were concerned. Until just before Dot and Guy had left Criehaven, there was always a store; if the harbor was too rough for the *Mary A.* to come down from Matinicus, someone came down in his lobster boat with the mail and freight.

Oil came out in drums on the mailboat; in the earlier, palmier days when Mike McClure ran the store, an oilboat came and filled the big tanks on Sunset Point and in the storage shed, and one bought oil from Mike. There was almost always someone else to worry about transporting food, fuel, and mail; telegrams came by way of the government telephone in the store.

And so we were three innocents. It seems to me now, looking back, that we were rather shiftless about the oil situation at first, though it's a handy thing to use the war as an excuse and say it was impossible for us to add to our handful of five-gallon cans. . . . Guy got a fifty-gallon drum and had it horsed up on the rise above Leslie Young's wharf, and when the oil truck came to fill Leslie's drums, conveniently and *luxuriously* placed in his cellar, it came down the road to the wharf and filled our barrel. Then Guy took the cans over and filled them, and brought them back to the fishhouse. And though he was forever repeating this procedure, the oil cans in the Lazaret were always at ebb tide, and the ones in the fishhouse were lacking altogether.

Other fishermen suggested rolling the filled drum onto the stern of Guy's boat at high tide and bringing it across to the island. This seemed a sensible idea; eminently so. But Guy apparently had other thoughts on the subject. A gregarious soul, he liked to have an excuse to go often to the other side, where he could usually find a group working around in Leslie's fishhouse salting bait, and ripe for conversation.

Anyway, we were continually conscious of the tank behind the stove; we were never sure of an adequate supply of oil on the island to take us over a bad spell of weather. We had two hurricanes the first fall, and had discovered how uncomfortably rough the Gut could be. A strong northeasterly or east wind blowing down the Gut could, conceivably, hold a light skiff in one place no matter how hard a man rowed. So there were times, after all, when to all intents and purposes the Gut was as large and inhospitable as Penobscot Bay.

In the interests of economy we kept the needle as low as it would go, thus keeping ourselves chilled most of the time. Guy wasn't chilled, since he could always have a wonderful fire roaring in the fishhouse stove as long as he kept wood in it; and on his trips to the mainland he could always find a cup of coffee or a nip of something stronger in a warm kitchen.

There seemed to be an unwritten law of chivalry that said Women Weren't Fitten Critters to Lug Oil Cans. Dot and I laid all sorts of plans in which we would simply pick up a couple of empty cans, row across for the mail, and incidentally get some oil. Each time, Guy foiled us. We strode down to the fishhouse, Smokey running in circles all around us, and engaged Guy in conversation.

"How about keeping Smokey here with you while we row over and get the mail?"

"O.K.," said Guy amiably, putting a new traphead into a trap.

"Might as well fill up a couple of cans while we're about it." Casually, Dot picked up the cans.

"No need of your doing that," Guy would inform her. "I'm going over pretty soon—got to ask Roy to do some soldering for me—and I'll tend to the oil."

"Why don't we get two, and you get two or three?" Dot would ask brightly. "Then we'll have a little extra."

"I'm not going to have my wife carrying oil cans," stated Guy. "What would people think? Around here, women don't do things like that!"

"No, and I'll bet they don't have perpetually blue fingernails, and chattering teeth, either," said his wife. "I'll bet they don't measure oil out by the teaspoon. I'll bet. . . ." Wisely, she never went any further than this. On the few occasions when we did succeed in sneaking across the Gut to get some fuel, because Guy was out to haul or in Rockland and couldn't stand guard over his oil cans, we discovered that the drum was practically empty.

Thus, by the power of suggestion, Dot and I became convinced we were not able to lift five-gallon cans full of oil. We waited staidly for Guy to lift them. This also led to disadvantages, as the winter came closer and closer, and there were days when even among the Georges Islands it was too rough to haul. When the weather man promised two or three days of storm, Guy went to Rockland. We couldn't blame him too much. He was a born extrovert, for whom the Gay's Island winter was sheer torture. Here there was no one to drop into the shop and sit whittling and spinning cuffers with him while he worked. Dot and I both had our daily stint at our typewriters; we both liked to read. Guy was as restless as something caged.

So off he went, sometimes on the spur of the moment because he could get a ride to town with Dana Herrick or Roy Seavey, leaving us in possession—he said—of plenty of oil. But when the temperature dropped below freezing overnight, and we realized that we had plenty of oil only if we wore as many clothes indoors as we would have put on to go outdoors, we found fault with our present method of fuel supply.

It wasn't until Guy had gone back to Criehaven to lobster, with Dot's brothers, that we discovered we *could* carry full oil cans. Two of us lifting one can from the skiff wouldn't suffer any acute damage, and the cans could always be wheeled up to the house by the wheelbarrow. We had a good path through the alders now.

So we began to get our oil down the harbor, at Mr. Dunn's store. This precluded having to remember when the oil truck was due; we could get oil whenever we wanted it. At first we rowed down with two or three cans, on windless mornings when the tide was on the rise. We were accustomed by now to the twice-monthly tide that flooded the wharf, and were charmed by the idea that we could make it work for us. Coming back we could beach our skiff at the edge of the grass, tie it to an alder a good distance above our usually rocky landing, and then carry the cans to the fishhouse.

Next, as we added to our fleet of skiffs, we began to take nine or ten cans at a time, towed in a skiff behind us. Now we could get fifty gallons at once. Young Dana Herrick, when he married Dot's sister Bette, brought with him a dowry of cans. Nothing could have been more delightful. I used to measure wealth in terms of cash; now I see it in piles of new yellow lumber, in a bright, shiny lawn mower, and oil cans. To have fifteen cans, all full at once, in one corner of the fishhouse is to bring out the miser in me. I gloat and gloat. So does Dot. Seventy-five gallons of oil lasts an incredibly long time and is transmitted into eternal glory when it boils lobsters and warms the house and burns brilliantly in the shining chimneys of our lamps.

Dana, bless him, when he and Bette used Tide's Way for their honeymoon, brought the old drum from the mainland and filled it as well as the cans, running back and forth down the harbor in his powerboat. He started us off on our new regime of plenty, and we're very happy to have him in the family.

As with the getting of food, this pursuit of fuel has also become inextricably blended with the social side of existence. Rowing down to Dunn's for oil means usually a call on Mr. Dunn (he is "Rich" to all of Pleasant Point), a retired shipbuilder from Thomaston. His big white house looms up against the woods. He's past eighty, a short man with lively dark eyes and a big white mustache. Last year he helped Ken Sevon, who works for him, to build a barn to house the milch goats, the sheep, the pigs, the chickens and the ducks that Melba Ulmer takes care of as well as him. Melba's dog runs down over the terraced lawn to meet us; a nanny goat bleats from the edge of the woods. The Sevons live in a tiny green house across the yard from Mr. Dunn, and the big grassy yard usually presents an interesting assortment of several families of kittens, a couple of visiting dogs, ducklings, and Sevon children.

If Melba has time, she sits down to talk with us in the big

kitchen at Dunn's. Melba's just my age; she has beautifully carved features, like something on a coin, and the clean molding of them gives her a strength that belies her slight build. She's always hustling. It's quite a feat to get Melba to sit down.

Melba shames us often. We stroll into the kitchen on a warm day in July and sink into chairs. "I'm exhausted! I don't know why. . . ."

"This weather *is* tiring, isn't it?" Melba stops in flight to look at us with sympathy. "Have you seen my boarders? I told them when dinner would be ready—I wonder if they're on their way home. . . ." She lifts a rack of steaming jars out of the canner. "Mrs. Lane's berries—I do most of her pickling and canning for her. . . . Thought I'd get them out before I start dressing those chickens. . . ."

She flies out the back door, pursued by Lady and Judy, the dogs, and little Sandra Sevon. Mr. Dunn, who sits unperturbed in the middle of the bustle, asks if I've got a new book coming out soon and what it's about. He raps his stick at an adventurous kitten who's too interested in the kitchen table. Melba returns again, smiling and eager as she always is.

"Will your father get down again this year? . . . Aunt Sue and I'll be over to get some blueberries this afternoon, and I want to see that fancy new well curb he's built for you." She has pies in the oven. For the Grange supper. She thinks she might get to go, if her boarders decide to go.

That's Melba, from one year's end to the next. There's always a project. If it's not boarders, she's papering and painting the kitchen. The baby and the little boy playing around belong to a young couple who can't get a place to rent yet. "Take them in if you want to," says Mr. Dunn. "It's all right with me."

While Dot crosses the yard to see Ken Sevon's new electric guitar, I might go over to Maud Stone's, at the other big white house, and thank her for the pictures she sent, last winter, of the harbor frozen solid. She's getting ready to plant some flowers. Her son, Charlie, posed several years ago for N. C. Wyeth's "Young Maine Fisherman." Maud is another sample of the wonderfully resistant persons bred in Maine; like Leslie Young, like Susie Davis, like Jim Seavey. When she is eighty she will no doubt go skating over the frozen harbor as she did last winter. (The Will Maloneys are of the same breed.)

Maud tells me about her skating, and then brings me a Patient Lucy to take home. She's gay and chipper; she rakes blueberries in the summer for the Goulds, and picks cranberries in the wet bogs in the fall, because she enjoys it. I wish I had her staying power.

Meanwhile, Ken has filled our cans, and we cast a long glance over the shelves in the little store, and stock up on flashlight batteries, ginger ale, candy bars, and so on. We row homeward among the punts and dories at the moorings; the high tide floats the yellow rockweed on the ledges, the harbor brims; the dark spruces of Gay's Island on one side, the white houses and tall wharves of Pleasant Point on the other, make constantly changing arabesques on the tranquil water. High tide and high noon and a sunny silence; or the silvery gray hush of a warm cloudy day in spring or fall. It may rain, presently, and the drops will fall on our heads and dimple the water all around us, making a pleasant sibilant sound. We don't hurry. The skiff in tow slides along behind us like a docile pack horse. Nothing to worry about. . . . And if it should turn cold tomorrow we shall be blessedly, extravagantly, *wonderfully* warm!

Jim Seavey came up to the house the other day with a message for me. Jim was seventy about a month ago. He is a little man—both he and his crony, Leslie Young, are short and wiry. Jim has bright, humorous eyes above lean-fleshed high cheekbones, and one hand is continually reaching into his hip pocket for his package of plug tobacco.

When he came up the path the other day, he had for us a slack-salted codfish, and the news that I had a telephone call from New York. It had come to his house, because no one was home at Leslie's. The fact that telegrams and long-distance calls reach Gay's Island at all is entirely due to the perspicacity of the telephone exchange at Thomaston—Clara Spear knows everybody on the Point—and the enduring interest and kindness of people who will hop up from their dinners, launch a skiff, and row over with the news—often bringing a gift along like the slack-salted fish, which is the world's finest chewing along with hard red apples on a stormy night.

We used to worry about causing trouble, but fortunately the Pointers temper their willingness-to-oblige with practicality. When my friend Anne, with rare foresight, telegraphed me that she would be on her way to Maine the next day, Leslie didn't rush right over to bring the message. He knew her train wouldn't arrive until after three the following day, and he had plenty of time to get in touch with me.

"Long's you knew in time to make up a bed for her and have a skiff over here," he told me, his blue eyes twinkling. "Makes a good surprise too, doesn't it?"

But when Jim came the other day, he said, "Came right over . . . sounds urgent. Not bad news, though," he added in reassurance. We rowed across, and I made my call and had an interesting conversation that would have provided a week's material for the whole town of Cushing had the Point been in the habit of abusing their fifteen-party line. But in all the time that I've made and received telephone calls at Pleasant Point, no one has ever interfered or listened in. Everyone is unfailingly courteous about the right of others to private conversation.

So while I talked with New York, Jim and Olive talked birds with Dot. When we came over to the Point again, late in the afternoon, for the mail, Dot brought along her Audubon book of birds and a couple of stubbies of beer for Jim. We felt very rich to have had them on hand; one of her brothers had been down a week before and had left half a dozen bottles of beer for his next visit.

It was a warm afternoon and Jim appreciated the beer. "Next time the telephone rings, Dot," he told her solemnly, "I'll be right over."

"He won't even wait to see who it's for," said Olive.

"Nope! I'll come down on the shore and let out a war cry for ye."

"What kind of a cry is that?" asked Dot.

"All his cries are war cries," said Olive.

Jim was having a little trouble with one of his ears; an abscess or something which made him temporarily hard of hearing. He spat into the coal hod, which he carried tidily about with him in Olive's shining kitchen, and looked at her owlishly. "You c'n talk about me," he told her. "You c'n insult me all you've a mind to, and I won't know a thing about it."

At first, long-distance telephone calls were ordeals that left me drenched from the skin out with perspiration. So-called friends who in their horrible ignorance thought it would be much quicker to reach me via telephone than ordinary three-cent stamp ran a constant risk of being cast off by me for life. There are still such occasions. The call to New York was a shining exception; it stands out in my memory surrounded by a visible aura.

There was Anne, who called me—by way of Leslie Young's —from Scituate, Massachusetts. She left her number, and when I came across for the mail, with a thunderstorm rushing rapidly toward us from a blackening west, they gave it to me. Since various attempts to call people who'd left their numbers had left me psychically scarred—created a trauma, probably—I approached the telephone in a mood that was by no means enhanced by the fact that the Youngs were having a big family reunion and everybody was just sitting down to a lobster supper in the room where the phone was.

I called long distance, and gave Anne's number, and discovered again why some people feel impelled to shout over the telephone. The thunderstorm broke overhead at that moment; maybe the operator was as startled as I was. We were both shouting at each other pretty soon, and I found out that Scituate was absolutely the most unintelligible word to pronounce or spell over a telephone when thunderbolts were rolling along the wires like tight-rope bicycle riders.

All this time the Young family was showing commendable restraint in not discussing their lobster aloud; or perhaps they were enchanted into silence by my end of the conversation, which was strictly from idiocy. The familiar sensation of trickling sweat began. The lightning flashed, and the telephone took on symptoms of life.

By the time I was put through to Scituate, relayed along a bevy of girls who must have all been hiding under their switchboards from the storm, I felt indeed as if I had been "put through," and stirred up to a lather by an electric beater. . . . I then discovered that Anne had given the wrong telephone number, or presumably she and Bob were living at Scituate under an assumed name.

There was a long delay here, kept from being monotonous by a number of strange sounds, and my compulsion to say something into the receiver at intervals so that nobody would shut me off. After a time a brisk young-male voice said, "Hi. Who's this?"

"Who's *this?*" I asked belligerently.

"Roland. Can I speak to my mother?"

Dumbly I motioned Madeline to the phone, and she had an animated conversation with Roland, who was up the road somewhere. . . . I wouldn't have been surprised to find he was up on a pole, tapping the wires. After this the telephone remains more of a mystery than ever, and I sometimes see it as strictly black magic. . . . Because no sooner had Roland hung up—or slid down the pole—than Anne was on, screaming at me joyously.

"I would have called earlier," she said, "but we had a terrible thunderstorm here!"

A crash of thunder right overhead made me feel like Chicken Little. I am afraid I was not very gracious. "What do you want?" I screamed back at her.

"I'm driving up tomorrow," she shouted. "What are you doing to that telephone? It sounds as if you were teething on it." There was a sound like a buzz saw and then complete silence. I found myself wishing uncharitably that Bobby had found the scissors and cut the wires.

I apologized to the Youngs for spoiling their supper. They assured me that I hadn't spoiled it. Possibly I had been more entertaining than I knew.

I went out into the storm and let the cool rain drops revive me, and then I could begin to look forward to seeing Anne.

There was also the time when my former publisher was arranging an autograph tour through Maine for me, and had sent one of his young men to make contacts. The ambassador was making jaunts from city to city and naturally thought the simplest way to keep me informed, and find out what dates were best, was to talk to me on the phone. Fortunately, Sybil Young, who looks at us as quizzically as does Leslie, her husband, was more entertained than annoyed by this performance, and it guaranteed her an hour or more of our company every few days; Dot talked with her while I struggled to keep up with the young man. The principal cities of Maine disappeared from this stratum of existence whenever I attempted to call him in any one of them. Once, to be sure I reached him in Bangor, he sent a message that was telephoned to Thomaston, thirteen

miles from the Point, and then given to Ray Noyes, local taxi
driver, to bring to the Point and deliver to me in person. This
necessitated Jim Seavey's bringing Mr. Noyes over in his boat;
we met on the path and he gave me the message in the solemn
tones of a diplomatic courier handing over a packet of sealed
papers. I was to call Bangor at two o'clock.

That was the beginning of a cozy afternoon in the Youngs'
dining room. Without the thunderstorm to harass the operators
and me, we were disturbed by another noise which seemed to
have definitely supernatural origins. I wondered if somehow
we hadn't tuned in on the cosmic ray, or the planet Mars; maybe
the telephone was really a time machine. Between crackings
and buzzings I was rerouted all through Maine. I toured the
state from the edge of a rocking chair that afternoon. I met
more nice people! In the rare intervals of silence bright young
voices came: "Hello! What can I do for you?"

"I'm calling Bangor," I answered politely but with dying
hope.

"Oh." Manifest bewilderment. "Well, this is—" It was always some place not anywhere near Bangor.

Understandably, people on the local line tried to use their
phones; they listened first, heard nothing, or else the ghostly
crackling, and rang in. My eardrum felt as if it had shattered.
Holding the receiver at arm's length, I repeated with growing
meekness, "The line's busy." I began to suffer the humiliation
of being a nuisance, and I grew more and more limp and hot,
until suddenly Bangor was on the line.

The young man was not where he was supposed to be. While
they were looking for him, the spectral noises grew louder and
louder. Finally he was there; I recognized, dimly, a human
voice, male. That was all I did recognize. His words were fantastically garbled, as if the unseen forces were jamming them.
I shouted over the din, "Why don't you write me a letter?"

"All right, I will!" he shouted back and we hung up with

mutual pleasure. Sybil must have been entertained, but with rare tact she didn't even looked surprised when after an hour of struggle to get the man I simply shouted a half-dozen un-gracious words into the transmitter and hung up.

But all long-distance calls haven't been like that; it's just me. My flesh creeps at the thought of one, and if I am actually forced into a position of having to make one, by the time it is successfully completed I am limp and quivering.

To me, the mail driver is the hero of our existence here. And as far as I'm concerned, he shall *not* be unhonored and unsung. In wintertime and in mudtime, he drives up and down the roads delivering mail, giving rides to town to anyone who happens to be waiting at the mailbox for him, doing errands in Thomas-ton—many has been the manuscript I've left in the mailbox for him to deliver to the Railway Express Agency for me. Between "Mr. Wink"—he's one of the Friendship Wincapaws—and Mrs. Stevens the postmistress, we are very well looked after.

Again the personal touch enters into our existence. Friends supply the oil, the groceries, deliver the mail; we have mutual interests. The new black road the town of Cushing built last year—we all paid for it. The raise in taxes was voted at the Town Meeting, and as soon as the frost was out of the ground the work on the road was begun. We saw Cushing men work-ing on the road; and the rest of us, who didn't actually wield a pickax or run a bulldozer, knew our money was doing its share, and when we drive over that road we say "*our* road," and mean it.

CHAPTER ELEVEN

THE TEMPERAMENT OF THE TIDES

Some day, when I am in a suitably poetic mood, I am going to write a poem about the Little Tides of Pleasant Point Gut (called "the Intestine" by a ten-year-old friend of mine). Of course, it's my personal belief that the water between Pleasant Point and Gay's Island comes and goes according to its own occult schedule, which has nothing to do with the neat tide tables that hang in everybody's kitchen. Whenever the tide happens to be high at the hour specified on the list, I experience a distinct and pleasant astonishment. I feel tempted to say, "Hey, whaddya know?" to everybody.

Since that first day, when an extra high tide and the worst thunderstorm of the season combined to give us a cataclysmic welcome to the island, we've never reached a working agreement with the highs and lows, floods, ebbs, neaps, and that dismal phenomenon which occurs every few weeks and is known as "low dreen tide." It is as uninspiring as it sounds.

As far as the Gut itself is concerned, we have understanding *and* respect. There was a time when we felt that because the island was so deceptively close to the mainland we were entitled to bask forever in its delightful calm. The shining harbor, without a ripple except when passing boats sent small curling waves to wash musically against the shore, was like all the streams of poetry. So we basked, for a few summery weeks, in the pure and proverbial bliss that is attributed to the ignorant. Rowing was *fun* after the dusty and discouraging hours spent in house cleaning. Dot had been rowing all her life; as a youngster she often rowed a doryload of younger brothers and sisters along the rugged shores of Criehaven, where there was always a surge and swell. They'd land in a rocky cove, fill the dory with driftwood, and then she'd pile the kids back into precarious balance, threatening them with battle, murder and sudden death if they happened to breathe an extra deep breath, and row home. She liked to row a skiff out of the harbor when it tossed in the tide rip like a chip. That was the sort of rowing *she* was used to.

Well, I could make the oars go in some sort of synchronized motion. But I still didn't know enough about it to trust myself in the harbor at Criehaven, where anyone was likely to dash by at any moment in a thirty-foot powerboat with the throttle wide open, stirring up a wake that looked like a tidal wave. So the Gut at Pleasant Point offered untold possibilities for both of us. Dot had never played around on such consistently tranquil water before; and it was a good place for me to get used to rowing, since anyone who couldn't handle a skiff was going to be immured on the island like Mariana of the Moated Grange.

I could go on and on about evenings when the sun set directly at the Friendship end of the Gut, and turned the water peach and rose and lavender, and we dipped the oars in pure color as we rowed along, leaving eddies of gold behind us; the birds made sleepy sounds in the alders and birches that grew down close to the water, and the fish hawks from Howard Head soared and piped high in the sky, on the last foray of the day, while the gulls flew homeward two by two. I could go on about the silvery quiet of a rainy day, or the mornings when we rowed over to the mailbox while the land fog was burning away in opalescent shreds, and the water was the pale blue one sees in some types of sweet peas.

I could go on, too, about boats. We had only two skiffs at first; Guy used one for a tender, to row back and forth from his mooring down the harbor, and we had the other one, to use for our various errands. Dot's Uncle Peter had built it, long ago. He had died before we'd ever heard of Gay's Island, but like the work of any true artist, his work lived after him in the boats he had built: from the big sleek powerboats for lobstering down to nine-foot skiffs like the one we used. To launch her, to fit the oars into the oarlocks, was to evoke Peter Mitchell before us. That was the anglicized version of his name, and what the Danish version was, we don't know. But we do know that the little dark man who married Ellen Anderson was a scholar and a dreamer. He had been educated on a Danish school ship; he had sailed everywhere; for years he had been an officer on the White Star Line and had crossed the ocean count-less times. What path led him to Criehaven, I don't know. He was small and unassuming, always smiling, always agreeable. He loved to go fishing almost as much as he loved to build boats. He was a pilot; when some big vessel lay off the islands, hooting mournfully for help in finding the Penobscot rivermouth, Peter often went out to show them the way.

Peter has a sort of immortality, passed down in his sayings. He had a sly humor, all the more effective because of his soft voice and Danish accent, and an unfailing good nature.

We never failed to think of him when we slid the skiff down over the rocks, gently so as to save her all we could. She was perfectly balanced and easy to handle in spite of the sturdy construction necessary for Criehaven boats. Close as we were to the water in her, we felt that she had a certain integrity of her own, like her builder's, and would do her best for us.

As a mark of distinction—and also because it was the only

kind of paint on hand when the spirit moved us to paint her—
we stained her a darkly luscious shade of red, with gray for the
inside and the seats. Guy was humiliated beyond words. He
hated the color red with a ferocity that would have interested
a psychiatrist, and if we were ever afraid he'd want to swap
skiffs with us, we didn't have to worry after that.

"I wouldn't be caught drowning in a skiff that color!" he
announced savagely. Of course the red had worn off and we'd
replaced it with green by the time he took it back to Criehaven
with him. And it seemed appropriate for Uncle Peter's skiff to
go back to the place where it was born, so to speak.

The charming possibilities for rowing were balanced by the
mud flats. The mussel beds which filled the Gut looked convincingly solid until we saw the clamdiggers wading knee-deep
—well, *almost* knee-deep—in them, and pulling their feet out
with a truly horrifying effort.

And the speed with which those mud flats emerged was horrifying, too. One moment things were at a nice half tide, allowing plenty of water for getting over the bar, and the next
moment—oh, fifteen minutes later—when you arrived at the
wharf flexing your muscles, prepared to slide the skiff down
the rocky slope and into the water like a trick boat in an amuse-
ment park, there wasn't any water. At the foot of the rocks
there was mud. *Muck.* And as you looked, more mud appeared.
The tide was running out and there was nothing left but a faint-
hearted channel that made no attempt at all to pass near the opposite shore.

We made a forced acquaintance with this muck during the
early days of residence at Gay's Island, when everybody we
knew was bent on coming down to see how we'd got stung.
They would arrive on the other side, a gay party out for an
afternoon's ride, all dressed up. This in itself was enough to
disgruntle us, because we'd probably all be up to our necks in
some particularly obnoxious task like dragging old bedsprings

away from the house, or gathering up the insides of the wood choppers' quilts, whose entrails had blown all through the tall grass when we threw the bedding out the window.

Invariably these callers came at half tide just before a low dreen tide, which meant that we'd be stuck with them for hours and hours and nothing extra to eat in the house unless they, with admirable forethought, had brought their own liquor, in which case they wouldn't need anything to eat. And we looked terrible, and so did the house, and they were disgustingly well dressed, and probably sneering.

Or else they came *just* at low tide, which meant giving the skiffs the old heave-ho across the stretch of mud between the landing and the channel; directing the callers by shouts where to stand so they could be picked up, this against a crossfire of supposedly witty greetings on their part, which successfully drowned out our directions.

We learned early what mud flats could do to shoes. This stuff was a particularly disagreeable, odiferous, black, and adhesive substance. We learned by sad experience (some of it not so sad, since it was also the experience of our blithe and tidy callers) where to step. It was *not* safe to step on a cluster of mussel shells under the impression that they were on a rock. You went in up to your ankle with no effort whatever on your part.

Our high, slanting rock beside the wharf appalled us when we first realized we had to push the skiffs down over it and then haul them painfully up again, over the steep surface crusted with barnacles and dotted with periwinkles that rolled perilously underfoot. We found, too, that wet rocks here were a different matter from wet rocks at Criehaven. The mixture of fresh and salt water in the Gut made a slippery coating over everything.

It was nothing at all like having a smooth pebbly beach, *always* smooth and pebbly no matter where the tide was, and we crept and crawled around the ledge with care, regarding the barnacles as Heaven-sent helps. At half tide the water just off the rock was far over our heads, and all of us were true island-ers in one respect—we'd never bothered to learn to swim in the bone-freezing waters around Criehaven.

But with each lovely and shimmering high tide we forgot the disadvantages and somehow became deluded that the Gut would be like the maid on the Grecian urn. . . . Forever would we row and it be fair. . . .

Until the fall winds came—the west wind that sounds so well in song and story. You know, "a warm wind, the west wind, full of birds' cries." It came racing down from Friendship, send-ing whitecaps scudding across dark blue water and thence into the Gut, where the swiftly flowing tide added its five cents' worth. It rushed through the Gut, feather-white, and slopped loudly around the spilings of our wharf.

It was then that Dot and I realized that no stretch of water ever stays peaceful and pellucid. The first time it was borne in upon us we had walked nonchalantly to the shore, intending to take a handful of letters to the mailbox. We felt the lusty autumn wind hit us when we reached the wharf, but out at Criehaven the wind blew all the time, and this rough breeze against our faces seemed only natural. We saw the whitecaps turning the water to tossing silver outside the far end of the Gut, toward Friendship; we saw the water in the Gut racing toward us, splashing around the wharf. But these were such teensy, weensy waves, you couldn't even call them waves. They were hardly worth noticing.

So with an air of complete indifference—a rather debonair sort of indifference, with flourishes, because there were some people standing around on Leslie Young's wharf at the time, and who knew but what they might be watching us?—we pushed down the skiff. The tide was at its height, so we didn't have to push the boat more than a couple of feet. I nipped in and sat in the stern seat. Dot swung one foot in the bow, gave a good rousing push with the other foot that should have shot us out into the Gut, and hopped forward to the rowing seat.

Immediately we learned Lesson No. 1 about the Gut and Us in a westerly. Always have the oarlocks in place and the oars ready before getting in.

Belatedly I grabbed for the oarlocks to put them in, while Dot slid the oars out from under the seat, but already the wind was driving us sidewise against the rocky shore, the waves were slapping loudly at the side of the skiff and splashing all over us. Dot tried to push us away from the shore with an oar, but she admitted afterward she was scared at the moment and couldn't think what to do. The wind and the swiftly running tide meanwhile had taken us along the shore, banging us the whole time, and the rocks were pointed and sharp as they gouged away at the side of the skiff. Dot poked and pushed with the oar as best she could, and finally we came to a sandy spot. There she jumped out, grabbed the painter, and pulled the skiff up to dry land.

One of those teensy weensy harmless little waves slapped in over the stern and drenched me, and I leaped out with a yelp. We stood there watching the swiftly moving stretch of water between us and the mainland. It was such a small space, but at that moment it was as big as the twenty-five miles of bay we thought we'd left behind. And no Cap'n Stuart Ames to see that we got across, either!

We were marooned until Guy came in from hauling, and even then we each refused an invitation to go across, with him at the oars. Dot brooded about this for all of a week. After all, anyone who had landed a dory on the steep shores of Crie-haven, with breakers tumbling in behind her, does not take it kindly when she's bested by a nasty little chop in a harbor that isn't even pure salt water, but partly fresh. There was a science to it, and she was determined to learn it.

So with me for a willing audience and passenger—as long as I could stay within grabbing distance of the wharf—and with Guy safely out to haul so he couldn't offer to show us what to do, and with no spectators on Leslie's wharf across the Gut, she experimented. Blackie, the lamb, during his first few months at Gay's Island, was convinced that every time anyone pushed a skiff down he was about to be marooned on this alien strand where walking pincushions peppered his nose with quills, and woodchucks with big buck teeth popped out from under the barn to disconcert him. So our experiments were carried out to the accompaniment of Blackie's frenzied bawling. He would gallop after us down to the shore and watch suspiciously as we untied the skiff; he clattered up and down the face of the landing while we launched our craft; and once we were aboard he set up his lamentations.

We practiced launching; we practiced coming ashore with the wind trying to beat us to pieces against the rocks, and with each departure Blackie bawled, and with each return he went stiff-legged into the air like a very *young* lamb, bounced around us a few times, and then fell to eating rockweed and old grapefruit rind cast up by the tide, as if he'd been on a hunger strike for the five minutes we'd been away from the shore.

We soon learned to have the oars poised in the oarlocks, so that we'd be ready to push out into the Gut before the wind and tide could swing us ashore again. The Gut is at its roughest when the wind is west, but once we're out in the stream we can manage, and soon we're in the lee of the mainland. Coming back, we have several alternative landing places along the shore of the island if it seems too loppy at the wharf; that delightful, shallow little cove between our fishhouse point and Charlotte Gray's camp, for instance. And we know that a northwest wind will blow us nicely home in no time, so that if two of us have to bend to the oars on the way over, we'll come home with no effort whatever. And the things we can do with a nine-foot skiff!

We learned, too, how to save our backs by leaving the skiffs at the bottom of the landing if the tide was low, coming back later to haul them on when the tide has brought them halfway up. Now the nightly inspection of the skiffs is a routine thing, and we have evolved a system for putting a stern line on them so they'll be held in the lee of the wharf if the wind should change in the night. As long as it's southerly—which is the prevailing wind around here in spite of our struggle with the westerlies—they stay off the rocks when they're only tied but not hauled on. But any other wind strews them all over the landing area at high tide and there they are stranded for us to tug around into position.

With Guy around to do the heavy work we didn't think much about it. But lately Dot put beckets in the sterns of all the skiffs, and that helps in hauling them around as much as in putting stern lines on them. The skiffs we have now—three of them—were built by Fred Killeran, up the road at Broad Cove, near Fales' store and Olsons' sawmill. They're light and we've got the knack of handling them without danger to sacroiliacs and such. We are as fond of them as we are of Tristi and Smokey and Blackie. They are sturdy and reliable, ride the tide and fight the wind with the tenacity of the Morgan horse who never turns his back to a gale.

The largest one is known as "the Pink Punt." Men like her because there's more room in her than the others. She transports an immense amount of luggage, cartons of groceries, full cans of oil, and still rides the water like a duck. We went berserk on her and painted her strawberry-ice-cream pink, with pale yellow interior, and lovely grass-green oars. Dot restrained me from painting small winged cupids on either side of the bow, holding garlands and loops of blue ribbon, pointing out that such decoration might cause understandable mirth among the neighbors. Instead, we painted blue-winged teals in flight.

The smallest skiff is called "the Run-About," and skims the water like a mussel shell. She runs back and forth for the mail and makes herself generally useful. Young-fry guests, suitably attired in one of the red lifebelts we found in the ell chamber, learn how to row in the Run-About and are surprised and delighted at their progress.

During the summer, the middle-sized skiff called "Salome" dances at her haul-off out by the weir, on the seaward side of the island. She got her name, obviously, because she dances. She is never still for a moment out there, bobbing in the faintest breeze. We use her when we want to row along the outer side of the island, or to go beachcombing in the coves, or to try for pollock beyond the ruins of the weir.

The dory came into our lives a year ago. It was a pig in a poke, though the figure of speech is hardly descriptive of the massive craft unloaded from a truck at Leslie's wharf and left for us to discover. It was such an unlikely thing for *us* to be rowing that we walked by it every day for a week, never guessing it was ours; Leslie was away, so there was no one to break the cruel truth to us. And then, when the bill came from the young man who had brought the dory from the shipyard in Waldoboro to Pleasant Point, the light dawned. We went to look at the new baby.

"She's very well built," Dot said bravely, after an intensely silent inspection. "Look at all those reinforcements."

"She's got nice lines," I contributed. We prowled around the dory, secretly wondering how we'd ever launch her on the mainland side and haul her up on the island side.

"She'd be a humdinger for the Grand Banks," said Dot, and all restraint was gone. "I didn't think she'd be so *big!* She's longer than fourteen feet—she *must* be!"

"I may be feeling a little tired from all the work we've been doing," I said, "but somehow I can't imagine us rowing her . . . but she'd be awfully good for an outboard motor."

Since the money expended on the dory had shot a hole in any chance of getting an outboard motor right away, we weren't any farther along. We sat down on some logs by the fishhouse and contemplated our pig. Dot smoked a cigarette. If I'd been a fingernail chewer, I would have been nibbling away for dear life. It was a bleakly bright October day, cold as midwinter. There was no one in sight anywhere. Margaret and Roy Seavey, who live in the little shingled house right above the wharf, had gone to town.

After a long period of meditation, Dot said, "We'll have to ask somebody to get her overboard for us." This was the darkest statement yet. We knew, suddenly, what comments must have been passed about this steel-enforced Leviathan of dories during the week we hadn't recognized it as our own; we could imagine all too vividly the twinkles, the wry comments, the faint but unmistakable grins of the launching crew. And our own defiance. . . .

"We knew she would look like this," we would say bravely. "This was what we wanted. Something substantial."

"She's substantial, all right," Leslie would say, looking at us with the particular kindly indulgence reserved for drunks and four-year-olds. "You'll wear out before she will. . . . I give ye about a week."

"Hey, why don't you teach that sheep of yours to row?" somebody else would ask.

Worst would be the silent head-shakings of the rest. . . . I sprang up and said brightly, "Maybe somebody'll offer to buy her from us. She'd be good to lug herring in."

Dot said nothing. We went home to begin to gain strength for what lay ahead. But because of a succession of minor ailments (psychosomatic, no doubt), and the pressure of work, we didn't get the dory launched. And then it was almost winter, and Leslie came to our rescue as he had done a hundred times before and offered to put the dory in his fishhouse loft for the winter.

He was kind, too. He didn't say half what he could have said. And we were so thankful for his offer that we wouldn't have bridled a bit, either, if he *had* said something.

So the dory went into the loft, and winter went by. Then came spring, and Dot said, "We really ought to get that dory out of Leslie's fishhouse."

"He's out at Monhegan," I replied happily. "We'll have to wait until the next time he comes in."

She fixed me with a stern eye. "Eighty dollars," she said. "What are we going to do about it?"

"Let's look at it again. Maybe we remember it wrong. Maybe it isn't so big as we think. . . . Maybe Dana could fix the stern for an outboard motor. . . ." I was babbling like a marijuana addict, to whom nothing is impossible. "Maybe one of us'll sell a short story, if we work like mad this spring, and then we can buy an outboard. . . ."

"Eighty dollars," mourned Dot, "that we're not going to get any enjoyment from."

"You think too much about money," I said.

The dory rested comfortably in the fishhouse throughout the spring and well into the summer. Nobody mentioned her after a while, preserving a tactful silence. Then one night Dana came in, glowing like a sunrise. He had seen the perfect dory up in Camden; he knew the owner; he had described our overgrown problem child to the owner, who said she was exactly what he wanted, and he'd swap his dory for ours.

"She's the littlest dory I ever saw," Dana said, "and she's

pretty, too. She's made of cedar, and is light as a feather. You can get her up and down those rocks as easy as the skiffs."

Another pig in a poke . . . but Dana vouched for her, and so she came to live with us. She is everything he said she was, a miniature dory, slim and light, as delicately curved as a mussel shell. For one person rowing alone in her, the sensation is marvelous. She skims the water with no effort on the part of the oarsman. Loaded with full oil cans and towed by a skiff, she exerts no pull whatever, but follows along as if she had a separate life of her own to guide her across the water. Pulled up on the landing in front of the fishhouse, among the chunky skiffs, she appears like an adult Shetland sheep dog among ordinary collie pups, who are almost as big as she is, but obviously immature beside her small-sized but grown-up perfection.

But a dory is a chancy thing. Two dories built exactly to the same design by the same craftsman may have widely different personalities. Dot speaks with affection of her father's dory, the one in which she loaded driftwood and children indiscriminately. She wants to find another one like it. But she never will. So, knowing the vagaries of the sisterhood, we weren't surprised to find that our new darling was tittle-ish. This word belongs expressly to dories, and it has a rakish sound, reminiscent of high-stepping horses. At least it has for me. In print it's picturesque, but in a dory it's a little hard on the nerves.

We spent many bright afternoons in the little cove between the fishhouse and Charlotte's camp, where the sandy bottom gives the water a green-gold brilliance, and a huge birch leans over its reflection in the shallows. We rowed the dory around and around. Whoever wasn't rowing tried to take the other by surprise by lunging suddenly over to one side, which sent the dory rolling down on her gunwales. We stood up and moved around in her. We changed places. We broke all the rules, trying to capsize her, but we couldn't do it.

She still rolls if you shift a foot or take an extra deep breath, and getting aboard calls for the balance of a toe dancer. Certain people eschew her as if she were the Typhoid Mary of the waterfront, but we know what she'll take. This doesn't mean that I've stopped imbedding my fingerprints in her gunwales, or that Dot stands up frequently to do a clog dance on the narrow bottom, but she's earning her keep.

She fits magnificently with sixteen-year-old boys like Herbie Schmitz, who stayed with us ten days last summer and couldn't be induced to part from her. He skittered around the Gut like an autumn leaf; he did errands; he transported vast quantities of luggage; at low tide he rowed among the mussel beds looking for skates that had been stranded on the mud, and in the resultant excitement, whenever he found one, the dory performed more acrobatic feats than one could ever expect from a creation of wood, nails, and paint.

Now, what with knowing the Gut pretty well, and knowing the idiosyncrasies of our boats, we do not very often sit wistfully on one side and would we were on the other. Not very often . . . but sometimes. When those darned tides go off schedule again!

CHAPTER TWELVE

SMALL CRAFT WARNINGS DISPLAYED

We still make some memorable crossings. At least they're memorable for us. Like the time we'd been invited to a baby shower. We awoke that morning to a gray day, and a brisk southerly gale turning the channel to a nasty gray-green streaked with white and howling around the house. And this wasn't the worst of it, the weather man said it would reach its height some time in the afternoon.

Well, we had the present for the baby shower, all lusciously wrapped in pretty paper and pink and blue ribbon; and we wanted to deliver it. So, with breakfast out of the way, we decided to take the present to Leslie Young's house, and his daughter Madeline could deliver it for us when she went to the shower, since we didn't expect to be able to get off the island that afternoon. We would dash over and back and hole up for the day.

We dashed over, all right. We dashed wonderfully, with the southerly wind coming over the island and swooping down on us from behind and blowing us straight across to a little sandy beach directly opposite the fishhouse. We gave the present to Madeline, talked for a few minutes, and came back to the shore. The wind hit us in the mouth with all the unsubtle persuasion

of a baseball bat. The Gut looked worse than usual because the
tide was low, and water was breaking in little waves over even
the meanest mussel bed.

I was understandably reluctant to shove off in the face of
such opposition, but Dot motioned me into my usual seat.

"We've got to get across," she said. "The wind is supposed
to be increasing all the time—we can't sit on this side all day.
. . . You can give me some help with the oars."

She gave the skiff the usual shove, hopped in, and we went
nowhere at all. We were grounded. The water was too shallow
for the skiff to float with both of us in it. Without appearing
hasty I got out, while the wind smacked water against the skiff
and soaked Dot. "Maybe we can't get across," I said doubtfully.

"We've got to get across," said Dot. "The oil burner is going
full tilt and food cooking on the stove. . . . Go out on those
rocks there," she commanded me, "and I'll pick you up."

Muttering, I went out on the rocks, while the gale tried to
push me back into Leslie's meadow, and she rowed toward me,
shouting, "Hop in here, quick!" The instant she let up on the
oars the wind wanted to drive her ashore again. I hopped in
and leaned forward to help with the oars; while I pushed, she
pulled, and after a horrible moment of standing completely
still, we got out into the stream. The important thing was to
keep the bow into the wind, and we were so perilously close to
the water in our little clamshell that if we swung sidewise at the
instant a gust hit us, the whole Gut seemed to come aboard with
the greatest of ease. . . .

As the crow flies—though not as the crows were flying that
day—it was a very short distance to the wharf. But not the
way we did it. We tacked, drifted with the gusts, rowed madly
when a gust let up, and concentrated on keeping that bow into
the wind. Eventually we reached the wharf, hauled up the skiff
with a flourish, made it fast for the day, and went home. Later,
when we turned on the radio for the weather report, we heard

the announcer from Portland describing the sixty-mile-per-hour gusts that were raking the Maine coast.

We looked at each other. We'd been out in a sixty-mile-per-hour wind; we'd rowed a nine-foot skiff into the face of it. . . . Well, almost into the face of it. I think at that moment we were convinced there was nothing we didn't know about crossing the Gut, and the days of trepidation were past forever. We wrote letters to all our relatives, adding the news of our feat in casual postscripts. "By the way. . . ."

The baby shower was a great success, for us especially.

Yes, indeed, we thought we knew it all . . . until the rainy day we started out innocently enough for Rockland. We had called up George Harvey and his taxi the day before. The rain was expected, but we always picked rainy days to go to Rockland anyway, having got used to the fine art of dressing to cross the Gut in a shower, with a change of clothes in a bag. While we were getting ready, we noticed the wind had a particularly disagreeable howl around the house, but it usually howled when there was any strength to it. We fixed the sanitary arrangements for the animals, made sure there was plenty of water for them, and were at last ready, only to discover the tide gone so far that we could land only at Leslie Young's wharf—which meant rowing into the face of a northeast wind.

The Gut had its nasty look again. There was no shelter as there would have been with a southerly wind. Even to stand by the rocky landing was to face a raw wet gale that whipped tears into our eyes.

We stared at the wind-whipped water with distaste. Neither of us can swim, and although the last part of the journey would be across shallows that were white with foam, we couldn't feel very safe, for who could walk in the soft mud that came nearly to one's knees, if the skiff capsized during the short period when we would have to row broadside to the waves? Yet, we felt that we should make an effort to get across. There was no way of telling George to turn back.

We stood in the shelter of the fishhouse and looked out on the stormy, dirty-gray harbor and listened to the wind keening like a whole family of banshees, while we raised our courage to start. Then we dashed out quickly and launched the skiff.

The Run-About struggled against the wind as soon as she touched the water; she poked her nose down and threw showers of spray against Dot's back and into my face as we dug into the swift-running waves with the oars. We could barely make headway; the strong tide kept us almost at a standstill, while the wind made it very difficult to lift the oars from the water.

We'd been almost four years on Gay's Island and had become used to all sorts of weather; I hadn't believed it held any more surprises for us, or that I'd ever be nervous in the skiff again. But now I was scared. Not scared enough to be weak, because I was pushing on those oars like Billy-be-damned. I was also beset with those wild regrets that always come out in such a situation. We were so silly, so idiotically brash, to be out here risking our lives for whatever we'd planned to do in Rockland.

It seemed years of struggling before we could stop rowing against the wind and tide and turn the nose of the skiff toward Leslie's wharf.

The white-crested waves rolled down on us and tipped the little skiff up on her side, but at the same time they drove us with racing speed toward the wharf. At once I stopped being scared. We weren't going to be capsized, not if our little duck of a Run-About had anything to do with it. The water slapped at her sides, and spray flew over us, and rain dripped from the brims of our sou'westers; in our relief at knowing we were making a safe crossing we began to laugh like two idiots, and the skiff bobbed along beneath us with a gallant and irrepressible gaiety.

Dripping and gasping we landed on the shore and hauled

the skiff up. We were both trembling when we climbed to the wharf where George stood waiting, but we were also feeling very drunk with relief and pride.

As we walked up the beach Dot said, "I was so scared I didn't know how I was going to keep those oars going. But when I realized we weren't going to roll over any time and be drowned in a couple of feet of water, I felt wonderful!"

There have been other bad crossings, like the first time we encountered ice in the harbor. We came back from Rockland one dark night, and realized with a bitter inward chill what made it so hard to row in the windless evening. The harbor was beginning to freeze, and we hadn't bargained on that. We hadn't bargained on waking to mornings when the boats lay mirrored on a still, glassy surface that looked ironically like the tranquil blue water of summer, and the whole world was bound in a hard, glistening silence; there was a crystalline beauty about it, but it was a strangling beauty. The mind immediately leaped to potential disaster; someone falling and breaking an ankle, and no means of getting across ice that was too hard to row through and too soft to walk on.

Sometimes the ice broke up and went out with the tide, and the next day it was back again. But we intended to stick it out as long as it was possible. Once the three of us—Guy was there that first icy winter—went away for overnight. It was during a mild spell, with no ice. We were to meet at Leslie Young's house at three o'clock the next afternoon. We had left the oil tank full so that the stove would go until after our time of return, keeping the animals warm.

But there came a swift drop in the temperature, and at three o'clock the next day the air was like a sharp knife against the skin, although there was not the slightest breath of wind.

Glowing from my visit, I arrived at Pleasant Point at the appointed time. The afternoon was a lovely, shining thing, all white snow and blue sky. Dot was at the Youngs', waiting.

"The harbor is covered with ice," she told me like the voice of doom. "Guy's gone back to Rockland. He says for us to come along, or we can stay here at Leslie's for the night. He says we can't break through the ice today."

I didn't want to go back to Rockland, I wanted to go to the island. In spite of the Youngs' protests that we couldn't get across, we walked in the deep snow down to the shore and looked at the harbor.

Someone had broken through the thick glassy shell near the wharf, but otherwise it was polished and whole. Across the harbor, Gay's Island lay under the late sunshine, its spruce woods dark above its snowy fields. We saw Blackie roving around.

"It's almost time for the fire to go out," I said, and Dot nodded.

"I keep thinking of that," she said.

We were having visions of the water freezing in the drinking pan, Smokey whining and shivering. The cats could curl around each other, but what could Smokey do?

"Damn it," I said angrily, "I'm going home if I have to wait till dead low water and plow through Leslie's field and walk across the Stepping Stones." Then there'd be another long walk through snow-filled woods on the island. It was an exhausting prospect, but it was possible.

Dot kept looking thoughtfully at the broken ice around the wharf. "Somebody did that," she said. "It's not too thick. It only formed since yesterday." We looked at each other, and then at our skiff.

Madeline Stimpson arrived, having followed us down from the house. "You're not going to try crossing, are you?" she asked us.

"We sure are," said Dot, untying the skiff. "It's either that or walk, and I think ice-breaking would be a lot easier." Dot has an enthralling phobia about walking which leads her to complain in a paranoiac tone of voice that I am always starting her off on brisk jaunts. Add to this her dislike of snow, and we have a very willing ice-breaker.

We got into the punt, while Madeline hovered anxiously at the edge of the wharf. "Do you think you *should?*"

"Why not?" I asked hardily, since from the stern seat I could not reasonably be expected to do any ice-breaking. "If it gets too much for her—for us—we can come back."

Dot said nothing. Standing up in the skiff, and looking like a gondolier, she grimly cracked ice with an oar until she had an open space ahead of us and on either side for as far as she could reach. Then we rowed a few feet, Dot pulling and I pushing from the stern, until Dot had to stand up again to break more ice. Fortunately there was no wind. The day was a weather breeder, fantastically beautiful, the land looming, the farther islands clear and blue against the sky; the sun was very bright.

It took us a long time to get across. I was the cheering section. "We're the North Atlantic Patrol," I said. "We're an ice breaker, going to rescue destroyers and stuff." Halfway across Dot sat down and lit a cigarette.

"You're no help," she said darkly. "And this is what we get for having *pets*." She uttered the word with loathing.

But the reception at the house was enough to make up for everything. The fire hadn't gone out, and we caught it in time. Smokey went around in hysterical circles, yelping and crying. The cats went to the well with us, running sidewise in the powdery snow, pushing their noses through it like miniature snowplows, crowding back in the house to climb all over us and say again and again how they'd worried, and was it really us, and how about moving supper up an hour or so by way of celebration?

Late that evening, Dot stood looking from the back window of the kitchen down toward the fishhouse and wharf and the dark frozen harbor beyond. At the wharf there was suddenly a tiny flare of light, as if someone had lit a cigarette. In a few minutes Guy burst into the house to regard her as some species of superwoman.

"What did you come across for?" he demanded.

"Somebody had to," said Dot with an air of simple nobility.

He had come across much more easily than we had because the channel we had broken was still open. And the next day we awoke to a blizzard. If we'd stayed on the mainland all night we couldn't have come across in a howling snowstorm.

"Darned cats and dog," Dot muttered. "What we go through for them!" But while she said it she was lying on the couch with Smokey across her feet, Soldi on her chest, and Tris curled smugly against Smokey's back, so I don't think she minded the ice-breaking episode too much.

Once in that same icetime, Madelyn's husband, Brad, came home on leave. So they bundled up the baby and a new chocolate cake and came down to Gay's Island. Roland Stimpson brought them over, landing them at a point down below Charlotte's camp. He tore up somebody's outdoor picnic table and laid the planks over the frozen mud flats for them to walk on, and then they tramped up through deep fresh snow to the house, to hand us the cake with a flourish as if they'd just gotten out of a taxi before the door. We're always flattered when someone arrives like that. It shows they really *wanted* to come!

Eventually, after a long spell of bitter windless cold, the ice in the harbor became too thick to break, but it was too unstable for walking. We decided in five minutes flat one morning to get off the island while the cove in front of the house was still open, and a space at the far end of the harbor, between Flea Island and Mr. Dunn's wharf. It was a splendid morning, and the water between us and the islands was as blue and gently rippling as it had ever been in summer.

There was an hour of complicated scrambling, during which Guy dragged a punt across the Neck by the fishhouse and rowed it around to the cove by the house; Dot and I threw what we intemperately called "necessities" into suitcases, later finding that we had practically nothing we needed and a lot of utterly useless gear like summer blouses and a bird book. We packed the firmly resisting cats just as firmly into their baskets, put Smokey on his leash, grabbed up our best coats, and tramped down through the snow to the beach. We were lucky in that there was no wind. It was another weather breeder of course, and temporarily everything was as calm and bright as silk. With three adults in a ten-foot skiff, two cats, a dog, suitcases, and assorted junk, we needed quiet seas to row out around the island and into the narrow stretch of open water at the distant end of the harbor. There was slush ice around Mr. Dunn's wharf when we came up to it, and the next morning the harbor was frozen over completely. We had gotten off the island just in time.

The ice doesn't catch us now, but the tide still does. It keeps us in a sufficiently humble state by chastening us every time we get overconfident. I suppose this has been happening since the First Man decided he'd at last gotten the better of Nature, whereupon Nature promptly drowned him with a flood or swept him off a cliff with a hurricane. When we Gay's Islanders get that omnipotent feeling, the tide does something absolutely unscheduled and uncalled-for.

Like the time when we went to see *Great Expectations*.

I am a Dickens addict. Dot isn't. I attribute this lamentable state of affairs to the fact that she didn't read Dickens in school, nor did she have a Dickensophile mother. She had not been driven to reading *Oliver Twist* at a very early age on a day when there was absolutely nothing else to do, and it was snowing outdoors; she had never gone around obsessed with the troubles Little Dorrit bore so uncomplainingly. And when I was in the eleventh grade we teen-age sophisticates were knocked brutally out of our shells of boredom as Mr. Smoyer read aloud from *A Tale of Two Cities* and left us sitting unashamedly tense and chilly with gooseflesh. He had wrung tears from the more impressionable girls with *David Copperfield* and commanded fascinated attention from the boys.

So, with *Great Expectations* showing in Rockland, I was ready to see that Dot became enlightened. Her idea of a cozy evening's reading is *Gamaliel Bradford's Journal*, or a book of essays that first appeared in *The Atlantic Monthly*. That was fine, but I wanted her to know Dickens, too.

We left the island on a bonny high tide. The season was autumn, too early for ice to form in the puddles. Fine, crisp, frosty weather. . . . We tied the skiff to an alder above the high-water mark, just below Hilda George's cottage, instead of making her fast at Leslie's wharf. We'd be back at the next high tide and could go directly across to our wharf as effortlessly as a chip.

We stayed later than we intended, but after hasty calculations we decided that the tide wouldn't be too low; no lower than half tide. We'd only have to get the skiff down over the rocks into the water. The rocks were uneven and covered with barnacles, but they were solid underfoot, and downhill.

It was just coming dark, a chill clear dusk, when the taxi driver let us out, and we went optimistically along the narrow path through the field, between banks of dead meadowsweet and hardhack, and came out on the shore. We could see the faint glimmering of the water far below, and see the line of rocks, frosty white with barnacles in the dimness, and we knew with a horrid certainty that the tide was much farther out than half tide. A great stretch of mud flats reached from the rocks to the water. The tide, with its customary lack of dependability, had rushed out with the speed of the Tidal Bore of the Petitcodiac, and there we were. Stranded.

Surely, when it was as low as that, it must be on the point of returning, we argued. If we started to tug at the skiff now, by the time we got her down to the last rock, the water would be high enough for us to get her overboard.

"You and your Dickens!" Dot mumbled as we pulled at the Run-About. Light as our little companion was, tonight she was as unmovable as a ton of pig iron, and I could feel the vertebrae in my back clicking merrily in and out of place like castanets. I could think of nothing but to reply, snappishly,

"Well, you liked it, didn't you?"

"Not so much that I think this is.worth it," Dot said obscurely. We were dressed up for the occasion in high-heeled shoes and good suits; we could hardly see where we were going, we slipped, skidded on the rockweed, and nearly fell down. At last, winded, we sat down on the side of the skiff and looked at each other. We said nothing. We did not even blame each other—me for insisting on the movie, Dot for insisting that the tide could not have gone down too far. Our frustration was too great for words. We were tide-nipped.

The cold breeze that had been blowing icily around our nylons was a lot colder all at once. We had to find a lee spot somewhere. We could have gone up to Leslie's kitchen where it was warm and bright with lamplight, but we didn't feel like holding conversation with anybody. We wanted to sulk in private.

So we walked around the shore to Leslie's fishhouse, making heavy weather of it on account of the dark and the uneven footing and our high heels. And when we got to the fishhouse we didn't want to sit in it. It was too dark to find a place clean enough to sit on, where we wouldn't get fish scales and gurry on our clothes. We walked down the beach to the end of the wharf that loomed high and dry above the tide and sat in Leslie's skiff, lying there aground in the shelter of the wharf. We saw with growing dismay that the tide was still receding and wondered if we were about to witness some new phenomenon, when the entire harbor would go dry before our very eyes.

"*Great Expectations!*" said Dot. "That's what *we* had! And look at us!"

"It was worth it," I said through my chattering teeth. "Remember when Pip was running across the marshes, and the gibbet was creaking in a wind like this one?"

"I know it was wonderful," said Dot. "I'll concede that. But please stop talking about it till we get home."

"If we ever do." . . . We turned back to studying the water, only faintly visible now. At last we could tell that the tide had turned, and as we stared intently it crept toward us. It was in no hurry to come back *in*, after its headlong and unreasonable speed in going *out*. It had to sneak about twenty-five feet over the mud and float the skiff we were in. It came with agonizing slowness; the stars began to appear and were reflected in the water. The wind blew up briskly, and finally, when we were so stiff we creaked, the skiff floated.

We rowed home in it, passing our own darling perched high and dry on the rocks. Blackie came to the door of his house to look after us as we went up the path. Smokey heard us coming and began to bark.

Home was warm; home had a teakettle humming to itself on the stove, an eager dog, a purring cat; warm slacks and sweaters, socks and moccasins, in place of city-going high heels, nylons, and dressmaker suits. Home was hot cocoa and thick satisfying sandwiches, and hungry animals racing through their suppers with loud sounds of enjoyment.

Warmed and fed, our snappish mood departed for one of

bland contentment. We discussed the movie, which Dot had enjoyed after all. We were expansive and smug. And all the time the tide was rising. The wind had slacked off when we went out to row Leslie's skiff home and get our own.

We rowed slowly. The harbor was without sound or motion, except for the faint *chunking* of our oars, and the way the star reflections broke and shimmered as the blades shattered the surface of the water.

"Isn't it beautiful?" we asked each other. And it really was. The loom of the dark woods against the star-dusted sky, the trembling images of the stars in the water, the endless quiet and solitude of the moment, had erased completely the long discomfort of chilled and hungry waiting. Being just fed and warmed, we could afford to relax and be admiring, and rather complacent, as if we'd grown the woods ourselves and personally planted the stars.

So you see, Tide's Way is a good name for this house. The tide rules our way of living. There is no fighting it. It goes its own way, irrevocable and silent. Though Yolande, the new Dodge, is stabled on the mainland side now, we still must cope with the tide before we can reach her. So she can't spoil us as much as people say she will. We shall always have the tide to keep us in line, to remind us that not for everyone has life reached a point where it is completely on wheels. We shall still have the use of our arms and legs, in spite of Yolande.

And I, for one, am completely satisfied that we can't drive her right up to the door. Oh, there will be times, no doubt, when it would seem eminently satisfactory to be able to drive the groceries home, instead of loading and unloading a skiff with them, and pushing the wheelbarrow up the slope from the wharf while fending off Blackie, who has discovered the apples and doughnuts. But because we've learned—almost—how to live with the tide instead of fighting it, it doesn't present us with too many battles. It helps us get our oil home when it's high, and when it's low we dig clams. When it's high we row far up the Gut and imagine peaceful English rivers; when it's low we watch cranes and herons picking their way across the purple mussel beds.

And it's nice to have a high tide when people come for the first time, so they can't see our mud flats. You have to live with mud flats a long time before you can see their beauty as we do.

CHAPTER THIRTEEN

IN THE DOORYARD

There are no trees close to the house on Gay's Island, though the thirty-three acres more or less consist almost entirely of woodland. The house sits prim and white on its rise, with wide open spaces all before, and the alders kept at a decent distance behind. We can claim numberless birches, a few maples whose red buds against a spring sky give rise to all sorts of lyrical emotions in us, and thousands of spruces. We can walk through deep woods that look like the Gustave Doré illustrations in the book of French fairy tales; one expects momentarily to see Hop-o'-My-Thumb pop out from behind a giant toadstool, or to discover that the little clearing ahead swimming in green-gold light is really the entrance to the castle of the Sleeping Beauty. Tristan, wandering among great trunks and over silvery mosses with his yellow coat glowing in the shadows, might suddenly make a metamorphosis into Puss in Boots, and if Smokey should all at once address a remark to one in a perfectly intelligible voice, it would not be surprising.

But there are still no trees around the house, and at first we grieved about it. The old wind-twisted apple tree, with all its boughs gone from one side, which stands halfway to the shore, became strangely beautiful to us, along with the tall feathery rowan tree on the edge of the bank, whose roots are washed almost daily in salt water. A wild apple tree, thick and misshapen, made a little clump of green near the rowan tree. It wasn't much to see at first, before we knew it could be a great rich bouquet of pink and white bloom in the next spring. These were all we had for trees near the house, and to reach them meant fighting through an armored thicket of raspberry bushes and thistles that had been allowed to flourish unhampered for hundreds of years, by the looks of them. We could well believe that the thistle helped the Scots repel invaders.

Trees bring and hold birds, and that was another reason why we missed having them close to the house. Interest in birds is a highly contagious disease and I had become a Bird-lover simply because Dot had such a good time getting excited about chestnut-sided warblers and such. But having to make special trips away from the house, up the hill or down over the Neck, was rather different from watching the antics of kinglets and sparrows over morning coffee, as we did on Criehaven. And besides, at first the woods seemed very forbidding to us. Even while we were entranced by the golden shafts of sunlight slanting through the loosely woven roof of boughs, and felt very spiritual and breathless about the whole thing, an unidentified rustling could freeze us momentarily with fear. Even if the rustle turned out later to be Smokey, we were still nervous.

Not having trees around the house, we had to settle down and make the best of it and convince ourselves that even if we didn't have trees, we at least had a View. Nothing stood in our way in any direction. From the back windows we could see the village of Friendship with its nestling white houses and its street lights twinkling at night; and from the front we could look across the river at Port Clyde, with its sardine factory and wharves and boats at anchor. With the field glasses we could pick out, among the woods, roofs of intriguing appearance that probably belonged to palatial estates staffed by Filipino house-boys. Sprawled around on what we hoped someday would be a lawn we enjoyed this vicarious contact with the idle rich and speculated without malice on how it would be to live in a spot-less house like an illustration in *House Beautiful,* and never be as dirty and tired as we were.

Turning slightly we could behold the line of islands march-ing out to the open sea, with Monhegan standing high and alone at the end, and then if we turned back toward the mainland we could see all the boats of our own harbor, resting like quiet gulls above their reflections in the dark shadow of Mr. Dunn's woods.

That hill of his, covered with spruce and maple, has become very dear to us. In the spring, the banks of the Gut are a series of paintings by Corot, with all the delicate greens that could be imagined, and here and there the misty white of a wild cherry tree, and somewhere else the spray of rosy buds that mark a maple. In the fall the colors blaze and sing. The oak trees still have their russet and tawny leaves when the others are gone. The birches are always lovely even while they are bare. Our own trees, seen from the house, have for us an inexpres-sible charm because they are our own. Our twisted apple trees; our rowan where the crows sit and in whose boughs I saw my first sparrow hawk; our little maples growing beside the stone wall, whose buds we hail each year as if they were a sort of annual miracle, which perhaps they are. Our birches, some of which are bigger than I ever knew birches could be. Our groves of spar spruce, in which we sometimes hear the whispering voices of baby crows, and always the chipmunks. Our fragile, maidenly poplars, all trembling silvery leaves. Our wild cherries and small pines.

And our alders. Properly speaking, alders are not trees. Alders are a scourge. Everyone who has ever lived in the country knows about alders. They will steal a pasture while your back is turned. They seem to grow with the bewitched vigor of Jack's beanstalk and aren't nearly so useful.

We cut a few back, with the intention of making a clear vista down to the Gut. It was a sort of Strength-through-Joy movement. Equipped with a brush-cutting implement that sprained my wrists every time I used it, axes, and machetes, we used to lead our guests out to the alders and warn them not to cut each other's legs off.

We did manage to get a path cut down to the Gut behind the house, and after that everybody was reluctant. Now, probably because there's nothing else we can do about it short of spending all our days hacking away, we like our alders. We have cleared a wide neat path to the fishhouse, and on early mornings in spring, when their branches are shining with dew and their tassels hanging in fragrant golden clusters, we swear there has never been a sweeter perfume, and it is ritual to linger on the path to breathe deeply, and close our eyes at the same time, because that makes it even better.

Two friendly little couples come each spring to make their nests there, and when we catch a glimpse of the little masked Maryland yellowthroat swaying on a topmost twig, we are enthralled. And as soon as his madrigal is finished, from the other side of the path comes the song of the yellow warbler, and we turn to see a tiny golden bird flying to another branch whose tassels are no brighter than he is.

The alders behind the house shelter warblers of all sorts, vireos and flycatchers and bobolinks; and there is a catbird who talks to us all day. He gives a creditable imitation of the robins, if only he wouldn't reveal himself with his ill-tempered whine on the end. In spring and fall, when the chickadees and sparrows and juncos are practically the only birds in the alders, the bushes are like banks of violet smoke when we see them from a distance, and the white trunks of the birches shine with an ivorylike gleam among them.

Following our policy of liking what we can't eliminate, we have even found an excuse for thistles. We fought them vigorously until the goldfinches came.

"What, get rid of our thistles and drive away the goldfinches?" we now exclaim, round-eyed with horror. This gives the impression that we planted the thistles expressly for the goldfinches, and suitably quells any remarks about thistledown blowing over the lawn.

We always think of it like this, in capitals: THE LAWN. We never thought we'd have one. Occasionally, for want of something else to do—though such a situation rarely arose— one of us would languidly gather a bushel basket full of tin cans from the tall grass. If one escaped the can hazard, one could fall into a camouflaged hole left by Hazel. We were a long time finding out what made all the various-sized hollows in the front yard and down over the slope.

"Sometimes They (the former tenants were always referred to as They, like the Forces of the Other World) dug holes and buried their garbage instead of saving it," one of us hazarded.

"Maybe They were digging *for* something," someone else said. "Water, or. . . ." Flash of inspiration. "Don't you have to dig for truffles?"

The rest sneered at that. "They thought somebody buried treasure at one time or another," was a third suggestion, delivered in a tone of authority meant to end the whole matter. "So They dug up the whole place looking for it."

"It was Hazel," Charlotte Gray told us one day. "Hazel was a pig. She belonged to Them, and she was the largest pig Pleasant Point ever knew. She adored picnics, and whenever someone came down from Thomaston for a picnic, Hazel smelled it out and ambled graciously right into the middle of it."

Hazel was a Gay's Island character. She rooted her way merrily around the fields, and the scoops and hollows that give our lawn its delightfully scalloped look we owe to Hazel.

We used to wish that we had a hundred sheep like Blackie to do something to the area where we wanted a lawn. Failing that, we longed for the courage to burn off the fields during those still, silvery gray April days when the scent of other people's fires filled the air. But the wind had a nasty habit of springing up suddenly and carrying flames from one thick mat of dead grass to the next. It wasn't until one of Dot's younger brothers, Oscar, came down to stay a few weeks with us that we actually took the job in hand.

We must have been a great trial to Oscar, who had been a first sergeant in the Coast Artillery and was used to Getting Things Done. He told us what he could do on Gay's Island if he had a working party, and we felt glummer and weaker by the moment.

"Why don't we make him Overseer?" I suggested to Dot. "Like in plantation days . . . he could see to things for us."

"Where's the working party?" she retorted. "*Us.*"

And that's how it turned out. One night at dusk he rushed us out with a great fanfare, equipped with brooms and buckets of water, and before we knew it the field was ringed in fire and we were burning off. His assurance was contagious. We stopped worrying about the wind, which didn't come up anyway, and realized we were starting THE LAWN.

After a few rainy spells the grass began to show up. Led on by visions of velvety greensward, we decided on what we could handle for lawn, and planned to let the rest come up in wild strawberries. This was a lovely and purely poetic thought, because we've never had more than a cup of wild strawberries from the field yet, but anyway, the rest of the idea worked.

It was then that we came into possession of a lawn mower. Guy brought it home from Rockland, where he had found it in someone's cellar and paid ten dollars for it. Guy is a small man, and the lawn mower was almost as big as he was. It was incredibly ancient.

"They should have given you ten dollars for taking it off their hands," Dot said, and Guy stated the unanswerable premise that it was better than no lawn mower at all.

This was true, because Blackie didn't like to eat grass that needed cutting, but grass that was already cut. He followed *behind* the lawn mower, preferring his salad tossed, as it were.

The lawn mower was about as heavy as a Juggernaut carriage and as unwieldy. It ran with a particularly erratic, sidewise motion and a disconcerting sound of gears, as if it were working up to the moment when it would suddenly fly apart and disintegrate completely like the Wonderful One-Horse Shay. One might say that we actually mowed the lawn six times at once, because we had to push the thing forward a foot, whereupon it stopped short, then draw it back and push it ahead ten or twelve inches. Even with such a delicate and painstaking technique, the cutters were likely to stop without warning, and all the time that we thought it was working, nothing was happening at all.

After Oscar's visit, Bette came, and Dot's youngest brother Neil, about sixteen. Bette and Neil fought daily with the lawnmower. No doubt they banged their young stomachs against the handle fifty times a day when it stopped treacherously short, but they kept at it, racing—jerkily—over the slopes and hollows and yodeling at the top of their lungs, all the while looking like beautiful young blond vikings.

It is amazing—truly—to look back and see how we suffered and yet conquered with that old lawn mower. Without it, we couldn't have begun to clip the new grass; the grass would be tall again, harboring the vicious mosquitoes that could give the Jersey brand a run for their money.

But now, glory be, we have a new lawn mower! I never knew

Elisabeth pushes the wheelbarrow (the Gay's Island T-Bird)
past the remains of Blackie's house. A tree swallow's house
tops the pole in front.

The shingle message board is left on the door when Elisabeth and
Dot aren't home to let people know where they are. (Liz's typewriter
is parked here temporarily; this is not the writing table.)

The fish house, seen across a field of goldenrod and bayberry.
Flea Island and the mainland in the background.

Flea Island, at the upper end of Pleasant Point Harbor,
with the mainland behind it.

Looking down through the Gut to the Stepping Stones.
Low tide, revealing the mussel beds and clam flats and ledges,
has an infinite variety and irresistible charm all its own.

Liz has always liked to work outdoors, and the old wheelbarrow
is a veteran of quite a few books.

Dot and Elisabeth in front of the house.

Old lobster traps near the shore, with the house behind.

The mainland wharf and workshop, next door to Dennis Young's.
The island looms across the harbor.

The fish house and wharf seen from under the big birch
at the Office.

there could be such bliss in owning a sensible, utilitarian object like a lawn mower. I never knew I would ever bring one into the house, with such joyous reverence, before the dew could fall upon it, and get down on my knees like an adoring slave to pour oil into every possible place where oil could be poured and gaze with admiration at the rubber tires, the shining metal, the clean sharp blades!

Marvelously, the lawn began to resemble a lawn. We could hardly believe it at first. When visitors exclaimed, "Oh, how nice your grass looks!" we thought they were being graciously kind. Of course it looked good to *us*, but we were prejudiced. We remembered the cans, the mosquitoes, the rotted boards with nails in them, the thistles. But it was really getting to be a lawn, even out in the back yard under the clotheslines, where the pressure of your feet stirred up the aromatic cologne-scent of Jill-over-the-ground, and you had to steer the lawn mower carefully around a certain patch of strawberry blossoms, and a sea of tall grass rose beyond the straight edge of clipped green. Fog, moist southerly winds, and Blackie had all contributed.

Now we sprawl luxuriously on our grass, looking with professional eyes at the fruit trees that were a gift from my mother; in summer we watch cutthroat croquet that is full of devastating hazards because of the slope. Once a ball rolls to the foot of the lawn, the unlucky player spends the rest of the game trying to knock it uphill, only to have it bump against one of Hazel's hollows and roll down again.

No doubt as a reward for our labors with the lawn mower, sickle, and shears, my father set up a flagpole for us. He and my brother Kent cut down a tall slim spruce in the woods, trimmed it smooth, painted it white, and sank it in the lawn one Labor Day week end. The Schmitzes sent us a flag for it, and it looks wonderful, blowing against a backdrop of woods and water, and gives the place tone, besides. Lord knows we need tone!

When we're taking the flag down on a summer evening, and the cats are chasing moths across the lawn, and the sight of Blackie feeding leads us to make poetical allusions to flocks and herds winding over the lea, it is easy to have a sort of mystic assurance that all's well with the world, since we have attained a lawn, a new lawn mower, and a flagpole.

Nature's landscaping, now that we can keep it under control, works in well with our own. The catnip, for instance, that grows all around the back door; we don't know how it got there, but we have it, attracting clouds of bees with its pale lavender blossoms, and keeping the cats in a mood of alcoholic sentimentality. True, some uninitiated persons are prone to sniff with horrified interest and say, "I smell a *skunk!*" But since we know it's catnip, it doesn't smell like skunk to us. We don't mind the bees. In fact we have a great fondness for them, since they're in the family, as it were. We sit on the doorstep with the bees humming close to our heads, and trust them implicitly. Perhaps they trust us.

The catnip keeps thrusting up between our flagstones and having to be clipped back. This accounts for the shameless way Tris sprawls his yellow length across the flagstones and rolls and rolls, and purrs and purrs. Properly speaking, our flagstones aren't flagstones, but flat rocks from the beach, which we carried up two or three at a time and set in place. For a while we had quite a struggle with some young visitors who displayed an uninhibited desire to move anything movable and throw it away in the tall grass or down the well. We had to fight for our flagstones, which kept disappearing.

"I've put everything else out of reach," Dot announced, when a visit was due. "The ducks (decoys) are in the open chamber. I've taken up the border of quartz from around the delphinium, and gathered up all the tools. And I'll be darned if they touch those flagstones—I'll *sit* on 'em if I have to."

"It would be more helpful if you sat on the children," I suggested. But since this was not practical from their mothers' point of view, we didn't try it. We merely threatened them, quietly but effectively, and after Blackie chased them over the lawn, snorting, stamping, and leaping, they were really very good.

On the other side of our line, up the slope toward the southern end of the island, the blueberries grow profusely. If mind has any power at all over matter, they should be spreading with a positive rush down into our fields, because we concentrate deeply on this in blueberry season. It is not easy to forget that some day someone might be living up there who would not be very charitable about the blueberries.

Whenever he comes and whoever he is, he'd better hurry if he wants to save anything from the juniper. I understand that juniper produces the berries that sometimes flavor gin. This cuts no ice with me, however, and as far as I'm concerned, the juniper is the White Man's Burden. In our fields it gets short shrift from us, what with our horsehide gauntlets, our brush hooks, and the nameless (for me, anyway) gadget which snips off alders so efficiently. Everybody used to want to use it back in the days when we could get them all to work in the forestry department, before they became disenchanted.

As for that long stretch between the house and the barn, along which we used to shove wheelbarrows loaded with household goods and feel we were carving something out of the wilderness, Blackie has done a fine job at clearing it out.

Now the fields on either side of the path show an unbelievably lovely carpet of violets and strawberry blossoms in May, later giving way to the buttercups and the tawny hawkweed. Is there any color more burning, more intense, than those little spots of blazing orange along the path? Red clover grows amid the scattered gleams of rattleweed, and the daisies open in long powderings of white. Where the highland cranberry spreads its glossy dark green vines over the ground, their blossoms show like tiny pink-and-white tulips. We have blueberries starting to come in the fields now, and they are thick with waxen white bells. And then there are all the infinitesimal plants we don't know, small stars of white and yellow; and the bluets along the edges of the paths, and the blue flag budding on their bright green spears in the marshy spot below the well, the stiff-stalked evening primrose and bright orange jewelweed.

The island will always put us to shame in what it does without any help from us. But we're proud of our lawn, our sweet peas, our delphiniums, lupins, and phlox, which we set out in a rainstorm and watched for days like anxious relatives waiting for baby's first tooth. But when we discover violets we still act as if no one else had ever found a violet, white *or* purple.

The magazines are full of wonderful pictures, over which I can dream for hours. Formal gardens, informal gardens, vistas and arbors, terraces and pools. . . . Oh, lovely, lovely! But I look at them without envy, the way we used to peer through the glasses at the sumptuous roofs emerging from the trees across the river. We have our LAWN. We have a few perennials to grow in tall and vivid spikes of color against the white clapboards; we have two apple trees, a Winesap and a Red Delicious, a peach tree and a cherry tree; and there is the twisted old apple tree that gave us twelve apples last fall for sauce. The rowan treats us with white flowers in the spring and red berries in the fall, besides having a romantic name; and there's the wild apple tree with the gorgeous blossoms.

We have bull thistles alive with goldfinches down by the barn, and alders with tassels and bobolinks. I think we're doing pretty well in the landscaping department. It may be a little out of control in places, but on the whole, it's satisfactory.

CHAPTER FOURTEEN

OFF THE BEATEN TRACK

The lady back on Criehaven who used to flit in and out of the house doling out disagreeable prophecies, like the Cumaean sibyl without the chicken entrails, had a favorite refrain.

"You won't ever see anybody over there on that place," it went. "Nobody will ever find you. You'll be buried alive!"

Feeling like Dreyfus about to be exiled—I'll never forget the movie, where it showed him in his little hut on a barren sun-baked hunk of land—I always managed, nevertheless, to give her a calmly confident smile. At least she and her broomstick couldn't fly over twenty miles of ocean to drop in on us at Gay's Island, and that made exile seem very bearable indeed.

We did have our lonely moments, in that first hot, dirty, hectic month. There were times when we felt absolutely cut off from all that we'd known and loved. Everything seemed impossibly involved, and we were always just out of something vital like sugar or canned milk. What with ration stamps, and the fact that Port Clyde was three miles to the east, Friendship three miles to the west, and Fales' store seven miles up the road toward Thomaston and we had no car, the food problem practically dwarfed all others. When some of the Criehaveners came down, we did not fall on their necks with gratitude because their faces were familiar. We looked at them suspiciously, and wished they could have waited until things looked a little better around the house. After they had gone, our loneliness was more pronounced than ever.

Yet not one of us admitted to regret at leaving Criehaven. We must have sensed the possibilities of this alien territory and half guessed at what lay before us after the first exhausting struggle was past. Our low moods came from fatigue, not remorse. We loved Criehaven, but it had nothing left for any one of us.

One morning we all came to rest on the back doorstep—which is at the front of the house, only on the ell—looking like a pack of gypsies who'd just been run out of the last town, and began to get dinner. My mother and I were snapping some wax beans (donated), and Dot was cleaning clams for frying.

We sat there in the midst of our squalor, still in clamdigging clothes; with quilts hung out to air, the gasoline washing machine covered with a dingy tarpaulin, the chickens wandering absent-mindedly about our feet. Down in the field Patty tried, with a frustrated air, to eat her way through the tall grass, Blackie moving skittishly around her. Patty is dead now, and we remember mostly her little-lady ways, and the trusting nose pushed into our hands. But in the days of settling, her temper was as uncertain as ours, and Blackie never knew when he was going to be bunted amidships.

We must have been an unprepossessing collection of people and animals. And we knew it. With something like horror, then, we saw a strange man suddenly appear in the path from the fishhouse, a woman behind him. Even my mother, ordinarily never at a loss, sat there in a frozen silence, thinking, she said afterward, that here she was, caught at last in slacks.

The man was a hearty-looking individual dressed in tropical white and carrying a case, and somebody muttered, "Good God, it's a traveling salesman!"

Guy, who hadn't had time to shave for several days, looked furtive and did things with his cap brim as if he thought he could really hide behind it. Dot, resplendent in clamdigging dungarees that did nothing at all for her stocky figure, sat lower on her log and became very busy with the clams. No one seemed inclined to make a move in the direction of hospitality, and Nemesis in white slacks and sun glasses continued to advance upon us.

Remembering the Ogilvie motto: "To the End," I got up. Smokey came out of his coma, saw the strangers, and remembered his own motto, which is, apparently, "To the Barricades!" He rushed down the path barking, scattering the hens in a squawking flurry and stampeding Blackie, which so annoyed Patty that she bunted him soundly in the ribs.

Nothing destroys one's poise like having to punctuate greetings to a stranger with ineffectual commands to a hysterical dog. And in the midst of this chaos the strange man beamed at me, put out his hand, and said briskly, "I'm looking for Elisabeth Ogilvie. My name is Alton Hall Blackington."

"That's me," I said helplessly. The lady, who looked so cool and crisp that we felt even dirtier than before, was Mrs. Blackington. But they had a wonderful gift for putting people at ease, and they sat on our little square of tramped-down grass as if it were velvety turf at least two hundred years old, and explained what they wanted.

The exciting fact was that he was preparing a lecture about Maine authors, and I was one of them; in fact, he was classing me with Kenneth Roberts and Ben Ames Williams. I've never known how those gentlemen felt about it but I know that I was complimented to the point where I sat in a sort of smiling, imbecilic silence and did what I was told, wondering if he'd really use these movies he was so busily making, and if people would actually believe I was bright enough to write a book.

As for the others, they tried violently to back out of camera

range, but there was no escape, and so we've all been immortal-
ized on color film: my mother with her slacks, Dot in her
dungarees, Guy with his whiskers. But they stopped worrying,
because after we'd all eaten fried clams together, and Mr. Blackington had entertained us with story after story, we weren't
thinking much about clothes, the lack of permanents, and the
junk outside the windows that hadn't been carted off to the
shore yet. We were having fun. We were remembering, suddenly, that we were supposed to be Buried Alive, we were Off
the Beaten Track.

Obligingly I milked Patty for the camera. She was never
bothered by odd milking hours because ever since Dot had
owned her I was forever being called upon to show that I could
really milk a goat. I was the one who had to do it, because Dot
had to hold Patty up. Patty was never actively unpleasant about
being milked, but she believed in passive resistance and lay
down in the dish.

Patty also distinguished herself for Mr. Blackington's public
by driving Blackie away from her grain box during the milking. Blackie, exhilarated no doubt by the sudden carnival air
around the place, struck back. Patty sprang into action and the
whole battle was filmed, while the chickens descended happily
on the grain box and drank the milk, and I stood by looking
mutely distraught. My expression, which was entirely unre-
hearsed, is remarkably vivid on film.

Mr. Blackington came back again, the next year. He sent a
postcard in advance. We conferred; this time, the thing must
be done *right*. This time we'd be ready. We'd have clean
clothes all ready to put on the instant we sighted him. Daily,
from the arrival of the postcard, we dug clams, and when he
didn't come, we used them ourselves and dug fresh ones the
next day. We picked quarts and quarts of blueberries, and every
day my mother made blueberry pies. We ate pies every day.

We were as blue-tongued as pure-bred chows. And we were clammy.

"If anybody tries to scratch my back," Dot mused, "they'll be surprised. I'm growing a shell. If I start burrowing into the mud flats any time, please haul me out."

"I'll worry," my mother said, "when we all start washing in melted butter."

"God, for some beefsteak," Guy mourned quietly to himself.

Some friends, the MacLellans, arrived in the meantime and took up residence in Victor Whittier's little cottage across the cove. My oldest brother Allan, his wife Wilma, and the two girls, Pat and Katherine, drove up from Connecticut to take a look at Gay's Island and see what it had that could keep me from Criehaven. My second brother Kent's daughter Barbara and her chum Evelyn were here already. The island seemed crowded with people, especially little girls fourteen and under. There were cats underfoot, Tristan and Isolde, and my mother's cherished Alec, who Walked by Himself like Kipling's cat, and never spoke to anyone but my mother.

In spite of the throng, we kept preparing for Mr. Blackington. All the guests were enthusiastic about the pies and the clams, but the berrypickers and clamdiggers were getting a little tired. Suddenly our enthusiasm petered out, and we backslid.

Came a dewy morning when some of the men, with the exception of Allan, got up early to go hauling with Guy. Another summer day was beginning, calm and warm and bright, when from across the cove someone shrieked, "Fire!"

To our horrified eyes smoke seemed to be pouring out in white billows from Vic's little cottage. Fire, the constant terror that comes to live side by side with one's delight in owning woodland, was upon us. I raced down to the shore to catch the men before they started out in Guy's boat and screamed myself hoarse trying to be heard above the racing of the engine.

In the meantime my mother had gone around the outside of the house until she was below the windows of Allan's room and was calling up to him.

His wife heard her, just as Allan said groggily, "Whassa matter?"

"The house is on fire," said Wilma calmly. She is a tall slim blonde who would be tranquil through a tidal wave and earthquake combined.

"Oh," said Allan, scowling at her. "What time is it?"

"That hasn't anything to do with it," said Wilma. "You'd better get up."

And now that the alarm had been thoroughly spread, and the men were starting around the edge of the cove, the lady who had shrieked "Fire!" came out on the porch of the cottage to wave her arms and shout that it was all right after all. She was very apologetic later, and unhappy about scaring us all, but she'd turned the oil *on* instead of *off*, and had sent a terrific flood of oil into the burners. It was a perfectly natural mistake to make, because the dial wasn't properly marked.

We were all so relieved when we congregated in Tide's Way's kitchen that we were positively giddy. I don't remember how many people were there at once, but I remember the children flipping through the tangle like so many little minnows.

It was Dot who glanced out the window and said in a tone of appalled astonishment, "My God, here's Blackie!"

Nobody looked around. We thought that the sheep had broken his rope in the general excitement, and in a little while we'd have to go out and round him up. We went on gabbling about what we'd thought and done, and would have done, and what would have happened if there'd really been a fire, and Mr. Blackington walked calmly into the midst of our little private madhouse, set down his camera, and said, "Hello."

After the first look, I was resigned. This is the way it always happened; this was the way it would *always* happen. If we were expecting a visit from the President, and were prepared every day for a month, he'd be sure to arrive on the day when the oilstove had sooted the whole house and the dog had thrown up all over the sitting-room rug.

It seems to me that there was an incredible amount of confusion for the next few moments. Allan had to have his breakfast. He is tall, dark, and extremely silent at times; and he shares with me the Ogilvie trait of being unapproachable before breakfast. The children scattered out over the lawn, with happy trills of laughter. They were wound up for the day in good style. It wasn't every morning that you began with a fine rousing fire alarm. The adults, limp as old seaweed, prepared to be entertaining while they gave harassed thoughts to the state of their hair, their shoelaces, and the pantry.

The rest of the day remains formless in my memory. I remember Blackie and Allan in an involved conversation about heavy water and the atomic bomb, which gave me a chance to zip into my special outfit and brush my hair. Mr. Blackington's nickname is Blackie, and so everybody was confused all day. "Mr. Blackington" was a terrific mouthful to say in a hurry, but on the other hand, the sheep was also called "Blackie."

I remember Blackie—human—setting a gorgeous clump of goldenrod against the silvery shingles of the Cuckoo's Nest, the little shed beside the ruins of the barn, to make a sharp note of color in the movie shots. And while he and I posed in animated conversation about galley proofs, with Blackie—ovine —nosing us, Allan operated the movie camera. I remember Blackie—the man—and myself sedately pacing around a field holding hands and sharing an alder fork, looking for water, while the rest of the party stood looking on and offering suggestions as to why the forked twig worked and if it really worked at all.

It did turn downward strongly in one spot, and to this day I am thrilled by the memory of it. But I can't make a forked twig work by myself, and it's one of the sad spots of my life that I haven't got the power. The family gets into frenzied arguments about water dowsing, and I always bring Kenneth Roberts and Alton Hall Blackington into it as incorruptible proof that it does work—if you've got what it takes.

And I remember my state of sadness because I was doomed always to be in a state of unpreparedness when Somebody came out of the goodness of his heart to help me with my career. And I remember Allan seriously addressing the sheep. In order to lessen the confusion, he said, Blackie (the sheep) should henceforth be called Mr. Blackington.

Mr. Blackington (Alton Hall, that is) has plugged my books and shown movies of a distraught and disheveled E.M.O. all over the country. Patty is dead now, but she lives on film, and Blackie, who still kicks his heels over the lawn, has kicked them for many audiences. I must say Patty and Blackie were far more photogenic than I.

We loved having the Blackingtons, but my sole regret is that I couldn't have met them at the wharf, looked poised and literary and *soignée*, in crisply tailored slacks and shirt from *Vogue*, waving a pair of dark glasses with jeweled frames and followed by something exotic like a Bedlington or a Saluki.

I used to have a pleasant dream of becoming an established writer and having a salon rich in editors and publishers and other literary characters. In the dream, the weather was always mild and bright, this simple classic white house was embowered in banks of hardy perennials (they save a lot of extra work in the spring), and surrounded by rolling slopes of green turf. We'd all sit around the lawn in those upholstered wheelbarrows and stretchers and things that pass for lawn furniture, sipping drinks pleasantly iced. (The refrigerator comes in another ·dream.)

The conversation would crackle, and of course I—in the *Vogue* outfit from the Blackington episode—would be tossing off epigrams, like a whole string of ladyfingers. This pleasant imagery didn't exist in the wintertime, except as a way of putting myself to sleep when the wind was shrieking down from the north, and the harbor was slowly freezing over.

Before our first uncomfortable experience with too much ice, we found the house cozy and easy to heat, the island lovely in the snow. We had visions of investing in skis; from the brow of the hill above the house, down past the front door to the barn, there'd be a wonderful slope.

But the ice came in quick and early, and we knew at last what it was to be stuck on the island. It was beautiful clear weather, snapping with bright, eye-dazzling cold. Usually after a day or so the ice broke up, and then in a windless spell it closed together again. We weren't nervous, but we were beginning to think it would be wisdom to pack up the two cats and the dog and a few clothes and typewriters and take off, in the next spell of clear weather.

There was a lot to do in the house and we were living mostly in the sitting room and kitchen. At the end of one particular day, we hadn't been across to the mainland for a week, and, feeling safe from unexpected callers, we'd let a great deal of housework go for the sake of more important work. The groceries, while not uncomfortably low, had reached an uninspired selection. There was a sinkful of dirty dishes. To give me credit, I was just about to do them up, and perhaps if the Two Gentlemen from *The Transcript* had waited one more day, they would have encountered a shining house.

But our usual destiny was with us. The kitchen smelled pleasantly of the new trapheads piled in one corner, of pine for lobster plugs, of spruce for new hoops for the trapheads; half the kitchen table was buried in manuscript. It was getting on to suppertime and we were discussing, lackadaisically, what could be gotten out of the uninteresting cans on the Lazaret shelf. The heavy knock on the door startled the dog into a shriek, and the rest of us into momentary paralysis.

It was Dot who opened the door, to a perfectly strange young man very formally got up in a dark overcoat and pale-gray felt hat. Since nobody dresses up around here in the wintertime, that in itself was amazing. What made it more amazing was that Dot thought it was her brother Russ. I did too. The first moment of resemblance startled us, and probably startled him, because we stood there staring at him as if we'd forgotten what other human beings looked like.

He came in smiling, and asked me gaily if I'd forgotten him. There was another young man with him, who seemed perfectly serene and friendly. I said very stupidly that I didn't remember.

"Hugh Boyd," he said, and then I recalled the feckless child who stood up in the Problems of Democracy class and made remarks about graft that had the teacher shushing him in frantic haste.

"Oh, yes," I said dazedly. "Only you were sort of weedy then." So we got off to a fine start. The other man was Dick Higginbotham—to be known within fifteen minutes as Higgy —and they'd bought the Boston *Transcript*, it seemed, and had come to ask for an article for their first issue.

Considering that the night was very dark outside, and that they'd found their way down from Rockland over seventeen miles of curvy, uphill and downdale road, the last few miles of it a narrow dirt trail through thick woods, and had gotten Leslie Young to row them across the Gut in a bitter wind so cold it burned, with ice to be broken all the way—considering all this, their zeal augured well for the future of *The Transcript*, especially when they could have reached me much more easily by a letter with a three-cent stamp on it.

Hughie is tall and talkative and blond, and Higgy, short and dark, is perhaps the most amiable and well-informed character I've ever met. He can discuss anything from the care and feeding of babies to milking a wild cow, and he'd been with Grenfell in Labrador, and he knew the King of Siam. In fifteen minutes we realized that the clutter, the lack of a gourmet's menu, and the dirty dishes, didn't mean a thing. While they introduced Guy to a quart of "anti-freeze" they'd brought along, Dot and I rushed through dishwashing with a fine *esprit de corps* and an enthusiasm we hadn't had for days, and assembled supper. We all talked at once over the table, and later on Dot brought out her guitar and we all sang, Hughie leading off in a fine sweet tenor which he must have developed since high-school days, since his most noted talent in those years was for making subversive remarks about the school committee.

We had a wonderful time, and I must have been still under the spell of it a few weeks later when I wrote off an article about lobstering which still seems good to me whenever I read it, which I do whenever I'm entertaining doubts of my talent.

The next morning Guy rowed them back among the ice floes, and the visit from Hughie and Higgy provided us with material for letters for several days.

It was a far cry from the salon of my dreams, but they were publishers and editors after all, and I suppose there are salons and salons.

It was summertime when Betty Finnin of *Woman's Day* wrote that she'd like to drop in on us. We had a lawn, even without the fancy furniture and the blossoming banks of delphinium, etc. It began to look as if this occasion would follow more faithfully the conventional way of entertaining editors. My mother was here, and a friend of hers, Mrs. Dickinson, a tall stately lady with fortitude and a quiet sense of humor which refreshes us whenever she's on Gay's Island. This time we prepared to be prepared and relaxed at the same time.

But I had read the letter wrong, and thought it was *next* week, and it was *this* week, and the telegram announcing her arrival came one miserably rainy, bleak cold afternoon.

So relaxation, that beckoning fair one, was out of the question, and we all hurried around bumping into each other as we worried about clams and blueberries and things. The next morning the sun was shining, however, and Dot and I went down to the fishhouse to wait for someone to appear on Leslie Young's wharf and wave.

Every car that turned into Leslie's dooryard had us craning frantically, swapping the glasses back and forth, and then, at last, somebody came out on Leslie's wharf and waved.

"It looks like two men," I observed, thinking with remarkable perception that one lady editor couldn't possibly look like two men, but we launched the skiffs anyway, with a great racketing over the rocks, and rowed across.

It turned out, inevitably, to be Hughie and Higgy. By now we were saying the two names like one word, Hewienhiggie, and we squawked at them like a couple of gulls discovering a doryload of herring, while in our minds the Problems of Unreadiness were arising like specters. The laundry problem was one of them. We had enough sheets, but Barbara and her chum had just left and we hadn't had time to wash their bedding. We had clean sheets for one, or maybe two, but for two more. . . .

Still, our pleasure and delight in seeing the boys again was the more important thing, and we gave them a skiff to row back to our wharf, to the great confusion of my mother and Mrs. Dickinson, who were watching from the house and also wondering if either of these two mysterious figures could be the lady editor—in slacks, possibly.

We explained to the boys that we were expecting Betty Finnin. I began to explain who she was, but Hughie, beaming happily, said "Good old Betty! What a surprise!"

"Do you *know* her?" I gaped, I'm afraid.

"Of course I know her. What do you think?" This with indignation. I couldn't say what I thought then, besides thinking that I was pleasantly surprised. But I know what I think now. Hugh has a marvelous formula for putting people at their ease, and I think he should patent it, definitely. It consists of interrupting explanations of identities with excited cries of "Good old So-and-So! Well, isn't this wonderful!" Then when he meets good old So-and-So, whom he has never in his life met before, he spikes all guns by exclaiming so radiantly and convincingly about some mutual friend so that Good Old So-and-So spends the entire visit with his brow furrowed and his eyes distant, trying to recall said mutual friend, and sure that his own memory is failing, since Hugh is so persuasively confident about the whole thing.

Anyway, Hugh's approach makes for hearty if rather confused cordiality all around. So I was beaming away as incandescently as he was at the thought of our *both* knowing Betty Finnin. And while Dot and Higgie looked at us with bemused eyes, another car pulled into Leslie's driveway. The figures that got out of it looked very purposeful.

"I'll go over and see if that's your company," Higgie volunteered. "I can row. Don't forget, I've been in the Navy." He rowed away, and we yelled after him, "Look out for the sand bar."

"I've been in the Navy!" Higgie yelled back in reproof, as he ran aground on the bar. After some splashing and shoving he freed himself, reached the other side, and disappeared up the road. When he came back with Mr. and Mrs. Christ—Betty and her husband—they were old friends.

By the end of the day we were *all* old friends, and it was much more like a salon than I'd expected. Though I wasn't getting off any epigrams, here I was entertaining Literary Personalities. And I was beginning to realize that people who want to see you enough to take chances on ice floes, rains, high winds, or a low dreen tide, are usually fun.

Arthur Christ struck up quite a friendship with Hezzie, the tough little ram who was supposed to be a companion for Blackie, and who was taking down the barn, board by board. Why he didn't attempt to take Arthur down, I'll never know. My mother and Mrs. Dickinson and Betty talked as gaily as three members of the same sewing circle; Smokey was, of course, frantically cordial, and Susan Dachshund eventually came out from under the chair where she'd been growling most of the day. Blackie begged cigarettes from everybody. What with swimming and horseshoes and croquet, and sitting around in our antiquated lawn chairs, we looked like a real summer resort, and everybody was having too much fun to be scintillating.

We put the boys to bed in the upper part of the fishhouse, down by the wharf. (We kept extra cots there to take care of the overflow from the house.) They had to be up early in order to catch the North Haven boat, so in the morning, when every raspberry bush and alder along the path dripped diamonds of dew, and the air had the cool luminosity one catches only before 7 A.M. in summer, Dot and I walked down to tell them their breakfast was ready.

When they had gone, we took Arthur and Betty up to the Old House and showed them the view of Friendship across the Tinker Field. We wondered, again and again, why it was that we felt this appalling sense of a hundred things undone at the arrival of company, when all the time we *knew* how much we were going to enjoy our guests.

We've entertained, unexpectedly, a great many people on Gay's Island. The list of guests whose visits went off in well-arranged, conventional, but also delightful fashion, is long; but the other list is growing too. There were the two girls on their way home from a hunting trip in Elderbank, Nova Scotia, the stamping ground of the Ogilvies. Leslie Young brought them over, and they startled me out of my wits by bringing me greetings from Elderbank. I *know* I looked stupid until they explained. Then it was a charming surprise, like a mica-flashing rock or a perfect shell washed up by the tide.

There was the time when a yacht anchored in the cove, and we sat there innocently watching the dinghy come ashore and discovered that some nice people, cruising on rationed gas, had used up some of their precious rations to call on me and tell me they enjoyed my books. They were the Knowlton Hewinses of Augusta, and they came back a second year too. The second time, we were knee-deep in shavings from my mother's and Dot's woodcarving, and from the time we recognized the *Margie*, until the dinghy touched the shore, the brooms were flying, the dogs were shooed, the cats left in tremendous dignity. Fresh blouses came out of bureau drawers, hair was combed—and when the Hewinses and their friends came up the path, we met them with a sincere cordiality that probably hid our breathlessness.

There was that morning in the spring, when we'd been so isolated on our side of the moat for weeks of wind and rain, and also lack of money. We had felt our isolation more keenly than usual because the bad weather made every day seem exactly alike. Suddenly there was a man on our doorstep, who had rowed himself over from the mainland to call. He was a man of a few concise words. As a boy he'd visited Criehaven; now he'd read my books and they'd renewed his memories of the place, and he was going back. He had a cup of coffee with us, while he and Dot swapped stories of Criehaven characters; of John and Eben and Raishe Crie, of Barney Erickson and the rest.

Mr. Wadsworth has been back twice, once to find out the

names of some Criehaven people with whom he might board, and again to tell us he'd been there, and how nice Roy and Ava Simpson were; he told us he was having a boat built—not power, but sail—and some day he would sail into the cove here and take us for a little jaunt. Mr. Wadsworth always arrives unexpectedly—he is at the door before we know he's around.

We more or less expected the Telesforo Casanovas. Mrs. Casanova had written to me from her summer home near Rockland several times, and we'd at last made arrangements to meet. But we hadn't made arrangements with the tide, and when they arrived the mud flats lay in all their purple glory between us and them.

We launched the two skiffs and rowed over, having to go all the way around the bar. The Casanovas were beautifully dressed, intending to drop in at a cocktail party after they left us, and we shuddered at the thought of those lovely suede shoes making contact with our particularly black and sticky mud.

But we found the Casanovas ignoring the mud and in raptures about the mussels. "Don't you ever eat them?" they demanded. "Have you never tried *moules marinières?*"

We all walked up to the Old House and back and talked of hunting and reading and dogs and Maine people, and I didn't know until weeks afterward that Mrs. Casanova was also Grace Hegger Lewis. I was exceedingly embarrassed by my ignorance, and since then I have run into any number of people who are horrified by that same ignorance of mine.

Elizabeth Coatsworth Beston was a Semi-Expected. We had met by correspondence—she and Mr. Beston own Chimney Farm, near Damariscotta—and she was planning to visit us some nice day the early part of November. The stated date blew up with a storm, and thick fog followed. We were disappointed. We let the dishes go, and took out our sulks in a magnificent burst of laziness. We lounged in the kitchen, sticking close to the stove, while the fog pressed white and thick and clinging and wet against the house. It was a perfect fog, as fogs go. It couldn't have been any denser or wetter.

Dot set up her easel and worked on a picture. I propped my feet on the stove hearth and read a twenty-five-cent mystery novel, with a pleasant sensation of guilt because the story was not Worth-while Literature that would help me in my work.

Suddenly we looked up, in something like horror, to see strangers standing outside the window, beaming in at us. I'm afraid we gaped back. Miss Coatsworth had arrived, and with her a friend, Mrs. Sortwell. We never looked worse. We were never more acutely conscious of it.

But Miss Coatsworth was glowing. "To arrive on a strange island in the fog!" she exclaimed. "And to be met in the path by what is probably the largest sheep in captivity! . . . What a wonderful adventure!" They had their lunch in a basket, and Miss Coatsworth had a copy of her new book, *South Shore Town*, under her arm, with a special inscription for me. Roy Seavey had rowed them across the Gut.

We all had a fine time, and we have a new thing to tell people who look askance at stacked dishes. "We put first things *first*," we shall explain, loftily. And we have it on good authority. Elizabeth Coatsworth Beston told us so.

Later she sent us a little poem she'd written about Tristan. He really made up for the sinkful of dishes, when he sauntered across the floor with his elegant tail and his furry plus-fours. He has never been quite the same since the poem arrived, and when it was published in the *Ladies' Home Journal*, he was quite excited. Next, I suppose he will be wanting his portrait made.

In an entirely different category of guests were the Men Who Came at Dusk. We'd put in a hard day and were thinking about bed when we saw the strangers coming up through the alders, loitering along in a rather sinister fashion. We could just make them out, and decided we didn't know them and didn't want to know them. But there was nothing to do when they knocked but open the door, and Smokey responded nobly.

I held his collar as if restraining a bull mastiff at the very least while Dot opened the door. A large, blond young man in the dungarees and rubber boots of a fisherman, and a violently plaid shirt, came in, followed by a couple of nondescript companions. Perhaps they weren't really nondescript, but just dimmed down by the splendor of his shirt.

"Can we have some water?" he asked, and his breath was even louder than his shirt. It smelled like all the cheap vodka in the world.

"Certainly," said Dot with nervous cordiality, taking his bottles out to the pantry. He turned a glazed eye on me and I pulled on Smokey's collar and said, "Down, boy, down. It's all right, it's all right!" This was supposed to convey the impression that Smokey's straining and leaping were marks of a vicious and probably man-eating nature, and even if he wasn't very big, he was plenty fierce.

One of the nondescript characters peeked over the blond man's shoulder. He didn't seem to be as thoroughly steeped in alcohol as his friend. "We've got a little engine trouble," he said. "We're gonna stay tied up at your wharf for a while."

"I hope you're able to get it fixed," I said with great sincerity and a set smile. I was seeing headlines, announcing our deaths and the burglary of our most prized possessions. Offhand I couldn't think what those possessions were—I was more intent on seeing that they didn't discover Smokey had no teeth but the one he uses for scratching.

Dot brought back the water bottles, full. The blond leaned against the wall and showed a definite, though mute, desire to be friends; probably the vodka had paralyzed his tongue by that time. I understand it's slow but devastating. However, his explanatory companion said "thank you" for him, and steered him out.

We didn't know them and we didn't want to know them

"I think I'll sleep better tonight if I know where the shells for the .22 are," Dot said, and rattled through drawers with all the absorbed efficiency of a cat looking for a nest.

"The fishhouse isn't locked," I said hollowly. "What's in it that anyone could lug off?"

"Plenty." She gave me a look of foreboding. "But I'll be darned if we'll go down now and lock it right under their noses. If they're all right—and they probably are—it would be an insult."

"On the other hand if they *aren't* all right," I argued, "and they know we're two women alone except for a toothless dog, well, anything could happen."

Dot didn't answer. She had found the .22 shells. We locked the doors and after a period of uneasiness, went to our beds.

We heard later that the next day the Coast Guard had to be called from Burnt Island to the aid of a boat that had run ashore on the southern end of Gay's Island and was practically ripped to pieces. Our would-be friends, no doubt. Alcohol is a great thing where compasses are concerned, but I understand it has to float the compass to be useful, not the brain of the navigator.

Many people have had tea or coffee with us, while I wished frantically that I had yielded to a former impulse and had baked cinnamon crunch, or molasses drop cookies, or a marble cake.

But Dot's brothers have a pleasant habit of arriving out of the blue, laden with everything they can think of. One day the four of them showed up with the makings of a whole dinner, from steak to frozen strawberries, a sponge cake, and heavy cream. The other day Russ appeared in the middle of the afternoon, bringing half a case of beer, lamb chops, fresh mackerel, scallops, a cake, and a loaf of bread.

He said, in an offhand manner, "I didn't know just what you might have in mind for supper."

The "Expecteds" we enjoy in anticipation, in the flesh, and in looking back. But our "Unexpecteds" make their unique contribution to our Gay's Island existence. There's my friend Anne, for instance, who arrives with the same incipient hysteria, the same mutterings, the same air of having been shot out of a gun, with which she used to arrive at Criehaven when we were seventeen. Now that she has a husband and two children, she still shows up with her wet wash packed in a duffle bag, because she decided so suddenly to come.

Too late she laments, "And *this* time I was going to be poised and matronly!"

It is also too late for us when the guests are already coming up by the barn, and we've just figured out who they are. Too late for Dot to worry about her muddy sneakers and for me to wail that I never intended to wear these jerseys for public consumption because they make me look like a Displaced Person! Too late, when they catch us bottoms up in the clam flats, or wrist deep in greasy wool, shearing the sheep. But if they don't mind, why should we? That's what we get for living off the beaten track. Nobody can ever find us! Not much!

CHAPTER FIFTEEN

ISLANDERS IN THE MAKING

We divide all guests into two classes: Unexpected and Working. It doesn't follow that Unexpected Guests who stay over night don't help with the dishes or go to the well for water, or even slash away at the alders, the way Arthur Christ did. But generally speaking, Working Guests are the ones whose visits last long enough for them to become bored with *dolce fa niente*, and who latch on to a paintbrush or a hammer with far more gusto than they ever do at home.

We have some classic examples of Working Guests. Madelyn with her scrubbing, Bette and Neil wearing themselves to hungry frazzles with the diabolical old lawn mower and Hazel's Hummocks. My mother spends her summers cooking our dinners and redecorating Tide's Way's haphazard collection of furniture. In a frenzy of released inhibitions—she says she's never been able to paint as much as she wanted to—she turned even the ugliest articles into conversation pieces. Like the kitchen table, for instance, painted white with lobsters, mussel and clam shells, dories, deer, fish, and lobster traps strewn over the surface—and it does away with the necessity of using tablecloths.

On the wall above the kitchen table she painted an elm tree

—at least we think it's an elm, but everybody has a different name for it, so maybe it's a hybrid of several stately varieties. It has quite splendid autumn foliage on it, and an inviting little pond painted beneath it.

Frankie Herrick and Dennis Young, about ten years old, came to call one day and beheld our tree with reverent delight.

"Gee, what a good tree to have a picnic under!" said Dennis.

My mother, who says she did the tree in a moment of madness because Dot requested it, also—presumably—in a moment of madness, threatened to hang a discreet curtain over it, but everybody likes it, and it's a cheerful focal point in the kitchen on a rainy day in November. But she likes better the little Norwegian dancing figures on the cupboard doors in the pantry, and the picture story of the Tide books done à la Peter Hunt on the drawers of the old pine chest from the Crie homestead back on Criehaven.

My father is a charter member of the Working Guests Association. I'm expecting him to demand a union next, and I'm getting a little self-conscious about it. On his first vacation after the purchase of Gay's Island, he painted the house and tightened up all the windows. Our first step into respectability—a white house. Then he built a perfect gem of a doorstep over the wide, picturesque, but deadly slab of granite outside the kitchen door. This is a wonderful place to sit. The dogs think it's for them, the cats are sure it's for them, and Blackie has found that by pounding his hoofs on it he'll get all sorts of attention from the household.

Then, outdoing himself, Father took some of the marvelously thick, long planks from the barn and built a long platform extending from the doorstep to the corner of the house. When the doorstep is crowded, there's always the platform. Once a week we clean off the pile of rocks left by the last child visitor, sort out the tools, throw away the remains of mice which Tris was too surfeited to eat; and we rake out the debris which has been so conveniently hidden away underneath the bench.

This year Father built a new well curb. Or crib. He says crib and I say curb, and maybe we have both. I don't know, but it's beautiful and strong, and in its own way gives us as much unobtrusive elegance as the flagpole. For years we have been warning people to look out for rotten boards when they went to the well, and now we don't have to. Painted green and white, with a long pole to plunge the pail down into the dark depths fed by never-dying springs, it is a thing of beauty and will be a joy for a good many years, I hope.

Father is an indefatigable worker, and he takes the true craftsman's delight in his job. By profession he is in the insurance business, but his avocation is carpentry. Nobody gets any more tired than the rest of us when Father is working on a project, because we feel duty-bound to trot around behind him and admire. The admiration is sincere, because the work merits it, but there are times when we wish he were not so enthusiastic. We wish he could bear to leave his tools and sit down and be lazy for a while.

He makes out lists of what he will need, and we try to get the things from Rockland. Father needed a crosscut saw, and seven people crowded into a coupé, en route to Pleasant Point, managed to bring it along with them. I still don't know how they did it without severing someone's arm or leg, or scalping the driver.

Because of Father we now have all the tools we could possibly need, and this makes it easier for other Working Guests. If someone says, "I could do such and such, if I just had a splitting saw," we are happy to call his bluff by bringing out a splitting saw. We have a great many different saws, thanks to Father. We and Father practically supported the Henry Disston company last year.

This year, besides the well curb, he built what we sometimes call "the House of Parliament," and sometimes "the Little

Building." Properly speaking, he designed and started it, but everybody else worked on it before it was finished. Until recently we'd been satisfied with the Sears Roebuck outfit, but we'd begun to think that a small outdoor sanctuary, set charmingly in the alders a little distance from the house, would be nice, and very useful when there was a houseful of company. So Father planned one out, and then began a search for lumber.

We covered a good deal of territory collecting material. Dot and I are born beachcombers. In the spring and fall we roam the beaches, tossing anything we can find that looks even remotely useful up above the high-water mark. Many a good clean piece of lumber comes drifting in with the tide—boards, lengths of two-by-four, strong wide planks.

Eventually, after many treks in the July sunshine, we had everything collected, and Father went to work. His constant audience was Blackie. A sheep is one of the most curious animals in creation. When one of the women wasn't sitting on a rock in the shade of the alders, listening to Father explain the mechanics of building, Blackie was there, chewing his cud and following every movement with his jewel-bright eyes. Perhaps he thought the little house was for him. After it was built, he worried every time anyone went in and closed the door. One would hear his anxious bleat, coming out choppily around a mouthful of grass, and then the pounding of his hoofs as he raced up from the barn. He stood outside the door, muttering to himself, and waited until the occupant came out. The cats and dogs were equally fascinated. One could never expect to be alone; an animal was sure to materialize from somewhere and demand admittance.

Father's vacation was over before he finished construction, but he left us with careful instructions about hanging the door, a real door that had come ashore with the tide. The tar paper—spruce green—had already arrived from Montgomery Ward, and we'd bought hinges and the rest of the necessary hardware in Rockland. Dot and I were quite excited about hanging the door; it would be a professional job, we were sure, if only we followed Father's orders to the letter.

Meanwhile my brother Kent arrived, accompanied by the Parkers. They were to have the Periwinkle, one of the camps. We didn't know Walter was going to be a Working Guest, but that's what he turned out to be.

He is a large, broad-shouldered young man with a mild and pleasant manner which doesn't keep him from looking like the personification of the entire Marine Corps. He wears the Navy Cross for flinging himself down on a Jap hand grenade, which landed in a foxhole full of Marines.

Kent is somewhat shorter, but with a carriage that would mark him as a Marine even if his clothes—especially his green skivvy shirts—didn't.

"We will hang the door for you," they told us, but we protested.

"We know just what to do," I said. "Father explained. You boys have some fun. You don't have to act chivalrous if you see us go by with a stepladder."

They retired to the fishhouse, where they sat for long hours whittling out trick gadgets to baffle the women with, and drinking beer; they went sailing in the Gut in the nine-foot skiff, with a sail made up of an old bedspread. Whenever a power boat came through, Walter gathered the sail into his arms and Kent rowed the skiff, keeping her pointed in the right direction so they wouldn't be swamped; when they were safe, Walter let the sail go again. They had a wonderful time. Gerry, Walter's wife, took pictures of them, saying, "They don't even know they're grown up yet."

But the sailing palled, and we hadn't yet hung the door, so they broached the subject again. Still we urged them to have fun. They painted the flagpole, with an admiring gallery watching from the doorstep and saying at intervals, "I think it's dangerous up there. Look at that flagpole sway! Don't you think you ought to come down?"

Dot and I decided that the only way to get the door hung was to arise very early, while Kent was still sleeping and while Walter was far across the Neck in the Periwinkle. We got up early, and had breakfast, and before seven went happily down the path to the building site. The birds sang in the alders. The wild roses never smelled more sweetly. . . . Then Walter hailed us. He was coming up the path by the barn.

He too had risen with one thought in mind. "We might as well let them hang the door," Dot said. "When the Marines land they get the situation well in hand. Come on, let's go back and have another cup of coffee."

Not only was the door hung with skill and dispatch, but Kent evolved a weight system to make it self-closing. From an old bedstead in the fishhouse they took boards with ornamental carving and framed the door. They painted their initials and my father's on the big rock outside.

Later, when sixteen-year-old Herbert Schmitz came down, Kent put on the tar paper, and Herbie painted the cornerboards and the door and the fancy carving, all in snowy white. He added his initials to the others.

Kent cut a window in the back and rigged it so that it could be fully opened and hooked to the ceiling. Dot carved the all-important hole and whittled out the handle for the cover. My mother added the finishing touch by painting a trellisful of red roses all over the door. Her initials and Dot's are added to the rest.

I should really add mine. After all, I was pretty useful. I held nails, I fetched them, I carried beer, I came and looked when I was told to do so, and admired greatly. And what is any job without an audience?

I have told Father that this year he isn't going to work on his vacation, and I can't think of anything strenuous that the others will find to do, short of mowing the lawn. It's really wonderful, the way the lawn gets mowed in the summertime. Everybody, even my mother, leaps to the job as if it were a privilege, and who am I to deprive them of it? Dot feels the same way about it.

"Maybe they really like to shove the new lawn mower," she muses. "What do you say we enlarge the lawn next spring?"

Working Guests like, also, to go for the mail, and to row across and see if the Fales' truck has brought the grocery order down yet. They *like* to. It isn't work for them, and we appreciate the fact that they're enjoying themselves and also taking a little task off our hands.

Of course, this all sounds as if the instant someone accepts an invitation to visit we immediately begin to plan how they can make themselves useful. This isn't really the case. We don't mind if they want to launch Salome and sit out by the weir fishing for pollock all day, or spend hours sprawling on the lawn and sleeping; we think it's wonderful. The principal question is—do they look happy?

Eddie Schmitz, Herbie's father, plans to fish and paint when he comes. He has a good arm and back for the clam flats and he's not afraid of the muck; and he has the patience to sit in a skiff for hours, getting enough pollock or flounders for a houseful of people. But we like it best when he paints, because he doesn't mind someone breathing down the back of his neck. Temperament is unknown as far as Eddie is concerned, or it most assuredly would have appeared by now, what with all the times we've tiptoed around him, whispering reverently at the way he's got the old fishhouse down in color, or made a whole story about the red dory pulled up on the rocks.

Madeleine Schmitz looks forward to rest, and I think she finds it, even though she always seems to be washing the dishes when the tumult and shouting of a meal is over.

I think Anne comes for driftwood. Last summer we took

walks and walks, and Anne pounced ecstatically on any piece of driftwood that was portable.

"I'm going to put it on the mantel of my new house," she explained seriously each time. We began to wonder how long the mantel would be. From the size of the rapidly growing collection of gnarled pieces of wood, the mantel would have to be the size of the stage in the Boston Opera House.

"Can't you see how beautiful it is?" she would ask us earnestly, holding up a certain piece. "The empty places make the design. . . ."

"Oh, I see." Dot would be just as earnest. "It's not the shape it *is*, but the shape it isn't. I should think you could get the same effect by having absolutely nothing on the mantel."

Anne's children were also infected with the acquisitive desire, where driftwood was concerned. They came staggering home from their walks laden down with ambiguous shapes in weathered gray wood.

"How are you going to get it all home?" I asked one day when Anne was gloating over her largest treasure, a Daliesque shape roughly five feet long and armored with a great many hornlike protuberances.

"I can set some little potted plants in these hollows," she was murmuring, and then looked up at me like a startled fawn. "Good God," she muttered, "I don't know. Especially this one. . . . I never thought of it."

"If you put it in the back seat with the kids it'll stab them to death the first bump you go over," I went on unkindly. "What do you want it for, anyway? Some of the smaller pieces would look good in your fireplace—but. . . ."

"With all the junk you've got on *your* mantels, that's calling the pot a kettle," said Anne. Bob says the reason Anne never listened to Jane Ace was because she could go Jane one better without even trying. Anne is an extremely intelligent and well-read girl but possessed of a rather impetuous tongue, and after a week with her I am prone to say things like "He did it willy-willy," and "How are you ever going to get back into her good gracious?"

Bob came, he saw, and he said in his mild and scholarly accents, "I really think this stuff would make a nice bonfire on the beach some night. . . ."

Anne accused us of sabotage. But anyway, she had a wonderful time gathering her driftwood, along with fresh air and sunshine.

So far, everyone who has come to Gay's Island has found something he or she liked. I think particularly of the children; of thirteen-year-old girls sunning themselves on the rocks like seals, combing their wet hair in long, dreaming gestures, talking in slow soft voices. One minute they are very young, the next they are looking at you with emotionless, ageless eyes and know more than you ever thought of knowing. And the boys, diving, swimming, rowing, shouting. And the little children; Bobby and Susan, Anne's two, who have named the dark woods irrevocably The Growly Dogs. (We don't know why, but we all use the name.) They found a place they called "the Grassy Greenies," too, and "the Neighborhood."

As little Brad left behind him the pictures of himself that go along with clamming, with greening, with work in the fishhouse, two other little blond boys have left something of themselves behind. Enough so that when the long, golden days of October stretch toward dusk the island has a peculiar emptiness, and the beach below the house is oddly barren, and it seems as if, at suppertime, the lamplight should shine on the rounded foreheads and fair bangs of Peter and Douglas.

Peter and Douglas were used to life at the Great Lakes Naval Training Center before their father—Gordon, another of my brothers—received his three months' furlough between enlistments. He is a master sergeant in the Marine Corps. I found a cottage for the family on the other side of Pleasant Point for that summer.

Gordon went back to duty, at the Boston Navy Yard, the first of October, but he couldn't find a place for Mary and the boys. So they came to us for the month of October. We sent Mary up to Boston with Gordon for a week of fun-without-children, and in that week we became acquainted with Peter, slim, white-blond, talkative, and four; and Douglas, broad-shouldered, deep-voiced, rosy, and three. Like kittens, little boys are more fun by twos. These two were priceless.

Used to Marine Corps discipline, they obeyed without argument. Well, almost without argument. Peter could be eloquent when the occasion called for it, but with an air of sweet reasonableness, as if he were generously trusting to our intelligence to see what he meant. Douglas was a man of few words. He said, "Uh, huh," in a deep solemn voice if he intended to co-operate, and planted himself like a mighty oak tree and said nothing if he intended to differ.

Mary had provided them with red caps, useful for spotting them when they played in the tall grass below the lawn. They knew they must stay in sight of the house, but at that they had untold wide-open spaces for their hunting, which seemed to be mostly for wolves. With croquet mallets for rifles, they stalked wolves all day and came to the door bowed over and staggering under the burden of imaginary carcasses. They came in panting, Peter saying, "Where'll we put these old wolves?"

"Lay them in the corner until after supper," said Dot. "You can skin them after you eat." She whittled out skinning knives for them from thin pieces of wood, and there were never such marvels of knives. They had to be carefully wrapped in handkerchiefs every night; and every day began in a hurry, with no lagging over buttons and shoelaces, or their hot cereal and milk, because there was work to be done.

When they tired of wolf-hunting, they went to the beach below the house, where they sailed their small dories for hours at a time, and played endless, involved, absorbing games, all requiring a flexible use of the imagination. I think they would never be bored, wherever they were, and certainly Gay's Island gave them tremendous scope. The woods provided the necessary suspense and mystery children love; there was no telling what lurked in those dark trees marching over the hillside. (Dot and I hadn't grown so far beyond that stage, ourselves.)

Their play, which never flagged, was a fascinating mixture of coast and inland. Their summer on the Point had given them a large amount of information about lobstering, and Gordon used to take them fishing, so they were either playing at lobstering, or hunting, or building complicated airports.

"This is a miscellaneous mess," Peter observed, when we stepped over his materials on the doorstep. "But it's going to be something when I get through."

We gave them a couple of small hammers and a coffee can half full of three-penny nails, and while the nails were supposed to go into the small pieces of wood we found for them, most of them were pounded into the big planks of the bench. They rode the wheelbarrow which, turned upside down, made a very adequate boat. They went with us across the Gut for the mail, and sat very still in the stern seat, two blond gremlins with red caps and blue eyes, as eager and receptive and quick to be thrilled as we all were at the age of three, or four.

For a little while we saw the island through their eyes. Dot and I were doing a great deal of writing, but every afternoon before sundown we took the dog and the boys and went for a walk. Just a stroll around the cove was rich with miracles; a tidewater pool, in the hollow of a great rock, was a tiny sea all apart from the sea; a fish hawk, hanging in space and beating his wings before he plunged into the still clear waters for his prize; the gulls going home in the rose-washed sky; the solitude of the high-sloped island named Caldwell, where nobody lives; a boat coming up through the Gut, right out of the sunset, leaving a widening, fanning path of beaten gold.

When the boys sat at their supper in the lamplit kitchen, washed and angelic in pajamas, Dana came in to call on Bette. We saw him as the nice boy whom Bette was going to marry. But in the boys' widened eyes he was a hero. Their father was one kind of hero and Dana another. Dana had a boat. Dana wore rubber boots, not like their short ones; his could be pulled way up to his hips. Whatever Dana did was of breathless interest to them. He belonged to this island life which was becoming an integral part of them, to the sea which was all day mirrored in their blue eyes and in their young hearts.

Dana could not pass one of them without laying a hand on a flaxen head or touching the moist back of a slim babyish neck where the hair grew in a little drake's tail. When he did this, and answered their eager, "What are you going to do *now*, Dana?" he didn't know of course about his own little blond boy, Loren.

Loren isn't two yet, but he has come many times to Gay's Island; snug in his bunting, he has tilted his head back to stare, open-mouthed, at the big trees overhead as Dana carried him along the woodland path that follows the shore. He likes to be in a skiff and gazes with delight at the constant sparkle and movement of the water so close to him. He took some of his first steps on our lawn. Loren will know two islands as he grows up—his father's island, little Flea Island here in the harbor, and Gay's.

These, and many other children, have come to Gay's Island and in so doing have left little bits of themselves to people the lawn and the beaches and the wharf for us. But at the same time, paradoxically, they have taken Gay's Island with them. And because in every person who ever lived there is something that loves an island, they will never forget. We like to think it will be the same for everyone who has ever come to Tide's Way, child or adult. Simple as our hospitality is, the island has enough to offer to make up for it.

CHAPTER SIXTEEN

THE IVORY TOWER MYTH

As we gradually became convinced that we actually had thirty-three acres, mostly woods, to rove around in, the idea of a studio—or atelier, as we called it in our flossier moments—became very pressing. It grew and grew, especially when the house developed the habit of becoming suddenly full of people. Not that they bothered us, but how could you nail yourself to a typewriter when the happy voices of picnic-goers were wafted to you on a fragrant summer breeze, or sudden peals of laughter from the lawn demanded investigation? And who was fool enough to want to be interested in deadlines when the beach looked like a summer resort? Those Labor Day deadlines surpassed the Chinese water torture. Drop by drop—day by day the end creeps near.

"The trouble with us," I announced one day as I tore a particularly uninspiring piece of fiction out of my typewriter, "is that we have no ivory tower. Two hours a day of perfect quiet, out in the woods somewhere, would produce some good work, and leave the rest of the day free."

Dot leaned on her typewriter and gave me a long look. "Yes," she agreed dreamily, and we were off. We painted lovely pictures of ourselves, churning out Great American Novels by the dozens (magazine and movie sales taken for granted) in some rustic nook straight out of *Better Homes and Gardens,* while our assorted relatives frolicked the mornings away.

"If we threw in some temperament," I said, "we'd get some respect. We ought to have a place absolutely forbidden to the public. Nobody should be allowed even to walk by it when we're working."

"The Scout lean-to," said Dot, her green eyes glinting with new inspiration. "It could be done. Nobody bothers to walk over there very much."

There was no chance of doing anything on it then, but the following spring we began our project as soon as the snow was out of the woods. At one time or another, some Boy Scouts had been permitted to build a log lean-to on the other side of the island, across the Neck and facing the river mouth, the small islands beyond Caldwell, and the open sea beyond. The Scouts had long since grown up, and the lean-to had come into our possession. It was as isolated as anyone could wish. It was approached by a winding trail through birches and young spruce, and then through a grove of tall and very ancient spruces whose distant tops swayed in endless circles against the sky. Winter or summer, when we entered the grove we walked in a soft brown gloom, on a noiseless floor of dry spills. For some reason, whenever I come into that cathedral silence and somberness, I think of some forest in Spain, but I don't know why, having never been to Spain or seen a picture of a Spanish forest.

The path widens to an avenue among the old trees, rises upward toward the light, and finally comes out into an enchanting place, where the sunlight slants across jade and silvery mosses, and rosy lichens on flat slopes of gray rock. There is the lean-to, its logs red-brown against the rich dark green of the trees and the pastel carpeting underfoot. Beyond the lean-to, where the ground descends in a series of rocky slopes, spattered with blueberry and strawberry blossoms, to the jumbled stones of the shore, there is the sea again.

A perfect place, where the only sounds are made by the birds, the occasional staccato chatter of a chipmunk, and the wind in the tall trees. . . . We decided we could use the lean-to if we took out some of the bunks to give us space for a writing table. We spent an exhausting morning ripping out posts and pulling off boards, and then we decided to chink between the logs where the original moss and clay had fallen out. Just why this should have been so important escapes me now, unless we thought it would be pleasing to our artistic eyes.

So, morning after morning, through the first chilly days of spring, we left the house and hiked around the cove and through the woods. We carried buckets with us, and if we found an especially good patch of moss, we gathered it gloatingly in thick cushiony clumps.

We were almost always accompanied by Blackie. He was calm and gentlemanly when Smokey was left at home and not likely to come flying up on the rear. If someone stopped to look at a bird, and silence was essential, Blackie stopped too, and didn't even chew his cud, but waited politely.

Occasionally the cats went. They had a marvelous time, doing acrobatics on the two remaining bunks and running up and down the low shed roof switching their tails at reckless nuthatches.

"Can you imagine how it'll be to work over here?" we enthused to each other. "It'll be like another world, another planet! It's so still and peaceful. Just perfect for thinking." We could hardly wait for the chill to come out of the days, so we could sit at our typewriters and not get blue with cold.

When we were tired we sat down and ate candy bars, and at the rustle of paper Blackie stopped whatever he was doing and had some candy too. Since he has the sort of predatory personality that makes him take pencils out of pockets and snatch at pages of manuscript just for the sport of it, sharing candy was compulsory, so we usually took along an extra Milky Way for him, breaking it up into bits so it would last. Otherwise he was through before we were, and reaching forward with a twitching black nose to see what was left. Sometimes he lay down in the warm dry blueberry bushes and looked profound and extremely intelligent. Soldi, who had always loved him, lay under his chin, occasionally touching his outstretched hoof with a small white paw, as if to remind him that she was there.

We had a lovely time, and wasted plenty of it, before the day came when Dot seemed a little slow in getting back to work after intermission. She looked out at Caldwell with a faraway expression.

"You know we won't be able to leave our typewriters and paper and stuff here," she said slowly. "That means we'll have to carry everything back and forth with us, whenever we want to come over here and work. What a prospect!"

I played absent-mindedly with a handful of moss. "I was thinking—sort of—I mean, it's quite a distance away from the house, isn't it? Suppose something happened, and we were *needed. . . .*"

Dorothy was brightening by degrees, like the lights on a stage. "It's not as if all this has been wasted. With a little money we could make this lean-to into a nice guest cottage, for anyone wanting isolation!"

I agreed, enthusiastically. We stood up. "Come on, Blackie, Soldi, Tris. Come along, now." We were on the way home.

For all of a week, during which we wrote, and dug up garden spots when we felt the need of exercise, a studio wasn't mentioned.

"Let's go down and look at the office," Dot suggested one morning. "Down by the barn. That's away from the house, and yet it's handy at the same time."

We went down to inspect it, a very small building dignified by hand-hewn beams and a granite doorstep, like the house. The barn looming over it had been left a shell by a series of storms, but the corner posts were still stanchly set and there seemed no chance of the whole structure collapsing on the little building in its lee.

At one time long ago this small building had had a strictly utilitarian purpose, though it seemed an inconvenient distance from the house on rainy nights. It was probably then that someone with a wide paintbrush had inscribed the word "Office" over the door in big white letters. Inside we were admonished, with brisk courtesy, but in smaller letters, "For Prompt Service, Please Be Seated!"

But the necessary furnishings had been ripped out by one of our predecessors. No doubt the ones who had saved their garbage had needed firewood in a hurry. We'd kept the chickens there at first, and Patty. But Patty was dead now, and the chickens had all been killed and eaten.

The wall toward the barn was nonexistent. (This had enabled the chickens to run free, and lay their eggs in the alders, but they had come back to roost in the building at night.) When They (our predecessors) ripped out the equipment They'd taken the wall along too.

"All we have to do," said Dot with deceptive simplicity, "is patch up that open side with old barn boards, lay some sort of ceiling, and build a door."

"Do we learn to write in Braille?" I asked. "It's going to be awful dark in here when you close in that wall."

"Well, of course we'll have to have windows. . . ."

"How do you make windows and put glass in them? Do *you* know how?" I'm afraid I was a little suspicious, but Dot seemed confident.

"We don't have to think about windows right now. We have to think about closing in that open side and making a door.

Come on, let's start collecting some boards. Maybe there's some we can use in that pile down by the fishhouse."

We had quite a stockpile down there of planks and boards and pieces of two-by-four. With that, and what lay around the barn—torn loose by the last hurricane—we found enough to build a rough side wall. We laid loose boards across the beams and out of courtesy called the result a ceiling. So far it was easy, and I began to get enthusiastic too. We swept the wide planks of the floor, over which the rain and snow had beaten all winter and removed the traces of barnyard occupancy. I say, simply, that we *did* these things, but the statement doesn't encompass the aching backs, the bruised thumbs, the brittle tempers, and the rest.

The windows were our masterpieces. We used Guy's bit-stock and bit, which he had for boring holes in the laths and sills of his traps, and made a line of holes in the best walls. Then we worked a saw into the line of holes and sawed out two squares—one in the end of the building looking toward the shore and fishhouse, one on the side looking out at the path from the house. We had glass cut to measure, improvised frames, and became glaziers. We papered the walls with clean heavy wrapping paper in a nice cream shade. Narrow strips of wallboard gave a sort of Elizabethan half-timbered effect to the inside. Our chief expenditure was a square of cheap lino-leum—it cracked if you looked at it—for the floor. But it was bright and clean.

The door was the *pièce de résistance.* We used anything we could find for lumber, priding ourselves on using scraps and driftwood. We nailed and reinforced. Then, carried away by our success with the windows, and thrown into a creative frenzy by the sight of putty, we put a small window in the door.

It was a wonderful door. The first time we lifted it up, we knew how truly wonderful it was.

"This would resist an invasion by tanks," I said. "We ought to call this place 'the Vault' when we get through with it."

"There's no sense in having a flimsy door," said Dot.

It was my job to hold the door in place while she adjusted the hinges, and it seemed to me that I could feel my strength ebbing away with each breath.

"You seem to be taking a long time fixing those things," I said faintly.

"Don't carp," she admonished me. "We want them to work—we don't want people laughing at us."

"They'll never get a chance to laugh at me," I said. "When this door finally falls over on me there'll be nothing left but a flat impression. Like a gingerbread man. Only not so palatable."

"You'd better save your breath," she answered, "because I'm going to be quite a while on these hinges."

"Remember the ganglion on my wrist," I warned her.

She scowled at the hinges in a threatening manner. "When we get back to the house I'll drop a window on your wrist. That's how to get rid of ganglions."

After that I kept still. I was suffering for Art's sake.

We bought a lovely latch for the door, but since the door was slightly too much for the hinges—we thought for a while it would pull the whole front of the office down—the lock never worked, and we tied the door shut with a piece of marlin and told everybody we'd left the crack at the top on purpose, for ventilation.

We had plenty of ventilation through the ceiling, since the rain could beat in on the side where the roof was gone. So we covered the ceiling from below with glass cloth, that fabric so indispensable to people with henhouses. As the ceiling was not level, the rain ran off it and down the outside of the rough wall we'd put up, so we never worried about getting wet.

The cats loved to walk around on top of the loose ceiling

boards and sometimes curled themselves to sleep in a corner under the eaves.

With a long shelf made from a beautiful new board found on the shore, we had a place to put our paper and books; we made a workbench of stout boards, and a long bench to sit on; we put up cupboards made of beer boxes, and bright curtains at the windows; with a lantern for illumination if we ever felt like working there at night, and with one of those little round portable oil heaters for warmth on a cold foggy day, the office was ready except for a name.

So on a strip of white-painted board I lettered in ornate old English print, "The Cuckoo's Nest." This romantic and Victorian title was inspired by the cuckoos that flew among the alders across the path, but we were to find that other people gave it a more personal interpretation. The elegant lettering was a shade incongruous against the rough and hoary exterior of the shack, but we liked it.

After all the work we'd spent in making it a workroom, we found it difficult to accomplish anything in The Cuckoo's Nest. Whenever someone went past the windows on the way to the shore, we became obsessed with curiosity, which meant a recess of ten or fifteen minutes until the person came back again. If no one appeared at all, we decided that something indescribably intriguing was going on up at the house. This would consume us with a fiery interest and usually brought us to the conclusion that it would be better to find out what was going on and then get back to work, rather than just sit in idle wonder.

We were always hungry, too, now that the house was so handy. When one of us couldn't think of a word it was suggested that a cup of coffee and a doughnut or sandwich would help. We spent more time getting ready to write, and then being fortified by food, than we did writing. As I recall, it was a rather unproductive summer.

In the fall we took off that remarkable door and toted it to the fishhouse, where we nearly broke our backs getting it up-stairs. Then we turned The Cuckoo's Nest over to Blackie. We took out all the furniture to give him plenty of room to move around in but left him the linoleum. He is the only sheep I know who has linoleum on his floor.

"Another year," we assured each other solemnly, "we'll really have a place. A genuine studio." Intoxicated by dreams of a fabulous future, in which the major movie studios and book clubs fought for the rights to my books, we went on with our plans.

"A skylight," Dot said.

"Casement windows," I held out. "Opening into the woods. Imagine the birches and alders and bayberry bushes full of birds in the spring, and the big spruces swaying overhead. But you can have a skylight too, if you want it."

"Built-in shelves, lots of drawers," Dot dreamed on. "Pine paneling—"

"So knotty it looks polka-dotted," I said. (I adore knotty pine but whenever I say it, it sounds like *naughty* pine. Similarly our New England accents make *wobbler* out of *warbler*. Even now when I mention a yellow warbler I see in my mind's eye an intoxicated Chinese.)

"I'd like a warm brown siding to blend in with the tree trunks," said Dot.

The creation of this studio was delightful and restful. It was all accomplished without one blackened thumbnail, one short-ened temper, one kink in the back. Also, it was invisible.

But, having rested in the meantime, I didn't flinch percepti-bly when Dot announced one day that she was going to build a log cabin. I was even enthusiastic about it. We had found, as usual, the perfect place, in the woods just across the Neck, within calling distance of the shore. Trying to find a sheltered place to work in one day, we'd come across a small clearing, just a short way from the cove.

It was ringed fragrantly with bay, and the big trees pressed in from the deeper forest, headquarters for warblers in the spring and chickadees and nuthatches in the fall. There was one birch showing above some young growth, tall, slender, forever in motion against the sky. When we had first found the clearing, in the spring, the birch's branches were a fine amethyst-tinged lace. Later the leaves had set a cloud of green and gold about its head. Redstarts darted in and out of sight. The clearing had something else that was ineffably attractive to me, a flat outcropping of mossy ledge, with infant spruces growing up bright emerald green about it, and a few blueberry plants with their white waxen bells. In the middle of the clearing stood two slightly older spruces—adolescents—as if they were guarding an invisible doorway.

The decision was inevitable. "I'm going to give them a doorway to guard," Dot announced. "It's a fixation left over from my childhood. I've had playhouses all over Criehaven, I've built brush camps all through the woods out there. Now we'll have a log cabin."

"Fine, Daniel Boone," I said with some sarcasm.

"I've figured it all out. None of the logs will be more than five inches across, so they'll be easy to handle. I'll make a model first." She went ahead, serenely confident, and fashioned a model from little pieces of alder. By the time she'd finished, I had caught the fever. In a burst of enthusiasm I bought myself an ax in Rockland.

I don't know why I bought it. I never did cut anything with it. I had never cut anything with Dot's ax, either. All branches become bewitched, and manifest a peculiar diabolical personality of their own, when I attack them with an ax, and practically beat the tar out of me. This has led me to consider very seriously the idea of tree spirits. I have been known to limb out a tree, but only when somebody else had first laid it low so it can't rise up and hit me. Even then I'm suspicious, and lift my feet very high when stepping over the trunk.

But Dot had an ax, and I wanted one, so I could go around saying, "I went out into the woods with my ax this morning. . . ." Well, I could say it, because now I was out in the woods every morning with my ax. If people wanted to infer that I'd cut anything down with it, that wasn't my fault.

Dot knew just how many logs of each necessary length she wanted for her nine-by-fourteen cabin. We told nobody else about the project—Guy was still a Gay's Islander then—and we waited each morning until he and the rest of the Pleasant Point fishermen had gone to haul their traps. Then, about eight o'clock or sometimes earlier, we started out.

Fall was sliding on toward winter, and the woods where we cut the trees were on the northern shore of the island, in deep shade at that hour. Sometimes there was ice in the hollows among the roots. We worked for an hour or so and came home for a second breakfast and did the housework. *And* some writing. I regret to say that, when one of these projects was under way, the writing sometimes came under the head of necessary but hardly fascinating chores.

The sheep went with us to the woods, Blackie and Hezzie. At this time the little ram—no wether like Blackie—was about four months old, squat and serious, with long ropy wool like merino, the beginnings of horns, and a broad-browed, innocent face. He was very polite and had not yet found out his purpose in the world. He was still a baby. But in contrast to Blackie, who skittered nervously at blowing leaves, Hezzie was calm and well adjusted—like the psychiatrist's ideal of a perfectly secure child.

He and Blackie went with us and the axes to the woods. The cats went, yellow Tristan and three-colored Soldi. Smokey went. As we marched across the Neck, the lowest and most

open part of the island, exposed to the view of all Pleasant
Point, we fondly imagined that nobody saw us.

Because there was absolutely no way of getting away from
the house without being followed by at least two of the animals,
I had an important job that had nothing whatever to do with
my ax. In fact the ax was laid by as soon as we entered what
is now "The Growly Dogs." After Dot had the tree ready to
fall—some forty feet of straight slender trunk—I ran around
shooing animals. I shudder now to think how I managed all
five of them when two were cats, notoriously uncooperative
beasts, and one was Hezzie, who merely planted his hooves a
little firmer when I waved at him and stared at me without
blinking. Blackie scattered, snorting, and Smokey sat down
where he was told. He seemed to know what it was all about.

"These pesky animals!" Dot shouted more than once. "If
I could get anybody to shoot those sheep—"

"And drown the cats!" I yelled back, scampering through
the cold, shadowy stillness under the tall trees, with Hezzie refusing to be shooed, and Soldi flicking her tail at me as she
picked her fastidious way on little white paws across the place
where the tree would fall, while Tristi flattened his ears, widened his pupils, and made ready to dash at the Tree itself.

By some miracle they were always out of the way when the
tree came down, and while Dot sat down to rest a few moments,
I would take over, with as much éclat as Paul Bunyan, and limb
out the tree.

Sometimes, after all the shooing and shouting and warnings,
the tree didn't come down. These were embarrassing moments.
The trees were so close together that occasionally the tops were
enmeshed, and there our prize would stand, cut entirely free at
the foot, but clutching with its branches at its neighbor. Our
best tree, from which we'd planned to get a number of logs,
did this. Whenever a gale was blowing we looked at each other
furtively behind Guy's back and wondered if our tree had come

down. We got into the habit of taking walks across the Neck in the worst of a storm because our curiosity was so great. And if we saw anybody else walking into the woods, we were horror-stricken. What if the tree came down on top of him?

Finally we found it down, with as much triumph as if one of us had been personally responsible. The secret was still intact. Dot had dreams of presenting Guy with the *fait accompli*. The cabin would be built with no outside advice whatever, and her husband and the rest of the world would be properly dumfounded.

But, like our Mississippi kite which turned out to be a common, ordinary marsh hawk, the log cabin turned out to be something else not at all spectacular. We weren't getting much done in an hour a day, and we didn't have the time or the strength to put in more than an hour's work when we had a chance to go to the woods. The weather was getting more wintery all the time; Guy didn't go out to haul every day.

"We can't very well walk out of the house with a saw and an ax," said Dot, "and tell him we're going to pick cranberries."

"I'm getting a little tired of the forest primeval," I announced, "especially when it's equipped with a cageless zoo. You can't do a thing around here without those sheep getting in the way, and the last time I pushed Hezzie he pushed right back. He's growing up."

We realized that building a cabin entirely of logs was beyond our muscles, so now we planned out a little one-room shack in which our logs could be used for the frame. We could board it over with the odds and ends of stuff we'd accumulated on our beachcombing walks. We sawed the logs into the right lengths, piled them up close to the clearing, and then the snow came.

Early in March, with the delicious stealth of conspirators, Dot and I began once more to go to the woods. Now that we could actually begin to build something, we were excited. We made a foundation of logs, securely spiked together, and propped up the corners with flat rocks where the ground was uneven. But we needed a few more logs and took to wandering around through the woods for them, up rocky trails and slashing new paths through the underbrush.

Sometimes we were a good distance from the clearing when we found what we wanted. On the walk back, one of us at each end of the tree, many an innocent young sapling was mowed down. I couldn't swing a seven-foot stick nonchalantly to my shoulder and walk away with it, having the sort of bones which become unduly prominent at such moments and give the unpleasant impression that they are coming right out through my skin. I had to carry my end of the tree as best I could in my arms. I panted, tripped, and seemed to be forever entangled between tree trunks.

"I feel like an elephant toting teak through the jungle," I gasped. "Only not half so graceful. Do you realize that if we *had* to work like this we'd have all the unions out fighting for us?"

Something about it—maybe the way I looked draped over my log with my hair full of twigs—was too much for Dot. She collapsed, laughing like an idiot. So did I.

"It's just dawned on me how silly we look," she moaned between bursts of laughter. "So earnest, so fervent, falling all over ourselves to carry one certain stick half the length of the island, through a whole stand of good timber, to one certain spot!"

We couldn't carry anything else that day. We left our seven-foot sticks and went home for a cup of coffee and a couple of good books.

Finally we had the whole framework of the camp in place, but our courage and muscles gave out when it came to lifting a couple of fourteen-foot logs into place so we could have them to lay our rafters on. It was a sorry moment when we reached this tragic decision. We sat down on what would be the doorstep, looked sorrowfully out between the guardian spruces at the edge of the clearing, where Soldi was making love to a foot-high spruce, and were silent for quite a while.

"There's no way out of it," Dot said at last. "We'll have to tell Guy. He and Neil can lift those logs for us." Neil and Bette were visiting us.

I roused myself briefly. "I still think. . . ." But when I flexed my aching shoulder muscles, I knew better. "Well, anyway, Guy's away this week end, and we don't have to mention it to Neil until Guy comes back."

Anything to put off the instant when we had to admit we needed help. But the day came when Dot led Guy through the woods, up the path we'd made from the shore. I walked behind them. We had brightened considerably when we realized how surprised he would be.

He was surprised all right. He stood still and stared. Then he said in a low and prayerful voice, "My God! What's *that* thing?"

Dot, who had been prepared to smile indulgently at his amazement, bristled. "What does it look like?" she demanded snappily. "It's a cabin. Or going to be. We want you and Neil to put up a couple of logs for us. So we can have something to fasten the rafters to."

"I thought it was a hot dog stand," said Guy. "Well, let's see what you've done wrong."

We seethed, but silently. We were between the devil and the deep blue sea, and if Dot wanted this camp by summer, she had to have a roof on it, obviously.

Neil and Guy raised the roof, literally and figuratively. Who was it who said that no man will ever let a woman have the pleasure of poking a fire or putting a piece of wood on it? Well, no man will let a woman hammer nails and saw lumber if he can help it. Neil and Guy leaped into the middle of our project, and in the flick of Blackie's tail we were reduced to the status of carpenters' helpers, holding tools and handing out nails. We stood around emitting small, futile sounds of protest; we sneaked over and worked in secret.

But the camp approached completion a lot quicker than it would have otherwise, with our trying to keep house, write books, redecorate Tide's Way, and build at the same time. Guy was able to get some cedar shingles for us; he found out where we could get some good spruce boards and have them delivered at Leslie Young's wharf. He came home from Rockland, as some men come with candy or chocolates, bearing windows he'd found in somebody's cellar.

We found a door. We screened the windows with mosquito netting. We moved in a couple of old cots, a table, and chairs. There were even shelves for books. There was no pine paneling, but an interior of clean, bright spruce boards that smelled delicious. Dot christened the place "Spruce Bough-er" and I whipped up a dandy little sign to that effect in my favorite Old English lettering, and she nailed it to a tree at one side of the path.

Guy and Neil had thought we needed fewer rafters than we'd cut, and consequently walking over the roof was like walking over a trampolin. It was a little springy to the foot, and nerve-wracking to anyone over one hundred and twenty pounds. I came under that and to my delight I had full sway on the roof. I had a marvelous time shingling. Dot stood on a ladder and leaned on the edge of the roof to supervise, but the importance was still mine. I laid the shingles without enough overlap, and the first time the camp was officially used, the rain came in all night. Later we put on sheets of wallboard (a kind that is made for outside use) and fastened the seams with laths. Half of the laths were oak, and I bent double nine nails to every one I drove successfully. The mosquitoes enjoyed the project because I was so helpless. They came in happy swarms while I swore at them and the India-rubber nails.

It began to look as if we'd go on laying new roofs forever, till my father took pity on us and sent down three rolls of tar paper. Then I could rip off the wallboard and lay the tar paper, and again hammer myself into a frenzy trying to fasten down oak laths. But the tar paper was successful, and the camp has weathered a couple of harsh winters. It always smells dry and fragrant.

Truthfully, the Bough-er didn't turn out to be much of a studio; it's been of more use as a dormitory. Once Dot and Anne and I slept over there for several nights in early September. Between the drought and the constant succession of visitors, our sheets were few and far between, so Dot and I made up our beds with thin, very old blankets. Anne, being company, had the sheets. Also being company, Anne brought along a fancy nightgown, and while we others cannily decided to warm up our beds by lying in them awhile before shedding slacks and blouses for pajamas, Anne got ready for bed with due ceremony, and slid in between her sheets in her satin nightgown.

In the morning, when we awoke full of verve, Anne was blue-lipped and admiring. "I always thought I was husky but you two are more rugged than I am," she said. "I nearly froze."

"It must have been the sheets," Dot said innocently.

"Didn't you have sheets?"

"Yours were the last clean ones," I confessed. "We slept in blankets."

Anne sat upright in horrified indignation. "No *wonder!* Well tonight, by gosh, *I'm* going to have blankets. And socks. *And* earmuffs."

Her account of this "night in the woods" to her husband caused a justifiable confusion in her young daughter's mind. Susan intrigued not only her classmates at kindergarten, but also her teachers, by her disclosure, "*My* mother sleeps in trees!" Susan is quite proud of her mother's accomplishment. We haven't been able to find out whether she imagines Anne curled up along a bough, or in a hole like a squirrel, or in a nest with her head under her wing like a chickadee. But the neighborhood children have begun to regard Anne with new respect, as a sort of female Tarzan of the Apes.

The camp is a retreat when Dot wants to read; it's a gallery for her paintings; it's a pleasant place to take anyone for a quiet talk when the house is full up.

Sometimes in the spring or fall, when the yen for a trip comes over one or the other of us and we know we can't go, we pack up some food and go across the Neck into the woods. It always seems fresh and new, and rather exciting. A little imagination can transport us straight into the Great North Woods, toned down slightly for us timid souls.

Anyway, we now do most of our writing in the main house. And we don't try to write in summer. That seemed the happiest compromise all around. In case there must *absolutely* be some work done, there are plenty of places around the house where one can set up a typewriter and still know what's going on. We save a lot of time that way. No walking back to the house every hour to feel its pulse and drink coffee. I find that I work best when I'm not too far from the kitchen.

Of course the studio dream still persists, changing its form occasionally but remaining substantially the same. Perhaps it's wishful thinking; the desire for the personality which can retire to a spiritual ivory tower and put blithely aside the mundane details of mere *physical* existence.

CHAPTER SEVENTEEN

THE MAID PROBLEM

There is a barrier, of course, to keep either of us from ever attaining the cloisterlike Nirvana of perfect concentration. Several bars, in fact. One is a natural gregariousness, a genuine fondness for people. The silence of the island is a wonderful thing, and for days at a time one is content to let time slip noiselessly by; there is always something to be done, and each of us is absorbed in her own concerns. But there come the moments—especially in the fall after a summer of great goings-on—when we go suddenly stale. For a week, perhaps two, we fling ourselves madly into our work, piling up great sheaves of manuscript, and then fling ourselves just as madly into a skiff, row across the Gut, and go to Rockland.

Dot makes the rounds of her relatives. Some of them live in Rockland and environs, while her brothers go lobstering out at Criehaven. If she's lucky, the boys may be in from the island and she comes back to Gay's Island after a day or two, happy, exhausted, talked-out, and ready to take the vows of silence for another period. As for me, I have my own gadding to do.

But first, there is the ritual of coffee and fresh doughnuts in Ruth Brown's kitchen. Ruth is Dot's next youngest sister, mother of three big boys and a girl, and verily the jewel of her home. She is gay and forthright. She has a humorous sweetness about her that draws people toward her as irresistibly as clover draws bees, and she mothers everybody and everything that passes through her kitchen, from Carl, her husband, down through her children to Emmy, the big collie.

So after coffee and an hour of talk with Ruth—we're lucky if there isn't a constant procession of neighbors and relatives coming and going during that hour—I start off on my business. There's my visit to the bookstore where I always stop for conversation with whoever is behind the counter, Charlotte Gray's daughter Sally, or Rich Dunn's niece Mrs. Walker, or Mrs. Low, whose husband owns the shop. Thence to the Rockland *Courier Gazette* for typing paper and a chat with Raymond Anderson, foreman of the print shop (and Dot's uncle). An errand at the hardware store turns into a general buying spree, from which I emerge with an armful of sharp and shiny gadgets of which we already have too many. A visit to the furniture store for a cot mattress means trying out all the luxurious low chairs which would be far too big for the small rooms of Tide's Way. In the drugstore I spend long minutes studying the twenty-five-cent books in hopes that John Dickson Carr has a new mystery among them, or that I can find something as unheralded and deliciously unexpected as *The Scandals of Clochemerle.*

During all this I'm bound to meet a dozen or more people whom I know and my tongue is getting pretty well limbered up. It's really wonderful to *talk!* Dot and I usually have lunch or dinner at one of the local restaurants, and these meals are ritual too, since our island cooking, though nourishing, leans pretty heavily on vegetables and sea food. We eat meat when we go to town—steaks or chops.

I like movies, too. A good movie, whether serious or light, flushes my brain entirely clear of whatever I'm writing at the time and gives me a rest. And if I've come to an impasse and

I'm knocking myself out trying to find my way around an obstruction, the complete forgetfulness of a well-done movie often brings results in a new approach to the problem. My agent used to advise me to go to the movies frequently. I go perhaps once in three weeks, if there's something I want to see, and I find it increases my capacity for seeing my story in clear-cut scenes.

Of course, there are always the movies that plunge me into despair and don't help me at all. After *Hamlet*, *Henry V*, or *Caesar and Cleopatra*, I'm inclined to sulk. What I am doing has become, suddenly, worthless drivel. My brain has shrunk to the size of a pin point. I understand this is a natural and universal reaction to the dialogue of William Shakespeare and G. B. Shaw, but that's no help to me. My morale gets the best lift when I come squinting out of the theater, muttering, "If I couldn't write something better than *that!*"

All this is a long way of saying that I need frequent contact with the outside world, and Dot says the same thing goes for her. The island is truly paradise when we return to it, and if we have been away for only a day the homecoming is still an occasion for rejoicing. But neither of us has any inclination to take up the moat, as Anne puts it.

And the other barrier between us and the contemplative existence is the fact that we must struggle with fuel, with food (the getting and cooking of it), with washing and ironing, with cleaning paint and sweeping.

There is a dream which we both cherish along with the studio dream. It is the *maid* dream. It haunts us as the vision of the Holy Grail haunted the Knights of the Round Table. This maid would be the gem of our lives, lives which at her advent would suddenly mesh smoothly, silkenly, into gear and become six times as productive as they'd ever been.

We don't want much of her. Dot would like to think that the dishes would always be washed up, and dinner served at noon-

day without any effort on her part. My special yen is for someone to do the ironing. I would just as soon do the washing, if
someone would starch and iron all my cotton clothes and fuss
over my dress-up blouses without going mad, as I do. I love
blouses in soft crepes, yellow and aqua and rose and snowy
white. I love blouses with ruffles. I buy them as an alcoholic
buys liquor, knowing that I am a craven soul and will repent
this deed a hundredfold. So I want someone to iron for me. I
want a closetful of things so that I can change my clothes five
times a day if I want, without measuring up how many hours
of sweat and tears this extravagance is going to cost me.

We are both agreed that it would be heaven on earth to have
some help. Occasionally this domestic Joan of Arc changes
form. Sometimes she becomes a couple.

"I wish we had something to offer a D.P. couple," Dot said
recently. "We could find a lot for them to do, but they could
have a garden, keep a cow and have chickens, and he could go
fishing."

I agreed sadly, like Moses looking into the Promised Land.
"But it would never happen to us. Whatever we got, whoever
we got, would turn out to be like Hazel."

I didn't mean Hazel the Pig. I meant Hazel, the jewel of *The
Saturday Evening Post* cartoons.

You see, we once had a maid. Once, for a week, we knew
what it could mean. Strictly speaking, she wasn't a maid, and
that was the way we wanted it; someone who would be part of
the household, whom we could help as much as she helped us.

Bette, the kid sister of Dot's family, had come out of the
Waves and wanted to do something quiet for a while. She came
to make us a little visit.

"I'd like nothing better than to be with you and Liz here on
the island," she said to Dot, her blue eyes wistful. "There must
be a lot of things I could do."

Knowing the talent for housewifery Bette had exhibited when she was a round-faced, solemn ten-year-old, Dot said from the heart, "I know darn' well there is. So just roll up your sleeves and plan to stay awhile."

It was early fall. We had stacks of work to do; we were enchanted at the prospect of having Bette, someone who was in the family, who would laugh at our jokes and be charitable about our idiosyncrasies. She liked to read, she liked to play the guitar and sing. She had visited us earlier in the summer and made the acquaintance of young Dana Herrick and his family on Flea Island, and of most of the people on Pleasant Point.

So we started out, the three of us happy as larks. While the typewriters rattled away in the living room, Bette sang out in the kitchen, washing dishes, sweeping and dusting. When she called us to dinner we knew at last the bliss we had been seeking for a long time.

Bette was blissful too. Dana was coming over to call. They went on long walks, or they sat in the kitchen in the evening and talked. Romance was burning brightly in Dana's brown eyes and glistening in Bette's blue ones. He had been a Seabee, she'd been a Wave; both of them were clean-cut, rather shy, and not at all cocky about their experiences. In some miraculous way they'd both preserved their romantic illusions.

We hammered away at the typewriters and pretended not to notice what was going on. True, Bette began to be a little absent-minded now and then, but all we wanted of her was a cupboardful of clean dishes and a dinner at noon. The situation was idyllic. That lovely week, those seven days that were all too short. . . .

Bette came back from Rockland on a Saturday afternoon with a diamond ring. She was engaged to Dana.

"I can hardly believe it!" she caroled. "It's so sudden, but

I guess it's really true!" She looked at us kindly from her Olympian heights. "We aren't going to get married right off, so I'll still be here to help you out."

We were glad she'd chosen Dana. If she was more absent-minded than ever, that was all right. If, while she sang, "Ah, Sweet Mystery of Life," along with the radio, she swept the days' accumulation of dust and cat hairs under the chest of drawers and left it, we didn't cavil. Love had hit her hard.

Besides, she was still getting dinner for us. If the dinner hour came earlier and earlier each day, so that she could be ready to meet Dana when he came back from hauling his traps and spend the halcyon October afternoons wandering dreamily over the island, we didn't care. We always had ourselves a mug-up in the afternoon anyway and fixed our own supper. Bette and Dana usually had a picnic supper out-of-doors.

After discovering that the cache of canned tuna fish had mysteriously dwindled to nothing and that the catchup had disappeared, I said, "When we run out of anything, Bette, tell me so I can reorder. Things seem a little short around here."

Bette gave me a wide and pitying glance. How could I be expected to understand the misty mountaintops on which she was roving these days?

"All right," she said dreamily. "You didn't really mind if we used the stuff to make sandwiches, did you?"

"Nope." I was very hearty about it. "But just tell me when we get short of things."

Quite suddenly, the rift came in the lute. Bette seemed to have descended rather abruptly from the heights, as if her feet had gone out from under her. She wandered around locked in proud isolation; she disappeared into her room and stayed for long intervals, during which I surreptitiously removed whole litters of dust kittens from under the chest of drawers, and Dot did up a batch of dishes which had unaccountably been left un-washed.

We went to the well for water and discussed the new phenomenon.

"Do you suppose she's had a fight with Dana?" I asked.

"I don't know." Dot scowled. "She speaks to him nicely enough, and they go out walking. She looks a little sour when she comes in, though."

"She turned off the radio this morning when someone began to sing 'Falling in Love,'" I contributed. "She's sort of—slammish, if you know what I mean."

The problem of domestic unhappiness came between us and our work. Settling down over the typewriters, we discussed—in whispers—the latest development. "I'd like to ask her straight out what the trouble is," Dot brooded. "But Bette's not that kind. She's always been aloof."

"She's so aloof she's got me scared to death," I said. "I walk around her in circles. I feel like Smokey when you shout 'Well?' at him after he's run away."

The bliss had been short-lived. We were being intimidated, and we didn't know whether to giggle at the situation or to take the bull by the horns—the bull in this case being our lovely and ice-clad Juno of the kitchen. And Dana was looking a little confused these days, too.

Then, one day, the ice cracked. Dot had mixed herself a mid-morning cup of cocoa and left the empty cup in the sink. Bette saw it. She drew herself to her full height of five-foot-seven—more, with her yellow hair piled on top of her head—and said in frosty tones, "Please do *not* leave any dirty dishes in that sink."

"And whose sink is it?" said Dot. "What's the matter, Bette? What are you being a tragedy queen for?"

Bette looked past her into the distance—at Caldwell, to be exact. "I've decided," she said hollowly, "that I don't want to be married. I decided it a long time ago. I want to be engaged, but all Dana talks about is getting *married!*"

"That," Dot assured her, "is what usually happens after people have been engaged for a while."

"I'm going to give him his ring back the next time he comes," said Bette.

"If that's the way you feel about it, maybe it's the best thing to do," said Dot, and left it at that.

"I don't think she'll break it off," I observed when we were alone. "Do you?"

Dot shrugged. "After all these years I don't think I know Bette very well."

It was like following a soap opera. We got very little done that day, what with conjecturing and discussing. A pall of unnatural silence hung over the dinner table. Bette toyed with crackers and tea, and we felt crass and heartless as we ate meat loaf and baked potatoes and large helpings of salad. It seemed cruel, but there was nothing else to do but eat. Bette discouraged conversation.

We went out for a long walk in the afternoon to give Young Love a chance to steady itself. Our domestic routine was about to be shattered; it was pretty badly cracked already. We yearned for a return to that first week when we had been looked after like minor royalty and had a songbird in the kitchen.

But when we came back to the house the ring had been returned. Bette was maddeningly toplofty about it all.

"Dana," said Dot accusingly, "is a wonderful boy; you should not have gotten engaged in the first place if you weren't sure."

Bette shrugged, and sailed off to her room like Mrs. Siddons. The next day she was cheerful in a determined manner, singing loudly, and sweeping with more energy than she'd shown since she got the ring. No more lovely mists softened her eyes; she was the Navy, brisk, cynical, and efficient. We got rapidly out of her way. Hazel was now ruling the kitchen.

Then Dot came back from the other side of the harbor with

the news that Dana had left the Point. Bette looked indifferent, but we noticed that she went out on the doorstep frequently and contemplated the length of the harbor. Whenever she came in she was thoughtful and wilder with the broom than ever. The days began to creep by. Our work suffered while we discussed, pondered, analyzed. Meals became erratic, as Bette lost all interest in food.

She had a heavy hand with the salt. During the afternoons we made many visits to the water pails.

"Well, after all," I said, "if you're shaking salt into a lobster stew at the same time you're gazing down the harbor like Sister Anne, you can't be expected to know whether you're putting in a teaspoonful or a tablespoonful."

The fire of efficiency soon died out altogether, leaving not even a smolder. Bette didn't offer to share her thoughts, but such was her manner that the house had a funereal silence. And of course the spirits that are responsible for radio had the thing possessed; "Lover, come back to me!" it wailed, and Bette shouted from the pantry like a Valkyrie, "Turn that thing off!"

Whenever one of us turned it on, the same thing happened. "Who's sorry now?" it queried. Or, "You won't be happy till you break my heart. . . ." Perry Como really gave out on that one.

Meanwhile there was no news at all of Dana. Where he had gone, what he was doing, no one told us. So we conjectured, aloud.

"Supposing he's gone somewhere to look for a job," said Dot, "and walked in front of an automobile."

Bette's door crashed shut. When the vases stopped rocking, I said, "Look, I can't put my mind on my work and I don't dare even breathe loudly. Let's go to Rockland for a day and get a change."

But such was the state of affairs now that no one dared tell

Hazel, firmly, that we were going to town. Instead, Hazel went. "I'll be back tonight," she said sternly. "I need a change."

She was gone for three days. Dot called Rockland and found that she was staying at Ruth's, so she was safe anyway. We got our own dinners and played the radio when we wanted it and discussed the romance in tones above a whisper.

"I've got past the stage where I want maid service," I said. "All I want now is for this to end. I've known Bette since she was a baby, but I never knew she could be so ferocious."

"Neither did I," mused Dot. "The poor kid, she didn't bargain for this. It's hard on her, but it's also hard on us."

"We'll go to town when she comes back," I said. "We need a change too. We'll come right out and tell her, 'We're going to town on Tuesday . . . that is, if you're not doing anything special that day, and you don't mind if we go. . . .' "

We broke down in slightly hysterical mirth. We were as sorry for Bette as we could be and even sorrier for the absent Dana, who'd been dismissed with no explanation. But we were slightly sorry for us, too. Here we were with our Pearl, and we were working harder than ever before. We were scuttling out of her way like a couple of cowed scullery maids. But that didn't matter; all we knew was that we'd settle for a little sunshine and love around the house, the rapid departure of Mrs. Siddons' *Lady Macbeth* and the return of the tranquil Bette we knew best.

When she walked into the house at dusk on a crisp November night, with a sparkle in her eyes that hadn't been there for days, we were justifiably pleased; but when we saw Dana behind her, his eyes gleaming too, we all but fell on his neck.

Bette, blushing and bridling, offered a few words of explanation. "I took a chance and called up his aunt," she said.

"Did you give her a good spanking, Dana?" Dot asked him.

"I threatened her," said Dana. "She knows better than to try it again!"

Well, we had lost our Pearl. She still stayed on, she graciously remembered to feed us. But how could we compete with Dana? We didn't mind, because we had the sunshine and love around the house; we had so much of it that we occasionally felt *de trop*, but who hasn't felt like that when confronted by a love affair that has all the hearts-and-lace trimmings of a storybook romance?

Besides, whenever Dana came to call, he brought a couple of cans of oil up from the fishhouse; he got water for us. He and Bette went often to Rockland and took our grocery lists along. True, they were a little absent-minded about the shopping, but we managed.

Now, the burning issue was *not* a little help to make our writing easier, but the successful accomplishment of the marriage. Dana wanted to get married before Bette changed her mind again. Bette herself, though dewy-eyed and absent-minded, was noncommittal. We were permitted to put dishes in the sink, we could have the radio, go to town almost when we pleased—but she was making no positive statements about the date.

We settled back into a sort of routine. As a wedding present, we'd given them an acre of land on the island, where Dana planned to build a house. Every afternoon he and Bette went to the spot, where Dana cut down trees and cleared away brush, and Bette, no doubt, felt like a pioneer's wife.

"This is the way it should be," I said. "The husband-to-be builds a house with his own hands. Every tree he cuts down, while she watches, should make their approaching marriage that much firmer. . . ."

Dot agreed. "I guess we can take a long breath," she said. "I think that Bette is sure she loves Dana; she just doesn't want to give up being engaged. She never liked being rushed into anything."

It was that very evening, at suppertime, when Bette returned to the house walking slowly and thoughtfully. She contemplated us for a long time before she said abruptly, "I know you'll hate me for this."

Dot must have known what was coming. She said, "Well?"

"I don't think I want to get married."

Dot's calm was remarkable, considering all we'd been through. "Why?" she asked with great quietness.

"All Dana talks about is *kids!*"

Dot did not argue. She did not point out, as she might have, that the *kids* Dana mentioned would be also related to Bette; they would not be some little urchins brought in from the gutter. She simply took a long breath and stated with finality, "I think I'd better have a talk with Dana."

"What?" cried Bette, losing her poise long enough to yelp.

When Dana came that evening Dot collared him before Bette could and led him into the other room for a Long Talk. I don't know if Bette has found out yet what they said in that Long Talk; but I know that she was very anxious for it to end. A few days later she set the date at last for the wedding.

It's been two years now. I don't think Bette's ever felt like changing her mind since. We have a sort of proprietary interest in young Loren; Dot is his aunt by blood, but I feel like his aunt by virtue of all that we went through that fall.

But you can see why we worry about having a maid. It would be sure to turn out strangely. No matter how smooth-running her existence before she came to us, emotional crises would begin to pop up in her life and thus in ours. We'd begin once more to wonder who was working for whom; we'd tiptoe cautiously through our own kitchen, not daring to leave cups in our own sink. We would be so interested in helping her solve her difficulties we would neglect our work.

I think in the long run it's easier to wash our own dishes and do our own ironing, and forget the ivory tower; after all, who wants to write more than five hours a day?

CHAPTER EIGHTEEN

CLAMS, FISH, AND LOBSTERS

I have met people in the most unlikely places who have mentioned Gay's Island clams in reverent tones. It seems strange to me that I had never heard of the island before the day when we rowed across at dead low water with Freeman Young. And now, since it has become such a vast part of my life, I am continually meeting people who know the island well—or at least, they know its clams.

The clams deserve to be famous. They are tender, delicate, sweet. They are every flattering thing anyone could possibly say about a clam. This will leave non-clam-eaters cold, but the rest of the public will understand what a poem a good clam can be. They are enchanting when they are steamed; adding melted butter is like gilding the lily, and anything stronger, like vinegar, is a criminal offense against the integrity of the clam. The chowder has its own place—a real chowder, that is, with crisp bits of salt pork, plenty of onions and thin-sliced potatoes, and more clams than anything else. *No tomatoes.* The clams must be whole, too, for me.

Fried clams are a sort of epic version of the poem, at least the way Dot fries them. She doesn't serve them encased in a hard shell, but in a delicious clam-flavored coating, crispy on the surface and light as air inside. They aren't deep-fried, but they're golden, and she is always surrounded by admirers when she fries clams. There's something irresistible about the process.

When we first found ourselves surrounded by rich clam flats, we were delighted to know that they served some useful purpose in the world besides being desolate and smelly at dead low water. (This was before we knew the unique pleasure of watching a blue heron pick his way along the edge of a pool dyed apricot and lavender by the sunset.)

When we got over being very tired, and were only a little tired, we decided to go clamming. It was difficult because everybody, except my mother and the dog, wanted to use the one clam hoe at once. Our fervor usually petered out after an hour in the sun, with no wind to drive the mosquitoes away, but it was always fresh by the time the next low tide came.

From the first, our methods were highly individual, though we all started out with the dedicated intensity of dogs digging for rats, spurred on by the interesting fact that clams were selling for five dollars a bushel. Why, there were hundreds of dollars right in our own back yard! We built up immediately (in theory) a profitable business which could be carried on right through the year and make us all independently—well, comfortable. Money in clams, was there? We gazed at the sea of mud in awe, as if it were literally studded with silver dollars.

Guy was a passionate digger. He worked fast, having decided sensibly that there was no use in lingering any longer than necessary in the hot sun. He was usually alarmingly red-faced at the end of half an hour, and we found we could add quite a bit to our clam-rollers by standing quietly behind him and picking up the clams that flew aft.

Dot, when she had possession of the clam hoe, dug carefully and methodically, emitting small yelps of anguish whenever a tine crushed a tender shell, and brooding over each mangled clam. As for me, I was always sure of a hoe. I found one that nobody else cared to use—because it wasn't any good, they said

*That it is possible to look ladylike while
digging clams is sheer illusion*

—and I devoted my hours on the flats to proving that I could dig clams as well as anybody. I was so very delicate about it, not wanting to mash any, that I practically excavated each clam by hand, and I was black mud to my elbows by the time I'd got enough for a very small chowder.

Clams were very few on Criehaven and we weren't used to digging. So after a session we suffered from spots before the eyes, light-headedness, aching backs and trembling legs, and an agonizing stiffness the next day. We female diggers had one misapprehension: we believed it was possible to look ladylike while digging. This is sheer illusion. The only proper way to dig clams is to set the feet wide apart (in rubber boots or bare), elevate the stern toward the sky, and forget appearances. Dungarees are the best things to wear, rolled up to the knees, and never mind who might be strolling along the other side of the Gut.

Our Get-Rich-Quick scheme was stillborn, because none of us ever succeeded in getting more than a peck or so at a time. We ate them right off. Steamed, in chowder, or fried, they brightened our long days of labor and upset our digestions until we were used to them.

Whenever we had company, it became ritual to dig a mess of clams on the spot, and of course the male guests felt honor-bound to do the digging. Dot had an instinct for discovering the best places. When I was the guide, I tried to pick out spots that looked exactly like what she'd pick out, and have thus led warm and muddy men all over the flats in an unprofitable search. Eddie Schmitz set the hunt to music one hot day by singing softly behind me, "Mary Ann McCarthy, she went out to gather clams," to the tune of "John Brown's Body."

After that I let Dot do the leading with her invisible divining rod. We still feed all newcomers on Gay's Island clams and are justifiably proud of them. But we feel a constant pity for the professional clamdiggers, who haul their dories up on the banks and proceed to fill roller after roller. They can have their five dollars a bushel, and it ought to be fifteen. They earn it. It's sheer physical labor, stripped down to its most harsh essentials.

Until this spring, whoever picked up the clam hoe and a roller was always sure of a companion. Little Soldi, who never got to be a very big cat, but always looked like a Walt Disney kitten, adored clams; she followed anyone who dug, hopping from rock to rock and managing to keep her white paws exquisitely clean. Sometimes in her eagerness she was into the hole as soon as you'd got it dug; other times, more restrained, she lounged in the roller like Récamier and expected to be carried from one spot to the next. Cleaning clams for chowder meant one clam tossed to Soldi for every two that went into the pan, and the purring that accompanied the ritual, punctuated with little upward chirps and hysterical tremolos, was something to hear.

Soldi is over in the old garden spot now, between the maple and the stone wall where she used to lie and watch us dig. We thought that would be a good place to put her; she went there often by herself, to prowl through the bushes and watch the birds, and find out all sorts of secrets. When she came home she smelled deliciously of green grass and violets and strawberry blossoms.

We haven't dug so many clams this spring. Strange how easy it is to be haunted; to be so sure, if you looked around quickly, that she'd be there, counting every clam tossed into the roller.

We missed the little pollock that swarmed in the harbor at Criehaven, silvery-green and as sweet as trout. When we got around to fishing here, we found that everyone concentrated on flounders. Flounders! We wanted *pollock!* And apparently they were to be found, not in the harbor, but in the cove below the house.

With only one skiff to use, we all but wore the bottom out of it by dragging it back and forth across the Neck and launching it over the rocks.

We tied our painter to one of the poles of the weir in front of the house, where the shags perched, all huddled together like vultures or fanning their wings to cool themselves. There was a scarecrow on the weir but none of the birds had half the respect for him that I did. Whenever I caught sight of him, his arms outstretched in weird friendliness, I was startled. I have a fine idea for a murder mystery, in which a passing yacht stops in the night long enough to stuff a corpse into the scarecrow's clothing. And then a couple of innocent fishermen bobbing around the cove, like Dot and myself, would get a little close, and discover. . . .

Enough of that. . . . Once we caught six pollock right off at the weir, but it never happened again. (But Eddie Schmitz could catch them by the pailful, so there must have been something wrong with our technique, because he used clams for bait the same as we did.)

The shags had a fine time diving, and seals came into the cove and performed acrobatics right under our noses, but if they were catching fish, they did better than we.

We tied up at Victor Whittier's mooring—he has a couple of cottages on the island, on a point adjoining our land; the fish would bite for Vic, but they wouldn't bite for us. Exhausting every seeming possibility in the cove, we dragged the skiff back across the Neck to the harborside. We used up so much strength *getting ready* to do things that the waste appalls me, now that we've got the knack. And we must have looked pretty silly to the Pleasant Pointers.

We tried for pollock at different spots in the harbor, at all heights of the tide; we muttered about the current that swirled so quickly through. At last, after hours and hours of futile sitting and staring about us at the landscape while nothing happened, we let our lines go down and rest on the bottom and waited for a flounder to bite. Sometimes we got a couple, sometimes we didn't. But they were delicious, cleaned at once and rolled lightly in flour, and popped into the frying pan. We ceased to scorn them and began to look for flounder-spots with the single-minded passion of conquistadors searching for El Dorado.

Everybody used to fish off Walter Young's lobster car; this year, they're fishing off the float by Harlan Davis's new wharf. Having a definite belief about fishing—that it was something like reading, or painting, that you moved off to some corner by yourself—we continued to wander up and down the Gut, looking for a good spot to cast our lines. Then we heard one day about a flat sandy bank down the Gut toward the Stepping Stones, where the flounders liked to come and lie on the smooth bottom.

The day we chose to try it was warm and gray; the trees were showing the faintest mist of green and the first of the warblers had just arrived. With our lines, a handful of clams, a knife, and—prayerfully—a large box, we rowed down the Gut, far away from the harbor and the boats. We dropped overboard a large rock with the skiff painter tied around it, and there we stayed. It began to rain. A soft, tender rain, light and warm as tears, it pattered on the silvery water around us and on our sou'westers. We sat serenely, listening to the whisper of the rain in the stillness and the calling of the birds in the spruce and birch woods that came right down to the shore. I could at long last identify the songs of a few birds and was smugly pleased to note that the black-throated green warbler and the white-throated sparrow were predominant that day. I ignored the other tweetings and trillings that I didn't know. Dot froze into a sort of silent ecstasy upon recognizing something called a "yellowlegs" . . . and then the flounders began to bite.

I am not an easy person to go fishing with, I am not to be

trusted by myself. I love to go fishing; I gladly rearrange my writing schedule—which is extremely flexible anyway—to include an hour or two devoted to fishing. But it must be the atmosphere that attracts and the first wild excitement when something grabs my line. Because when I see the fish coming up through the green water, fighting every inch of the way, I immediately want to let him go, and I cringe with horror because he's swallowed the hook and must be slit open. And even if I wanted to do it myself, I could never hold on to a vigorously flapping flounder. The other day, for the first time, I picked a fish up by the gills and thought it was a thoroughly revolting experience . . . and the sound of a flounder thrashing around in the box makes me sorry for him, so I am always glad when the fish are cleaned and ready to cook. Then, once more, I love to go fishing!

Fishing eight lobster traps is a very recent project, and we do it from Salome, the skiff that we keep around on the seaward side of the island, toward the weir. People are kind; they don't laugh at traps which are twenty-eight inches long, and twenty inches wide on the bottom! I understand there are some localities along the coast where fishermen running big strings of traps object to the small fisherman who fools around with a handful, and that there is a bill in the Legislature to do away with such dilettantes. But it's not so at Pleasant Point. If the men are amused by the size of Dot's traps, they don't show it, and they've been interested enough to ask if the traps fish, and to offer bait when we run short of flounders.

The traps come up into the skiff with the greatest of ease, and they do fish. The first one we hauled had four big lobsters in it. It was a marvelous beginning, and we attributed it to the corned herring in the baitbags. The herring, little ones, had been driven ashore by big silver hake, and had been left by the tide, enough to fill a small barrel. It was exciting—and it gave a good start to our lobstering.

We brought those first four ashore and wrote down the catch

in a little book. Wildly thrilled, we could hardly wait to get more traps out.

"The cove must be full of lobsters!" Dot exulted. "There's so much kelp around the weir and along the shore, and that's where you find lobsters."

"If the price keeps up you'll make some money this summer," I said.

"Then I can start a bank account," she said optimistically.

There was no bank account. We never caught enough to bother with selling any. We had enough lobsters and crabs to eat, and this decreased the food bill. Eight big crabs make a pint bowl of delicious meat. Four crabs and a lobster are responsible for some beautiful sandwiches. Two or three good-sized lobsters contribute a chowder for three of us . . . and so on. And there's the fun of hauling on a day when the southerly wind makes a chop in the cove and Salome bobs up and down like a cork, and I have to keep her nose always pointed into the wind. I do the rowing, you see, while Dot hauls.

Taking Salome out in the cove at half-past six on a misty morning, I have discovered things that I never knew and never would have discovered on Criehaven. I know that a man who sets out to haul so early on a summer morning floats in beauty, whether it's the clear, liquid crystal of a cloudless day sliding over the horizon, or the milky opalescence of dissolving mist, turning rose and gold as the sun burns through it. And when the boat moves close to the rocks, the morning songs of the birds in the woods come out over the water, and whether or not you know a warbler from a sparrow, you know they each contribute their small portion of sweetness to the day. Even the hoarse conversation of the crows begins to have a comradely sound, and the crying and bickering and laughing of the gulls affects you like the first mad and wonderful skirl of bagpipes— that is, if you happen to have the kind of blood that responds to bagpipes.

The huge black-backed gulls steal from the herring gulls,

the small trim mackerel gull with its close black hood laughs above the racket, the little medricks come diving out of the mist all swallowtails and eager orange feet, their voices shrill and urgent and musical for all that. Our raven, from the far end of the island, cruises by, saying laconically, "Awk," and the crows go after him with no respect at all for somebody who's a sort of great-uncle of theirs.

The fish hawks are at work, piping away in a fashion that's ridiculous when you consider the powerful sweep of their wings and their deadly talons. High above the channel one of them hangs in space, great wings fanning the air to hold him in the exact spot, and then, in a plummeting dive that shakes your heart to see it, he drops to the sea and is up again with a fish in his talons. He circles homeward to the nest.

The tree swallows skitter out over the cove in a quarrelsome flurry. They're not at all like the tawny-breasted barn swallows, who love to live in crowded quarters, all the relatives together. Though we have houses up around for the tree swallows, we've been rather disgusted with them this spring. They're like some people we all know; to hear their comments, you can imagine one remarking to the other, "My dear, it's so hard to keep this neighborhood *exclusive!* Did you see that couple looking at Wellview today? Grackles, I'd swear it!"

"Oh, no! Really?"

"And you know grackles! What I say is, let *one* family in and you've got all their relatives, and the first thing you know, this is a grackle neighborhood! Well, I told Joe to go right over there and let them know we don't want trouble, but they'd better not consider moving in here!"

It's not only the grackles they don't like, or the cowbirds who whistle so entrancingly and keep Blackie company, or the sparrows and robins, but other tree swallows. All spring the battles rage, the air is full of combat, while the little women sit on the rooftops adding their five cents' worth, heads bobbing in every direction. "Now, don't fight about me, boys! Heavens to Betsey! Tee-hee-hee-hee!"

Then, even when they're paired off and have settled the sex question, the couples begin quarreling even before the honeymoon is over. He lounges on the weather vane, riding around in the breeze, while she lugs in the bedding. Now that he's fought for her, she can do the housework and jolly well like it.

Well, they all add their little bit to the lobstering, and perhaps everything that we gain out of it can't be put down in dollars and cents in a little book.

At the present, in our spare time, we're working on a gill net to put out in the cove. We've started counting the jars of small mackerel already and wondering where we can borrow a pressure canner. If we should happen to get herring instead of mackerel, corned herring makes wonderful lobster bait.

A pair of perennial optimists, that's all. But what a wonderful satisfaction in going to the woods and cutting spicy-smelling spruce limbs for bows for new traps, and at the same time walking the dogs and looking for birds through strong binoculars; in making a net of fine, smooth, strong white twine, from flat needles Dot whittled out of pine; in dropping a fishline over the side of the skiff into the jade-green shallows over a sandbank, where the young poplar leaves rustle coolly over our heads, and the warblers dart among the sprucetops like sparks of winged fire; or come to perch in the alders to watch us as Lowell described them—"a-tilt like a blossom among the leaves."

There is even a purely atavistic delight in squishing around the clam flats in your bare feet on a hot summer morning. We've also dug clams at twelve below zero, and enjoyed it, because it was such an ideal way to get the air after a day at the typewriters, and keep warm at the same time, and have a rather splendid supper in the lamplit kitchen after we got home.

CHAPTER NINETEEN

WE RETURN TO THE SOIL

During my first spring as a landowner I uncovered the solution to a great mystery. For years, I had been alternately indulgent and contemptuous toward those whose conversation, come April, ran inevitably on one subject: *gardening*. They tell you in tones of hushed ecstasy how many rows of peas they've planted, and about onion sets, and about the tomato plants they are raising by hand in a choice sunny corner of the dining room—conveniently placed so that the Uninitiated can scrape their shins on the box —and which must be trotted out for a few hours of mild sunshine each day, like babies in their prams, and then must be taken in before the air chills.

My father is a Gardener. Once, when fetching in his infant tomatoes, he fell down the cellar stairs, large window box and all, shaking up his babies considerably, not to mention himself. Did he blame his accident on his addiction to Gardening? Not a bit of it. He was far more concerned over his seedlings than himself. Like an alcoholic who refuses to admit that his liquor is what's causing his upset stomach and his trembles, Father refused to see that his lavish indulgence to the habit of Gardening had caused his mishap. And later, when the seedlings grew into the finest tomato plants he'd ever had, he spoke of that dangerous fall as the best thing that had ever happened—to the tomatoes.

No, I could never understand this attitude. I couldn't understand the unabashed candor with which Gardeners of either sex came right out and discussed things like manure. Nor the way they stirred up malevolent-smelling mixtures with the air of perfumers brewing attar of roses—or whatever it is you do with attar of roses—and breathed the fumes with reverent delight. What is worse, they made *you* smell them too.

Let a couple of these earthy souls get together, and the non-Gardener could jump from a tenth-story window without being noticed. To get any real attention from the Brotherhood you have to be a cutworm.

And then the Flower-Gardeners, who lead you to a dejected, leafless, dried-up stalk and say, with obvious pride, "Mock orange! It's doing beautifully, don't you think?" You smile feebly and make sounds of approval, but if you are an honest and uncompromising New Englander you can't come right out and be enthusiastic, can you? Not when you're entertaining doubts of your friend's I.Q.

But with my first spring on Gay's Island, I discovered the key to the arcanum. I say it without shame; I too became a Gardener. I became one of the mystic organization that spends so much of its time on its knees coaxing recalcitrant young cabbages and dealing with problem peonies. I saw, suddenly, a golden galaxy of blossoms on a dormant forsythia. I knew at last what it was to be pained by the indifference of those Who Did Not Care when we told them how we had created our garden spot out of a Gay's Island alder thicket, like the first settlers of the island, back in the 1600's. I was amazed—and continued to be amazed—by any show of indifference to the quality of the soil. Let me tell you about it! There's not a rock in it, and anything will grow. . . .

Yes. Well, the metamorphosis began on a Sunday afternoon.

We weren't going to have a garden at all. Our first year on Gay's Island presented too many other problems. Guy was busy building up his string of lobster traps, and Dorothy and I had several major projects under way. Painting the ninety-six-year-old house and building some kind of a studio were two of them, until that mild, deceptively calm Sunday afternoon. We were prowling around among the alders at the edge of the woods, on the hillside behind the house. It was a tranquil walk because we'd left Smokey at home.

Walking with us, Smokey keeps changing his personality, like a small boy. First he's a motorcycle cop, then a whole wild-west movie complete with Pony Express and Massacre by Indians, and then he's the Wabash Cannonball. He runs twenty miles to our sauntered one, and all the birds, on whose account we brought the field glasses, fly promptly across the state to New Hampshire, or right back to where they migrated from.

So we were listening to the song sparrows, looking for May-flowers under the thick moist carpet of leaves, and admiring the red-budded old maple that stands by the ancient, tumbled stone wall. That was when the Idea came to us. The alder thicket would make a perfect garden. It would be easier to chop down a few alder clumps than cut through the sods of the fields.

The hurricane had put the old barn beyond repair, and we used to look wistfully at the skeleton and wish it would fall down, because the ground beneath was free of witch grass and troublesome weeds. But the ruins still stood, and Guy hadn't yet figured out a way for one man to pull them down without pulling them down on top of him.

So the alder thicket it was; the soil was dark and rich and fine under a luxuriant blanket of humus. I suppose it was then that the virus really entered my system. Or maybe it had been there, transmitted by my father's blood. Dot had it from her Norwegian grandfather, who had turned a rocky swampy site on Criehaven into a bower. We decided that if we cut down about eight clumps of alders—they were widely spaced—we could plant among the stumps as the Indians did, and the sun would stream in all day.

We started work the next morning. Dot cut alders—she has a strong right arm with an ax—and I dragged them out of the way. I cut down one clump and worked harder on that clump than she did on all of hers. The ax bounced back at me in a lethal fashion, the chips flew like hail, and I ripped off the branches in sheer rage after a while.

In a week the spot was cleared, not only of alders but of dead leaves and weeds. We raked, chopped, dragged, dug. It was an ecstatic experience. We got up very early and were over there at six o'clock when the robins and sparrows were singing loudly and sweetly all around us, and the crows shouted hoarse and, I imagine, disrespectful comments over our heads—or should I say our sterns? That was what they saw the most of.

Against the clear pale morning sky we saw the gulls flying in to spend the day around the Gut, that smooth and pleasant stretch of water that divides our island from the mainland. In this light, the maple buds were blood-red, the alder tassels gold, the lichens on the big granite boulder at the edge of the garden were silvery lavender and silvery pink. At six o'clock in the morning the scent that arose from the turning soil and the roots of the golden rod, mixed with the elusive perfume of the alder tassels and a faint breath from the spruce trees, was like no other scent in the world.

We were Gardeners. Whether anything grew or not, we were addicted. We couldn't keep away from the place. On those early morning shifts the cats went with us, Tristan and Isolde.

They adored the garden. They loved to help dig. We planted nasturtiums at the front of the house—in a perfunctory fashion, since we weren't Gardeners at the time—and they superintended; afterward they gave the job a closer inspection, sure that we'd dug up all that nice soft dirt just for them. For a while we thought the nasturtiums would come up part pussy willows.

Tristan, bright red-gold with a perfect plume for a tail, made a ravishing picture when he stretched himself out along the rough gray bough of a maple and looked down at us from among the flame-red buds. When we audibly admired him—with a lot of nauseous baby talk—he shot rapidly to a higher limb and batted at a neighboring spruce branch to show how intrepid he was. Soldi wasn't beautiful and golden, but of a mixture to blend in with the stone wall that was her daily promenade. When she was tired she lay on a rock, and whenever we looked from grubbing after roots, we met her little white-streaked face with its kitten-big eyes and saw her small white forepaws, which she folded delicately before her, like a little girl wearing new white gloves to Sunday School and being careful and graceful about them.

Smokey took to gardening too. Now, at the venerable age of ten years, he has a great sense of decorum, but then he did what Dot's mother calls "rampsing." The word describes perfectly his progress through the woods. He left a trail of swearing chipmunks behind him and the sound of madly whirring wings. At intervals he came back to the clearing, rushed and businesslike, panting earnestly to show us that he was really Doing Something, not simply running in circles. He saw that we were still working, saluted us, and went back to work himself, with a muttered word thrown at the cats who confined their activities to walking the stone wall and climbing trees. And helping us dig.

The tireder we got, the more frequently we stopped to admire the beauties of nature. The white-throated sparrows came, and the warblers and the catbirds; the alders were full of them.

One day a porcupine came down to the wall to see what we were doing. It was our first porcupine. We were horrified to imagine Smokey with a nose full of quills or a kitten with a face full. Dot sent me back to the house for the .22, while she tried to corral the animals. She said she thought she had ten dogs and twenty cats. I raced for the house, feeling like a pioneer woman—Guy was out hauling his traps, and we were alone on the island. When I came back with the rifle and the shells, and took over the kittens and the dog, we dropped the handful of shells in our excitement and had to scrabble around in the leaves for them. The porcupine had gone up a tree, but we didn't know that he would stay there. We scratched around in the leaves for the shells in nervous haste, trying to find one and get it into the rifle before the porcupine took off for the other end of the island.

Coward that I am, I took the animals and left before the shooting took place.

Sometimes it seems cruel to shoot a porcupine, but as long as Smokey hasn't the sense to leave them alone, we have no other alternative. And they are destructive animals. There are many spruces on the island that are dying on their account.

When the first green showed in the garden we were beside ourselves with pride. I should like to be able to state that everything grew with a luxuriance that dumfounded all the visitors who had looked at us so pityingly. Everything didn't. Everything was stunted and miserable, and the only things that grew were the chives which we'd bought from a florist and set out full-grown.

We did have some nasturtiums, though. They were very lovely, growing around a big gray boulder in front of the house. They were lovely because I spooned a special mixture over them. To get this mixture I first went around with a pail and a big iron spoon, and wherever Blackie had grazed, I made a rich and redolent collection. To this I added rainwater, and spent a great deal of time stirring this concoction. If a visitor happened to come along while I was hanging over the pail, I waved the big iron spoon at him cheerily and said the word right out. *Manure*. Just like that. What's more, whenever anybody admired the nasturtiums, I told them about the manure, and patted Blackie's head, and told him not to eat the flowers he'd raised.

The failure of our vegetable garden didn't dismay us. That shows what a grip the habit had on us. But that time I could even understand my father's point of view about the tomatoes. Because the next spring, with the first mild breath in the air, we said, stubbornly, "No Garden. All that work and nothing to show for it." Then we took a walk, and came to a pause by the bank above the Gut. We said, dreamily, "Just look at this soil!"

Once more we cut down alders and dragged them away. We uprooted golden rod and raspberry bushes. This time, Blackie's shed being near, we put fertilizer under everything. We planted an abundance of cucumbers and summer squash, bush beans, Swiss chard, carrots, and two dozen tomato plants, with little cuffs around them to discourage the cutworms. Everything burst up at once, and we really felt sure of this one.

Well, it was a wet nasty summer, and the garden reached a promising stage of development . . . and stayed there. The carrots were dwarfed, and so were the cucumbers when they finally took shape so we knew what they were. The summer squash had skins like armadillos, and the tomatoes had a fixation that kept them forever adolescent and green.

Last year, like a couple of lushes who have fallen into the hands of Alcoholics Anonymous, we made a serious struggle to break the habit. We had too much to do, we assured each other earnestly. We would get our vegetables from Al Carle, over on Pleasant Point. We did. All summer long we ate vegetables that looked like ads in a seed catalogue and tasted like pure heaven. We congratulated each other on the successful solution of this overrated garden business.

This spring has been cold and wet. In fact, spring didn't come to this part of the coast until it was almost time for summer. And with the first whiff of green grass, the first beneficent rays of really warm sunshine, the old complaint burst out like a rash.

We are having a garden . . . in a new spot this time. We fenced it in with a primitive sort of rail fence that looks like something in the midst of the wilderness. The fence is to discourage Blackie, who hasn't yet discovered that he could fly over it like a breeze. We lamed our arms and dislocated sacro-iliacs with spading up witch grass and getting entangled with alder roots. Still, with the incorrigible optimism of addicts, we think we have things under control. We have limited the crops to cucumbers, Swiss chard, and lettuce. We watch warily for progressive symptoms in each other. At the first mention of tomatoes. . . .

Come to think of it, there's been a lot of talk about strawberry plants lately!

CHAPTER TWENTY

IN SEARCH OF OUR FEATHERED FRIENDS

We went birding from our garden, and in addition to becoming a Gardener, I turned into one of those characters whom I used to class with Gardeners . . . the ones who were likely to exclaim without warning, "Oh, a yellow-bellied sapsucker!" or something equally opprobrious. That always seemed such a disagreeable name for a creature purporting to be one of our Feathered Friends.

But the two diseases seemed to go hand in hand. By late spring we were pointing out patted-down places in the soil and saying to visitors, "That's beets . . . that's Swiss chard . . . that's carrots," and the visitors were casting frantically around in their minds for something nice and encouraging to say. And then when they said it, we hardly ever heard it, because one of us was likely to shriek suddenly, "Oh, an olive-sided flycatcher!"

Dot was used to birds—Criehaven is a way station for practically anything that migrates along the Atlantic coast. But the study of them was new to me, and in my enthusiasm I was forever looking up strange large birds which always turned out to be robins. And I reported geese at all sorts of unlikely times— for geese—until I discovered they were shags, or cormorants;

the same idiots that sat all day on Leslie Young's weir, looking very silly with their wings spread out.

A deceitful chickadee once led us to the discovery of a hidden apple tree, whose secret blossoming was the most enchanting spectacle I have ever seen. Be that as it may, that chickadee was an untrustworthy bird who was not content to make noises like a chickadee, but who tried to sound like a phoebe and a wood peewee. He succeeded too. True, the glory of the apple tree kept me from being too hard on the personality that *misled* us (pronounced by me for years as *mizzled*, and really a better word for the purpose, I think). But the behavior of that chickadee only confirmed what I have come to believe: that birding, practiced to any great extent, leads to exaggeration and prevarication on *both* sides.

The chimney swifts are back. As a consequence of their arrival, Dot has just informed me that the Swift Family Robinson has again taken up residence in the unused chimney. And this leads me to the consideration of something which is classed as a recreation or a hobby, but which is rapidly becoming as much of a mania as gardening. It is with me, anyway. I've gone around for months now looking as worried as a Thurber dog because I can't recognize a mad burst of song coming from—yes, a feathery little throat.

My idea of persons who went "birding," ostensibly for fun, and spent the spring feverishly compiling bird lists to see if they couldn't get ahead of somebody else—my idea of such quaint and innocent souls was so low as to be almost nonexistent. If a person mentioned birds as a hobby I felt kindly enough toward that person, but in a remote way. Better to go birding than gambling, I conceded magnanimously. Better to be a birdlover than a Wolf or a Loose Woman. But still—*birds*. . . . Oh, I was fond enough of our Little Feathered Friends, but why not let them live their own lives without all this prying and pussyfooting?

That was before I caught a glimpse of a small yellow character, with a jet black mask, staring me in the eye from a thicket of alders. I stared back, and there we were. I capitulated. Let them consider *me* quaint and innocent; he was darned cute! And he had a whistle, a warble, that I could recognize when I heard it again. He was a Maryland yellowthroat, and for a long time afterward he was the only one I knew by sight and sound, and whenever I heard him I seized upon the occasion happily to display my knowledge of the profundities of nature. At this time I was still freezing in my tracks at the sight of a robin, imagining it to be almost anything that was rare and shy, and never, *never* to be seen east of the Alleghenies.

Depressed by my deficiencies—I thought I'd never get by the Maryland yellowthroat stage—I felt it would be fine for my ego to discover something that would really startle the Old Guard. They were so darned bored by my enthusiasm, having listed everything from an American three-toed woodpecker to a *Helmitheros vermivorus*. That means worm-eating warbler, I discovered after thinking it was probably something left over from the visits of the Norsemen, and let me state here and now that I think it's pretty small of some people to pad their lists with Latin names. Quaint and innocent, huh? Well, there's plenty of Machiavellian tactics going on in this bird-list business.

By painful stages, and much frantic manipulation of the binoculars—I still manage to focus them on a bough ten feet away from the one where the bird is—I added a few more birds to my own list. I don't get fooled by robins any longer, but I've had the catbird listed under plenty of names, which would probably flatter him, since he nearly bursts his lungs trying to be everything in the book.

I suppose I'll be tottering around with a cane, but with an eye like an eagle, when I can catch at one glance all the vital statistics you have to have in order to look up something in the birdbook. When I see a bird in a tree I can't tell whether he's spotted or striped on his chest; and "buffy," a word much in vogue in the descriptions, is either white or gray or yellow to me, and if his wing bars are pale yellow, so what? I like my specimens to have some good bright blotches of color on them somewhere, because I become hopelessly confused after wading through a column beginning:

"Above, slate-gray, the crown and back streaked with black (sides of crown sometimes uniformly black); wings and tail, dusky with slate-gray edgings, the middle wing coverts broadly, the greater coverts more narrowly, tipped with white, forming two distinct wing-bands; two outermost tail-feathers with inner webs extensively white at the end (the white occupying more than the end half on outermost feather which also has the outer web largely white). . . ." And that's just the beginning. See what I mean?

I suppose it's a sign of a primitive and childish mind, but I prefer to paw over the color plates and find something that *looks* like what I saw—only to be told that it's a Prothonotary Warbler which practically *never* comes this far north. Seizing on this chance for fame, I cannily insist that I did see it and get more positive with each protest, but I never win out.

But Dot, for all her years of experience, can still muff a shot. One spring we grew wildly excited about a large hawk that was hanging about the island. We'd gotten pretty blasé about the marsh hawk with the white-banded rump, since the cats had grown past the stage when the marsh hawks hovered menacingly over them.

But this was something spectacular, streamlined and handsome enough to give us gooseflesh. He was mostly blue-gray with white underparts, and when he skimmed over the lawn he looked as big as an eagle. Dot and I promptly went into a tizzy and dragged out the birdbooks. We've got three of them; two are like the ones Cornelia Otis Skinner describes, about as

big as *Webster's Unabridged Dictionary*, and hardly the sort
of thing one would care to lug around through the underbrush.
We raced through the color prints—the Audubon prints first—
and after a period of wild thumbing of leaves, peering over each
other's shoulders, and head-shaking, we came to a really stupendous decision. The bird was a Mississippi kite, which had no
business at all on the Maine coast.

We went around gloating. We planned how we would drop
this into the conversation the next time we met some bird-
loggers who purported to have seen practically everything the
books could offer—but not a Mississippi kite. One of us could
say, casually, "There's been a Mississippi kite hanging around
the house . . . handsome, aren't they? Oh, you've never seen
one? Rare? Impossible, you say?" And then, with a superior
little laugh, "Well, perhaps it *is* impossible, but there he is!
Come down and see him some day!"

It was Dot who, weeks later, chanced to look closely at a
plate showing our old friend the marsh hawk and punctured
our lovely bubble. He was an adult marsh hawk, male, and
hitherto we'd seen only females and immature males. He *belonged* around here; he was not rare, he was not impossible. Fortunately, the blow came from Audubon, and not from those
we'd planned to devastate.

Just another sign that this bird business is anything but guile-
less.

There was an owl, too. We looked up everything and found
that the great horned owl was really something. We toyed with
that idea for a while. After all, it *could* have been a great horned
owl. But out of discretion, I'm afraid, instead of honesty, we
decided on something lesser, like the American hawk owl.
Anyway, the great horned owl couldn't have scared us any
more than this one did.

He was with us all at once, close to our heads on great, noiseless wings. Staring at him in horrified amazement, at first we

didn't see Soldi flattened against the ground, gazing upward with huge eyes as the owl circled noiselessly over her, dipping lower with each turn. Tris, of course, was 'way behind, padding unhurriedly through the alders.

I shouted and ran at the owl, while Dot went for her shotgun. As usual, the shells had been put away in the last house cleaning, and the owl had taken off in the direction of the wharf by the time she came out again. Soldi raced to the house and went under the stove. But there was still Tris to think of, down in the path near the wharf, his yellow coat glowing invitingly in the shadows.

We called and whistled, and finally he appeared, not hurrying; merely lifting his tail erect as a signal that he heard, and for heaven's sake, what was all the racket about?

Upon reading in the book that some owls come down from the Arctic Circle in November and hang around New England for a while, hunting by daylight because they're used to the midnight sun, we had to see that our mousers were in the house by late afternoon. It was quite a struggle. One cannot warn cats about large and predatory owls. Soldi soon forgot her fright, and Tris hadn't been frightened at all.

It's when I have to surrender something as glamorous as a Mississippi kite or the great horned owl, or even the prothonotary warbler, that I take the birdbook and dream over its luscious plates. Sometimes I try to imagine how anyone could possibly recognize a bird song from the way it's described, with the exception of the white-throat's "Sow wheat, Peverly, Peverly, Peverly!" and the Maryland yellowthroat (ah, there!) who actually says, "I beseech you, I beseech you, I beseech you!" But after having taken a wood peewee for a phoebe and then discovering it was a chickadee all the time, my faith in our little Feathered Friends has been somewhat shaken. That's as bad as using Latin names. It's not cricket.

But I can't help being fond of the little things. I still get excited over sparrows and thrilled about the wood thrush who sounds out of the deep forest like a lot of little bells ringing at once. The only thing is, I keep imagining hungrily how nice it would be to discover a wagtail, a pipit, a pine siskin, a dicksissel, a bridled titmouse; or an Arizona pyrryloxia, a Lapland long-spur, a coppery-tailed trogon, a groove-billed ani, or a marbled godwit. Or any one, she said carelessly, of the order of Lamel-lirostral Grallatores.

CHAPTER TWENTY-ONE

OUR HOURS OF EASE

"But what do you *do* with your time?" they ask, frowning and plaintive. "When you've done the dishes, and gone for the mail, and done these other things you tell about—don't you have a lot of time *left?* You can't be papering and painting and weeding *all* the time!"

"I do some writing," I remind them modestly.

"Oh, *that.* I know about that. But what do you do with all those hours and hours left of the day?"

At this point, explanations are useless. There is no point in making blueprints for a certain mentality to prove that under a heavy writing schedule, along with the mechanics of daily living, one doesn't have hours and hours left in a day. One might wish for them, however. One does wish, frequently, to have hours and hours left after the necessary toil is done. But the aching back and stiff neck and washed-out brain yearn for bed and a nonstimulating book.

But we've learned that everything goes better if we take off a day or two for sheer *dolce fa niente* every four or five days, and at least two months in summer when the island bears a vague resemblance to Times Square in the rush hour. And we don't have any difficulty in filling up "those hours and hours."

Walking is one of the things I like best. Smokey likes it too.

At his age he is kept close to the house except for well-chaperoned excursions, or else he'd be tearing off like a young rake to swim the frigid waters of the Gut and visit the Tail-wagging Set of Pleasant Point. So Smokey shares with me my enthusiasm for long walks over the island. Dot has a noticeable lack of fervor about foot travel; bound up, she tells me, with her inherited memories of Indians and suchlike.

Still, in the spring when the birches get a warm amethyst cloudiness around their boughs, and there's a delicious scent of green grass mixed with the odor of the sea wind blowing up from Monhegan, I get her out. Both of us revert to our childhood and discover violets, white and purple, with the old bliss; and she forgets all about Indians if she hears a birdcall that means the warblers have started to come back.

We have special walks. There is the network of ways we've found through the thick woods across the Neck; the little rocky clearings filled with pale green light and strange small plants, the groves of tall timber that make one-time lumbermen like my father stand and stare in something like reverence. Under these trees the ground is flat and smooth, and one gazes in all directions as through arched corridors.

There are the scavenging walks along the shore, hopping from rock to rock, examining everything that we find, from battered toggles to pieces of lobster crates. Once we found a whole crate, door and all! We pick up buoys with names on them we've never heard before. Once I found one that said "S. Bennett" and I stood staring at it for a long time with the hair prickling on the back of my neck. I hadn't known any Bennetts when I began the Bennett's Island trilogy. But here was a buoy that belonged to Steve Bennett, one of my own Bennetts from my "Tide" trilogy.

"Do you suppose it's big Stephen or Stevie?" Dot asked seriously, and then we looked at each other and laughed. But we carried the buoy home and have cherished it since.

We find blocks of pine, too; pieces of two-by-four; occasionally there's a real bonanza in the shape of a fine plank. If it's water-soaked we drag it up into the chip-strewn grass under the spruces. Then, some fine day when the water is calm on the sea side of the island, except for a gentle, glistening swell, we launch a skiff and row down along the shore, landing in every little cove to salvage what we found on the last beachcombing walk.

The beaches on the sea side are far different from the tranquil sheltered nooks along the Gut, where the birches and oaks can dip their branches into the water at high tide, and the shallows are silvery green. Here we can play at wandering along a riverbank, or rowing in the gently dimpling current of an inland stream. But on the other side there is the great, bright, salt-smelling wildness of the Maine coast. Even when the water is calm, the wildness is still there; the glittering beaches strewn with shells, the bleached and ancient wreckage of boats, the dried, fine porcelain cups of sea urchins where the gulls have fed; the wind-slanted spruces, the short sparse turf strewn with rockweed from the storms. There is the smell and the feel of loneliness, and our voices when we call back and forth seem small and ineffectual.

But only a little way from there—fifteen or twenty minutes in a skiff—and around a couple of points, there are the birdhouses, the domestic squabbles of the tree swallows, the flagpole, the lawn, the sheep.

It is rather wonderful to have a wild world and a tame world, a river and a sea, encompassed by boundaries we can travel in an hour.

Then I like to go to the Old House. That is a place where we take all visitors, but usually they see it in summer, when green fields surround it, birds are busy in the thickets, and the water between Gay's Island and Friendship is at its brightest blue. To get the real atmosphere, to sense its solitude and its primitive

grandeur—for there is a grandeur in that great chimney standing alone against the sky—one must see it in the spring or the
fall, when clouds rush over its head and the tall dead grasses
bend in the wind, and there are still traces of the wild animals
that use the place for their own.

Built, according to the sales advertisement, in 1694, the old
Gay house has a long history. But so far we have learned little
of it. Perhaps it's because everyone on the Point, being descended from or connected in some way with the Gays, knows
the story of the house so well they take it for granted.

We saw the house the first day we came on the island with
Freeman Young. We saw the wide, stone-walled driveway
along which the oxen had been driven, and tried to populate
the hot bright emptiness of the afternoon with the people and
animals of that faraway time. The house, that day in 1944, was
in good repair, and if someone could have put carpenters to
work on it then, it could have been saved. But the hurricane
that struck that fall played havoc with the weakening timbers,
and each strong wind since has done its bit, twisting and prying.
Now the main roof has fallen in, and the great chimney with its
many fireplaces and big ovens stands bare and bleak to the rain
and the sun. It rears high above the ruins, the heart of the house,
first to be built and last to fall. The bricks are the small, very
old sort brought from England.

Beneath the house there is a fine cellar, with field-stone walls
and hanging shelves; what food it must have known, what
preparations for the winters when the wind and snow whistled
across from one side of the island to the other!

Some of the fields are still cleared, but they are much smaller
than they used to be, even within the memory of some of the
older Point residents. The thick dark woods are moving steadily
closer. Alders are springing up in the field that slants from the
walled drive down to the shore, over which we can look at
Morse's Island and Friendship. It is still a lovely meadow,

though, spattered with daisies and buttercups in the spring and hiding wild strawberries in the summer, sloping down to a charming, birch-bowered cove at the foot. A lovely meadow with a lovely name. We wonder who first called it The Tinker Field, and how long it will be before the somber spruce woods on either side encroach on it, and the fifth-column alders choke it out of existence.

What we *have* learned about the Old House is that its first people raised sheep and spun their own yarn, grew flax and made their own linen; and that the stone walls that wander everywhere, sometimes losing themselves in the woods, surely prove how hard those people worked at clearing the fields. And whenever we look at the stone walls, or sit on one for a moment's rest, we remember those men, whoever they were; we do not know the names of them all, but we know them through their work, and so the stone walls are their immortality.

The visitors, seeing the Old House for the first time, never disappoint us in their reaction as they stand staring at the tumbled ruins and the huge chimney stark against the sky. My mother has painted and sketched it in several aspects. Eddie Schmitz spent several hours in the windless heat of an August afternoon painting the house. "As Dot sees it," he explained. Dot had told him how uncomfortable she felt when she was in the vicinity of the place. And so he had painted it, with splotches of shadows that seemed about to quiver and a cruel brassy light on the faded red bricks of the chimney that pierced a hot and brooding sky.

We always point out the strips of birchbark that make a sheathing beneath the clapboards; sometimes someone picks up a wooden peg and carries it away with him in memory of the place. The wide roof and floor boards stir the imagination, and we try to picture the way they were brought to the spot—over the Stepping Stones by oxcart, perhaps—but it is all fancy. There is no fancying, however, the reason for the holes cut in the walls, like gun-ports; they were actually put there for defense purposes. Indians were a real peril once. There were people living in the house during the days of the French and Indian Wars, when Gay's Island was a disputed point between the English at Pemaquid and the French who came down from Castine.

Great flat expanses of gray rock, glittering with mica pockets, are laid bare in front of the house, and we think of the many children who must have played on those rocks, and what their games could have been. They must have welcomed the same birds we hear now—warblers, robins, thrushes, catbirds, and the sweetly trilling song sparrows. The gulls circled lazily overhead as they do now, the crows shouted from the woods, and the deer came out to nibble at the gardens.

When, in Ben Ames Williams's book *Come Spring*, we read how the sloop *Sally* anchored for the night in Gay Cove, we thought how the Old House must have looked down at the little ship, and that brought to mind, inevitably, what else the Old House must have seen. For the channel upriver to Thomaston is plainly marked with buoys, and we often see draggers and freighters pass by this cove. In the days of the glory and youth of the Old House, this channel must have been a real highway for the constant passage of ships coming down from Thomaston, newly launched from the yards that were so busy then.

It is enough to make the heartbeat quicken to think of the tall masts and billowing sails that must have gleamed and curved like gulls' wings against the high blue slopes of Caldwell as ship after ship made her way down among the islands toward the open sea. And when they returned from foreign ports on the other side of the world, how much salt spray must have whitened their bows and decks and darkened their sails before they returned to the dreamlike calm of this waterway!

There is no sorcery, no spell to cast, that could bring back the Old House from the heap of rubble around the chimney; but there is one thing that stands in little danger of change. No hurricanes, no rain or snow, no springing up of shrub or tree can take away those moss-grown stone walls that trail across the fields and through the woods. We don't have vandals here, but if we did, they'd have a hard time of it to destroy those walls. Here and there a few stones have rolled off the top, but otherwise they are complete. When we go berrying, or scramble through the underbrush in search of a bird, we never fail to stop for a moment when we come to a stone wall. And before we climb over it, we remember the men who placed it there. The Old House was a monument for as long as it could stand. Now it is tumbling down. But the stone walls are still there, quietly marking those days when to own land was a man's birthright, even if his land were only a few rocky New England acres out of which he must pluck the boulders with his own hands, and his sons' hands, if he was lucky enough to have sons.

Eloquently mute in its ruins, the Old House stands on its rise against the woods. It may be trite to say that it makes us think. But it does. A time of contemplation comes to all those who pause to look at it or to rest on one of its stone walls. It is a good thing for the soul to stop now and then, and think of the way things were *then*, and the way they are now.

There are so many reasons why walking counts for so much here; why I am perfectly satisfied to leave the car on the other side of the Gut where it can't tempt us to be lazy and thus cheat ourselves out of walking. Apple trees are one of the reasons. Apple trees on the edge of a rocky bank above the cove, where the salt water laps against the roots at unusually high tides, where the wind picks up the pale pink petals and drops them lightly on the sea, and the tide carries them off toward the distant horizons. Apple trees twisted and gnarled and bent toward the earth by the prevailing winds, so old they bear now only blossoms and birds for fruit; apple trees springing wild in so many spots on Gay's Island.

We had been here two years before we realized that the ancient and knotted apple tree in front of the house was not the only one. Oh, we knew about the one on the bank, practically growing out of the beach rocks. That one hardly counted, it was so small, and hadn't really begun to show what it could do in the way of blossoming. But last year it was a mass of bloom; this year it will be the same, and the fragrance spreading out from it, when we go down to the beach to push off the skiff in the early morning to haul the little lobster pots, is something you'll never find in the most delicate and expensive perfume bottle.

And the old tree, as if to outdo the young one which produced such an extravagance of blossoms but no fruit, gave us twelve apples last fall; twelve apples for sauce that tasted like none other. (I always thought applesauce was prosaic stuff until then.)

But it wasn't until the day we were following the sound of a wood peewee that we discovered yet another apple tree, a big one, hidden deep in a growth of alders.

We found an outcropping ledge first and climbed upon it to sit and rest. Here we could look into the tops of the thick old alders, silvery with age and still bare with winter. A chickadee, very impertinent in his black velvet cap, came and sat on an alder branch and let us know we weren't chasing a peewee at all, but Himself; he opened his bill and poured out the sad call just to prove it.

Then we noticed the apple tree growing near the ledge. It looked like any old apple tree, and after we climbed off the ledge and went back to the house, we forgot the tree.

But one day, after we had brought in an armful of fragrant, rain-wet branches from the tree on the shore, we remembered the apple tree in the alders. Having nothing else to do at the moment, Dot uttered the magic word "Walk" to Smokey, and we were off. We crossed the field and entered the thick alder growth, and made our way to the gray mossy ledge.

Here was no longer a twisted old tree with a mass of gnarled and tangled limbs, as if it had known nothing but agony since it sprouted its first branch above the ground. With its thick greenery and its hundreds of lovely blossoms, it became for us the most beautiful of apple trees, and smelled the sweetest. There it stood, hidden from all eyes except those of the birds, its trunk seeming to rise from a cleft in the ledge. When we stood on the ledge we could look down into the tree, which is quite a sensation if you have never done anything but look up into an apple tree.

The perfume from the roselike blossoms was not swept away by the breeze, but held in by the alders making a dense wall round about. It was as if no breeze ever came to this spot, and in the space around the tree and over the lichened shelf of rock the scent must remain, never to be dispersed, never to be breathed by anyone unless he came stumbling as we did, all ignorant, into the heart of this secret loveliness.

We have other things to do in "those hours and hours" which are scarcely strenuous. Dot has a fiddle and a tenor guitar, and I have an accordion. She plays both her instruments well. I play the accordion pretty well. It is so big that I have to feel exceptionally large and healthy before I hoist it out of its case. Still, we're able to make our own music, combining our talents in a repertoire that travels from "La Paloma" and the more melodious of the popular songs to the bucolic simplicity of "Little Brown Jug." Or Dot wanders off alone with her guitar to figure out a new chord or compose a melody for a favorite poem. Her version of Masefield's "Sea Fever" is always in demand, and it always gives me exactly the same sensation in my throat and under my eyelids. It's not just the way she sings. Her fingers

have a special way with that little and battered guitar, whether
it's an old minstrel song, a mountain ballad, something rowdy
and faintly ribald, or a fast popular song.

I am afflicted with embarrassment whenever anyone suggests
I play the accordion. My favorite method is to be sure nobody's
paying any attention to me. Then I can do as I please, wandering through simplified versions of Chopin, discovering weird
combinations of chords in a pseudo-Rachmaninoff fashion, and
make horrendous faces as I concentrate.

When my mother is here in the summer, she paints. Dot also
paints. My mother does tranquil, pastoral views of the island,
dreamlike pastels of the weir and the islands after rain, or sun-
sets down the Gut; Vic's old red dory hauled up on the beach.
Dot likes surf. To be shut in a room surrounded by half a dozen
of her paintings is to become acutely seasick, so much action
is contained in her boats rising to the peaks of huge seas before
they drop down into the trough, in the impact of water against
rock. She has found she can do quieter scenes, and her paintings
of the Bennett Homestead and the Sorensen House (from my
trilogy, though the houses are actual ones on Criehaven) are on
exhibit now in Rockland.

We have a drawer full of every conceivable sort of material;
papers of various textures, water colors, pastel, colored pencils,
charcoal, oils, layout pencils. Art gum. Books. My mother and
Dot keep them in constant use, and this year I expect textile
paints will be added to the collection, since my mother is doing
that now. I have dallied with everything, and have a few pastel
portraits to my credit, but I am incurably lazy.

One year during the summer months we lived in a snowstorm of shavings. My mother came down armed with carving
tools and some books on whittling; she was going to work in
wood. Dot caught the infection, of course. I tried it, sliced both
thumbs at once, and remained passive for the rest of the summer. Every night the shavings flew; every morning they were

swept up. When Fanny Davis, over on the Point, started up "Fan's Gift Shop," Gay's Island was represented by the little fishhouse-and-boat groups our whittlers made, painted, and glued onto rocks. These were done in great detail, even to chimneys on the houses and masts on the boats.

Dot abandoned this for a while to make the quantities of the small, brightly painted lobster buoys Fanny asked for, but my mother went on with the other idea, adding miniature skiffs with oars in them, buoys hung on the fishhouses—buoys the size of sweet-pea seed—piles of little traps. She made light-houses, complete with attached houses, sandpapering every-thing to a professional smoothness before she finished it. She went on from that to birds; everyone wanted perched gulls, it seemed.

So the shavings flew, and everyone but me was hysterically supplying Fan's Gift Shop and having a wonderful time at it, too.

This year it will be leather. You can't deny that we're a thorough bunch around here. I expect that during the hot months the place will smell like a tannery as my mother tools billfolds and purses and hands them over to Dot for lacing.

One project, which has been going on without cessation ever since we first came to Gay's Island, is interior painting. We are forever doing a room over; and when my mother arrives we turn her loose with a paintbrush, since my father keeps all his painting materials figuratively under lock and key, which is very frustrating to his wife. Being of an energetic nature she likes nothing better than to start on our old furniture; and we like nothing better than to let her do it.

This sounds as if we live in a *welter* of *décor*, but it's not really that bad. If Dot wants to paint the floors red, that's fine. It's a nice warm color. And I was the one who did the Scotch Blessing under the mantel shelf in the kitchen. You guessed it; old English lettering.

CHAPTER TWENTY-TWO

THE SEA! THE SEA! THE OPEN SEA!

The Pink skiff, which we also call "the Pink Punt," should really be called "the Picnic Punt," because that's the one which holds my mother, if she is here, and Dot and myself; Smokey, Susan the dachshund, pillows, blankets, paintboxes, lunch, and camera. Whenever the day seems to call for it we set forth to spend the day somewhere on the shores of the island. My mother establishes herself with her paints; Dot picks up shells—she has a miser's delight in collecting big mussel shells.

"They make nice ash trays," she says. She has a bushel or more of them now, but I've never seen her use one yet for an ash tray. Smokey and Susan gallop and explore. (If you've never seen a dachshund gallop, you've missed something.) I beachcomb. All islanders see beaches as sources of treasure-trove and begin automatically to paw through the rockweed whenever they land in new territory.

At the end of the day we come peacefully home, to be met by assembled cats who magnanimously forgive us for Sneaking Off Like That; to think happily of a good cup of coffee and a sleepy evening out on the lawn watching the sky until dusk (and the arrival of the mosquitoes) and then perhaps some special radio program. It has to be special, since we use the

radio very sparingly, believing we enjoy it more if we're dis-
criminating. Perhaps no one will touch the radio, but we will
go early to bed, to read, and then fall asleep.

That is the way a day's excursion by boat should be. Nothing
exciting, but something to relax the body and feed the soul.

And so, with this thought firmly in mind, we went one day
to Monhegan. For four years that high blue island, lying beyond the others but looming above them, had titillated our various imaginations. It was remote and imperious; it had, somehow, the look and shape of romance.

Even the photographs of the town in our many books on
Maine didn't violate my dreams of the place. They showed
little houses on curving roads, half-buried in the sturdy flowers
that bloom so magnificently in spite of constant winds; and
fields that made me think of English moors, and great cliffs of
dark rock, plunging down to wild and fantastic patterns of
leaping foam.

So we thought about the trip as a pleasantly exciting eventuality; but so vague an eventuality that we were actually
startled one summer day when Leslie Young said briskly,
"Want to go to Monhegan next Sunday?"

"Yes, yes, YES!" the answer came in chorus from the three
of us—my mother, Dot, and me. After the amazement was over
we were as giddy as children at Christmas. We were *going!* We
went home and studied the photographs of Manana, and the
harbor at Monhegan, and tried to imagine, as we are always
doing, how these sea-girt chunks of rock and soil looked to the
men from across the ocean. They say the Vikings reached Monhegan before they touched any other part of the country; it is
certain that Captain John Smith lingered there quite a while,
and built some boats there. It is a sure fact that the settlement at
Monhegan sent salt fish to the Plymouth Colony to help it
through its first terrible winter.

And we were going. There were a lot of crossed fingers

around the house for the next week, but Sunday dawned the sort of day that always makes me think of that verse in the hymn:

> Holy, holy, holy;
> All the saints adore thee;
> Casting down their golden crowns
> Around the glassy sea.

Between us and Caldwell the water was glassy enough. It was like a pale azure mirror, except that it looked softer than glass. Beyond Caldwell and Magee, Seavey and Davis, Allan's and Benner Islands, Monhegan lifted the proud head of a monarch. I remembered how, when I was little and we sang that hymn on Sunday mornings as the choir came in, I used to have a picture of all the saints, dressed in beautiful robes like the figures on ikons, sitting around a glittering sea in high-backed chairs, like the ones on the church platform for the minister and the deacons; and at a given moment they all took off their tall golden crowns and cast them into the sea. Ever since, this scene has symbolized for me the perfect, glistening, Sabbath calm of the Maine coast on such a morning as this—when we were about to start for Monhegan.

Smokey went over to stay with my friend Anne, who was in the camp called "The Periwinkle" at the time; we left milk and water under the bench for the cats and took Susan with us.

By the time we went out of the harbor at Pleasant Point, the glassy calm had given way to the gayest chop imaginable; the air was salty and smelled of the open sea, the water sparkled blue and green and silver, and we were all very happy. Leslie's boat was a narrow, low-sided, twenty-eight footer which bounced merrily across the channel paying no heed to the southerly wind that splashed spray all over her bow. Leslie has been fishing out at Monhegan on and off for years. I think he could find his way in a thick fog with no compass, simply by a gull's sort of instinct. That little boat of his had made the trip in all weathers.

We went out among the islands, getting a good view of all that Caldwell had hitherto hidden from us; the smaller Caldwells, and Teel's Island, which is distinguished by the largest, greenest, and most photogenic oak tree I have seen. There it rises from the heart of a flat and almost barren island, companioning the house in whose kitchen Andrew Wyeth painted Hen Teel. (Thanks to young Mr. Wyeth we are forever discovering Port Clyde and St. George neighbors in the most unlikely places; books on American art, *Time* magazine, the rotogravure section of the Boston Sunday *Herald*. Those are only a few of them.)

We passed Burnt Island, and the Coast Guard Station, which from Gay's Island is merely a white blob; and suddenly there was nothing to temper the wind, which until now had been merely a crisp and good-natured breeze. We were leaving the shelter of the islands and heading out into the last stretch between the Georges Islands and Monhegan.

"This part takes about forty-five minutes!" Leslie shouted at us encouragingly as we pulled on the raincoats we'd brought and wrapped Susan up in some spare sweaters. Her sleek hide didn't take kindly to the spray that kept flying aboard.

From that moment on, Leslie's boat was very small. Back in the harbor, and among the islands, it had been a perfectly normal-sized boat. Now it was a toy and we were in it, and the waves were very big, and Monhegan looked much farther away than it had ever looked from the sitting-room windows of Tide's Way.

"It is simply because we haven't been out in any rough water since we left Criehaven," I said to myself. "Except the day we were so scared coming from Port Clyde." . . . I decided not to think about that and watched the bow of the boat climb sky-ward on a big comber. It was a lovely morning, perfect for a sail. The boat slid down the other side of the wave and I loosened my fingers out of the grooves they seemed to be mak-ing in the underside of the plank where I sat. My mother and Dot were up beside Leslie, laughing when salt ice water showered them.

"Someone has to stay with Susan," I told them severely when they looked back at me. I remembered the dozens of trips this little boat must have made across this stretch of water. I re-membered the trips I myself had made out to Criehaven on the mailboat, when the shortest part of the twenty-five mile journey—between Matinicus and Criehaven—was often enough to intimidate all stomachs but the Captain's. And any-one who went up to stand by the wheel with him, in hopes of absorbing some of his imperturbability, soon discovered that his cigar could complete the job the elements had begun.

Occasionally we saw other boats; or rather the masts of other boats, since when they sank into the trough of the waves they were all but invisible. The sun glittered on the curling silver-edged crests, and all the time the island of our dreams loomed larger on the horizon.

At last we were there. The high, barren hump of Manana reared over us, and the boat-landing of Monhegan itself, with the Seacoast Mission Ship *Sunbeam* made fast alongside, awaited us with a welcoming air. Leslie had to unload us onto the *Sunbeam*, but there were plenty of hands to haul us up over the side, and Susan had been so cowed by the waves and the spray that she didn't offer to bite anyone.

Another step up, and we were on Monhegan.

We loved it. After having been introduced to a number of people by Leslie, admiring gardens (just like the ones in the photographs) and dozens of kittens, we went into the Odums' store and passed the time of day with Douglas and Harry. It still seems a strange fluke of circumstance that two brothers from Quincy Point—Quincy, Massachusetts—should be keeping a flourishing general store out on one of the most rugged Maine islands, but there they are, as comfortable on those steep and windswept slopes as a couple of gulls, and a lot more hospitable.

Their home is next to the shore, spacious and cool and quiet after the excitement outside. Oh, yes, there was plenty of excitement. There was the flood and dazzle of an August sun; and there was the constant surge and splash of water in what passes for a harbor at Monhegan. The southwest wind was growing stronger all the time and sending big seas crashing through the narrow gash between Manana and Monhegan. The boats pulled at their heavy moorings. We'd never seen such moorings. Even out at Criehaven, twenty-five miles from the mainland, they don't use such rugged methods of anchorage.

Sitting on the Odums' porch, while we talked with their mother and their sister-in-law, who were spending the summer with them, we watched the water that seemed near enough for us to feel the spray.

Later, on our own, we wandered over the island. There were artists everywhere. Of course, I didn't believe that the constant stream of people taking walks, strolling harborward or cliffward, were all artists, and we were very proficient at sorting out the natives from the summer people (being natives ourselves), but the island was undeniably spotted with artists. There was something refreshing about the sight of a man or woman working away at an easel, tranquilly unaware of passers-by and intent only on the scene laid out before his particular vantage point. It was refreshing, too, to notice the lack of curiosity on the part of everybody else.

One can set up his easel anywhere on Monhegan and cause no more comment than if he were waiting on a city street for a red light to change.

We finally sat down to rest and eat our lunch above a little cove into which the sea poured large and roaring combers. It was like many of the rocky coves on Criehaven; the thunder of surf and the glittering explosions of spray were familiar to us. Susan ran around on the short fragrant grass. My mother sketched assiduously and looked quite at home, like a real artist. Dot and I were lazy, and I acquired a magnificent rash from what I later discovered to be trailing yew. It is very rare, and Monhegan is one of the few places that have it. This fact would have impressed me more if I had heard it before I got the rash.

We talked about the surf.

"It should make me homesick for Criehaven, but it doesn't," Dot said. "I wonder why."

"Maybe you're thinking about the trip home," my mother suggested helpfully. "The wind's blowing harder all the time."

I brushed that off. "Oh, it'll be behind us. It'll get us home in no time."

Dot mused about the surf. "I used to miss it when we first came to Gay's Island. Now I'm sort of fond of that nice dreamy stretch between us and Caldwell."

"There's nothing dreamy about it in a sou'westerly wind," I said.

"Which is what we have now," said my mother, trenchantly.

The spray flashed like crystal, and the form made patterns of wild lace over the water's beautiful blue-green. It was a splendid day, and we liked Monhegan very much. But the truth was undeniable; we had to make the trip home, and we couldn't help thinking about it.

Later, down in the village, we met Roland Stimpson, who was spending the summer working on the Monhegan mailboat. We all sat down by the side of the road in the shade of some wonderful thick maples and talked and secretly wished that the wind would die down, even if it was going to be on our tail.

Eventually we caught up with Leslie, who is extremely social-minded, and after some final good-bys we boarded the

Artists everywhere, tranquilly unaware of passers-by

boat to go home. It looked tinier than ever, rising and falling in the noisy surge around the stone landing; and there was quite a trick in getting aboard in one piece, lowering ourselves onto the cabin roof just as the boat reared up on a particularly large swell.

And then we were out of the harbor, out of the shelter of Manana, and the sou'westerly was on our tail with a vengeance. We had all the faith in the world in Leslie, who had made this trip so many times and who knew just what his little twenty-eight-foot boat would do. But once we were out in that famous piece of water between Monhegan and Burnt Island, we realized just how much help the wind was going to be . . . or hindrance.

The tide was running against the wind; and the waves ran everyway, tumbling into us from all sides. Looking back was no good; we saw the dory we'd brought along for a tender riding high above us on huge seas that appeared like walls of blue-green water. Every time the dory-painter snapped taut, there was a chance of its breaking, and when and if the broken line whipped back into the boat, there was a chance of its giving one of us a terrific blow. And these great seas that shouldered us along—what if they should send the dory aboard? It had been known to happen. Even Leslie, whose blue eyes danced with mirth when we looked rather nervously at the boiling water along the boat's low sides, was apprehensive about the dory.

"Don't sit in the stern," he told us. "Can't tell about that tender."

Otherwise, he was entirely unabashed by the fact that his boat was being tossed like a chip from wave to wave. Once, suddenly, he slowed down the engine; there is nothing like that unexpected lessening of sound and speed to bring the stomach up sickeningly into the throat. While we rolled in a sort of cement-mixer motion, he investigated a floating log. It was nothing he wanted, and soon we went on.

In the morning, that far distant morning, we'd seen other boats out here. This afternoon it was practically virgin sea. In all my years of boats I have never felt quite so lost. My mother and Dot looked calm enough. I imagine I looked calm, too. But if their thoughts were anything like mine, we were three whited sepulchers.

I remembered, quite unwillingly, the only other time I had felt like this. I'd had to leave Criehaven for an important engagement in Boston, and the mailboat was broken down in Rockland and hadn't come for several days. Nick Anderson, Dot's cousin, promised to take me. "If it's too rough to haul," he stipulated.

Well, it was too rough to haul, and by the time we were heading out past the southern end of Matinicus I was sure it was too rough for anything. But the unfortunate thing about such lucid and practical thinking is that it always takes place when it's too late to do anything about it. For the first time in my life I was frightened in a boat. I knew what it was to feel weak with terror, as if all my bones had melted into a sodden mass. Nick, at the wheel, had been unconcerned. But not I.

Dot had watched with her binoculars from the back shore of Criehaven, and told me afterward how she had seen the full length and breadth of the boat's deck from bow to stern, outlined in its bright orange paint against the water as it rose up on a wave. And she had been afraid, watching.

Later I used this trip for a scene in *Storm Tide*, when Joanna went ashore with Owen.

Now, unfortunately, none of us were ashore. Leslie looked as peaceful, however, as if he were driving his car down the Pleasant Point road. The engine was wide open, pitting its speed against the erratic attack of the seas. *A wilderness of waves*, I thought. *Now I know what that expression really means.*

It was supposed to take forty-five minutes from Monhegan to Burnt Island. We did it that afternoon in thirty, the longest thirty minutes I have ever lived. But we made it, and I was drunk with relief when we entered the shelter of the Georges Islands and their comparative calm. My mother and Dot looked rather giddy too. Susan emerged from her wrappings and shook her ears hard.

"That was the fastest trip in rough water I ever took," Dot told Leslie, and he grinned.

"Were you scared?"

"A bit nervous once or twice," she said casually. "I was never out in such a little boat when it was as rough as this." Leslie nodded; he knows the Criehaven and Matinicus boats are for the most part big and heavy, as they must be for the constant beating they take.

"Out home they'd never dare slide down a sea at full speed the way you've done today for they'd keep on going till they struck bottom," she went on. "This boat is like a little duck."

Leslie was still grinning. "Well, it was pretty choppy out there," he admitted. "But she's been out in worse. . . . Anyway, the worst part of the trip is ahead of us."

We were too limp, at that, to do anything but look at him. "Between Caldwell and Gay's Island it'll be pretty nasty with this wind," he said.

We stopped relaxing. Every revolution of the engine was taking us out of this blessed calm and into more rough stuff; and I'd had enough experience already with the water between Caldwell and Gay's Island, when the wind was blowing against the tide.

But having delivered his block-buster, Leslie began to fiddle with the engine. "Been expectin' trouble with this all day," he said absently, and went into some technical explanations. We all looked at him very attentively, but I still don't know what ailed the engine. I simply remember thinking, If the line towing the dory had snapped . . . or the dory had come aboard . . . or a sea had come aboard and filled us . . . or the dory had filled and we'd had to stop to bail her out . . . or the engine had broken down. . . .

But we had been to Monhegan! And we'd have a story to tell . . . if Fate wasn't waiting malignly for us between Caldwell and Gay's Island.

Nothing was waiting but a blessed, miraculous shift in the wind. By the time we headed into the last stretch, the wind was west, and only a cheerful little chop riffled the water and chuckled about the bow. I have never seen the harbor at Pleasant Point look as radiant and welcoming as it looked at sunset that night, when we headed up the Gut toward the Gay's Island wharf.

We thanked Leslie with all our hearts. From the very *bottom* of all our hearts. We thanked him, aloud, for taking us to Monhegan and satisfying our collective dreams. We thanked him, silently, for knowing so much about boats and treacherous currents and violent winds, and getting us *home*.

Once ashore, we three stopped in the path and looked at each other solemnly. Susan rushed ahead of us to the house, seeing the cats on the doorstep. "How was it?" said Dot finally.

"I was scared stiff," said my mother. "So was I," said Dot. "I'm ashamed to admit it, but it's the truth." I said nothing, but suppressed a strong impulse to get down and pat the soil.

We still look at Monhegan. It has not lost its grandeur for us. We will not forget how it was, or the people we met, or the artists we saw so blissfully lost in their work. But this year, when we wish to go somewhere in a boat, we shall be faithful to the Pink Punt.

And let no outer-islanders cast doubts on the ruggedness of the inner-islanders and their waters.

CHAPTER TWENTY-THREE

GAY'S ISLAND GALLERIES

The Gay's Island Art Gallery I have saved for the last. It is a unique gallery, and certainly the most satisfying I've ever found, because the exhibits change not monthly, not daily, but hourly. We make the living, and the Gallery makes the living worth while. For example, it is April now on Gay's Island, and how cold April can be on the Maine coast, only an addict can know. But when I come up from the shore, with chapped hands and wet feet, and the seat of my dungarees soaked and chilly (I had to slide down a steep slippery rock to reach the skiffs before I could bail gallons of rain and sea water out of them), I know it is April because the exhibits have shifted while my back was turned.

The first tree swallow of the year has arrived to perch on the weather vane, and the sun coming out palely from behind the departing storm clouds shines on his steel-blue satin back; he is a picture all by himself, sleek and gleaming against an uncertain sky. Presently, when he takes to the air, he will become another sort of picture. And when he goes around investigating all the birdhouses, there will be still a third picture. Meanwhile, the cove has flattened out, a loon has come from somewhere, his breast and throat amazingly white. Caldwell lies in the rosy-gold light of a George Innes painting.

Tristan is a picture, coming up from the shore with the

leisurely pad of a lion secure in his own jungle. This morning there was a new sketch added to the rest; a little red squirrel— a little mother red squirrel, from the appearance of her clean white belly—stopped on the back doorstep to scold the world in general, regardless of the fact that a cat and a dog and two human beings were watching her from the window. We call her "Trixie Trollop."

We treasure the old squaws skedaddling and yodeling in the cove; a loon, who seems to walk across the water; porpoises doing somersaults out around the can buoy, and seals swimming in the Gut, their gleaming heads popping out almost from under the skiff and their irrepressible curiosity leading them to follow us when we whistle to them.

We keep for laughs the picture of Blackie racing on pogo-stick legs like a spring lamb; and we keep for sheer wonderment something that will never be on canvas but is indelible just the same.

One windy, boisterous night when we went down to attend to the skiffs, with the hope of intercepting Tris in his wander-ings and getting him home (so he wouldn't rouse everyone in the middle of the night), we stopped to turn the flashlight on the surf that was breaking with a fine roar on the little beach at the Neck. And there in the circle of light was Tris, crouched so close to the waves that the spray must have dampened his tawny coat. He was watching the water. We had seen him watching it in the daytime but never at night. How long he had been there we didn't know; but we tried to imagine how it must have looked to him in the dark, the gleaming phosphorus curling so high above him and then boiling so close to his paws. What was he *thinking?* For surely there is thought behind those eyes that look at me each day with a variety of expressions, complimen-tary and otherwise. Did it look and sound to him as it did to us?

There are some exhibits in the Gallery that can't be seen— not with the physical eye—but they can be heard, and in some mystic way they can thus be seen more poignantly, with the receptive eye of the mind. Like the wild geese flying so low over the house that they wake you from sleep and you lie there listening, imagining the long V-shaped flight, with your heart pounding in a strange excitement as if you are straining against invisible bands.

There is the music of the peepers; later on there will be the chiming of the maddeningly invisible wood thrush.

Today the Gallery presents a panoramic scene which takes in everything; across the water and fields to Friendship, down the Gut toward Flea Island, out over the islands to Monhegan. This scene must include the kitchen at Tide's Way. Through the windows we see the spring rain come down like a diaphanous curtain over the woods and houses of the mainland, and slant across the cove toward the face of Tide's Way. It splashes on the windows and fills the rain barrels with good soft wash water.

The Lazaret has plenty of supplies; the mailbox has recently yielded an armful of magazines, a book to review, some welcome letters. (There has even been a check, which adds considerably to the general harmony of the view.) The teakettle is pushed over to the front of the stove to heat for cocoa or tea. Smokey and Tristan dream peacefully, back to back on the couch. Blackie stands inside the doorway of his house and keeps an eye on the doorway of our house, to see if we venture out for a pail of water before dark.

The early and intrepid swallows have retired to a sheltered place out of the rain; the gulls and shags keep moving, and the loon is unabashed by the downpour. The sky and sea are the same shade of gray, but it is a soft warm gray, the shade of gray that is on pussy willows, or in wood smoke, or in the bark of an old apple tree, or on a mossy ledge in an open field.

The island is quiescent and totally at peace. And for the moment, so are we.

EPILOGUE

1950–1989. I won't name all the persons who helped to make this book and are now gone— some with long lives behind them, others much too soon. I won't list the four-footers who followed the tracks of Tris, Alec, Smokey, Susan, Mandy, Blackie, and Hezzie. But all these presences, great and small, are still there. Each contributed something to our particular history of the island.

And then there were the older people of Pleasant Point, who made us welcome. When we were able to buy a house over there for winter quarters (we can look across at the island all winter and visit it if we want to), we became people of the Point as well as islanders, and have tried to behave toward the newcomers as the Pointers have behaved toward us.

The Andrews and Robinson families are still our island neighbors, several generations of them. Charlotte Gray's grandchildren come to the Barnacle. Vic Whittier's point has changed hands very few times; the present owners, the Davidsons, have been coming here long enough for their children to grow up and make them grandparents. Dick and Barbara Lucas have connections from way back. The Saastamoinens' foothold dates from the time David and Donald were small. Barbara Ogilvie Mosher and her now-adult children live in the

Fish House whenever they can make it. Cheryl Bauguss Norton, whose father owned "the big end" of the island, is raising some young islanders. This year we have some new islanders, the Jamesons; they knew neighboring Morse Island well long before they built a post-and-beam house on the southern point of Gay Cove.

We're spread out over some three hundred acres, and it's a good walk from one place to another, but we are all bound by a common love of the island; the privilege of living on it is one of our dearest possessions, and it becomes more precious every year.

Life on the island is one long physical-fitness program. You may not jump up and down to music while wearing a fetching leotard, but you work out just the same—all the time. You go everywhere on foot, taking the rocky route around the shores for a change. Everything empty, such as water pails and wheelbarrows, goes down light and comes up heavy: lugged up the hill, pushed up the hill. The week's order of groceries is divided into manageable sections when we take it from the car over in the mainland driveway. This is the one time when a loaded wheelbarrow and tote bags go downhill, but once the stuff is into the skiff and taken across the moat, it is carried up over the rocks at the landing, and wheeled up the hill to the house. One reward for the work of bringing the food home: you burn up most of the calories from last week's order.

But when the last load is up and everything put away, and you sit down with a mug-up on the porch overlooking the water and the the other islands to sort the week's mail, you know that all the climbing up and down, lugging, bailing boats, painting boats, mowing, brushing out, is worth it. (And we do get help with the really heavy stuff from my grand-nephew Douglas, Dot's brother Oscar, and Paul Andrews.)

As for this house in which I write and have all those mug-ups, a great many people have slept under Oliver Chadwick's roof since he first shingled it sometime in the mid 1800s. Quite a few of them have slept under it in our time. The children of *Waters on a Starry Night* went to bed under the slanting ceilings for several months.

Returning now with their children, they say, "Thank God, nothing's changed!" The kitchen table is still covered with the largest assortment of odds and ends ever to fascinate the eyes of a child just tall enough to look over the edge. However, all these articles, useful and kept handily within reach, are not necessarily the same ones that were there twenty years ago —it just looks that way. We hardly ever eat at that table, but rather out on the porch. I also write at the porch table most of the time, and whenever anyone drops in and stays for a cup of tea, I stack my work precariously on a chair in the corner.

Dot knits trapheads from a hook in the sitting room wainscoting. She has her typewriter in there for her own work, and she also copies for me. In the years when there was always somebody else in the house in summertime, often quite a few somebodies, we wrote all over the place. I had a couple of favorite sites in the woods to which I'd lug my typewriter and paper, escorted by a cat or two who kept all the birds and squirrels in an uproar. We built a twelve-by-fifteen-foot office on the shores of the Gut for an indoor workplace where everything could be left spread out. Now it's a favored spot for certain guests to sleep.

My life as a writer is also my life as an islander. Criehaven, my first island, is responsible for the Bennetts. Gay's Island and this house are responsible for *The Witch Door*, *There May Be Heaven*, and *Waters on a Starry Night*. With some changes of terrain the island became the setting of *Weep and Know Why* and *The Dreaming Swimmer*. My nature descriptions, my acquaintance with four-footed wildlife from moose to mole, with birds, with Indian artefacts, and my knowledge of "messing about in boats," all spring from my existence here.

As a writer I've never done the variety of adventurous things that most others seem to have accomplished. I have simply written, during and since high school. Graduating in the Depression meant there wasn't much choice of jobs, but there were a few people who could afford child-sitters for overnight and weekends, and that's how I earned my pocket money. With the assistance of the public library (the whole family stocked up for the weekends) and the family typewriter, and with a thorough grounding in English behind me, I wrote and wrote. Finding authors I liked, I read everything the library had of theirs and tried to write like them, all the way from whimsy to romantic adventure to sentimental tragedy. Some of the results were awful—even I knew that—but some stuff was pretty good, and the whole experience was a great education.

I thought one had to arrive as a writer by doing short stories for magazines, and at that time there was plenty of magazine fiction published. So I wrote dozens of stories, aimed at *Good Housekeeping* and *The Ladies Home Journal*. Those early ones never made it. But the Bennetts were already in my mind, because Criehaven was such a huge part of my life, and my first short story, sold when I was nineteen to a small magazine that didn't live for long, was about a girl married to a Bennett.

High Tide at Noon was begun almost by accident. I was visiting Dot and Guy one early spring at Criehaven, and kept maundering on about the novel I'd write some time. Finally Dot said in self-defense, "Why don't you stop talking about it and just begin?"

Well, I did. By this time I had an agent who'd spent a lot of time reading my work, believing I'd "get there" some day, and he was enthusiastic about my first chapter but insisted that I plan out the book from there so I'd know where I was going. He and I parted long ago, but it's like remembering my driving instructor whenever I start the car; I never begin a book without remembering, "At least a dozen big scenes, and know where you are going." This rule is flexible, so I can do all kinds of things with the basic blueprint.

Besides islands, another grand obsession in my life as a writer has been Scotland. This was my mother's fault, or else it is in our genes, because my brothers were all the same. Our mother was in love with Scotland before she ever knew she had a Gaelic-speaking Highland grandmother. Then she married a man who was directly descended from an Ogilvie who fought at Culloden for Bonnie Prince Charlie. Father had grown up on that soldier's son's grant from the Crown. Father never seemed much impressed, but his father told my mother many things.

She never got to Scotland but she read a good deal about it all her life, and we also grew up knowing enough Scottish newcomers so that the accent was music to us. With family responsibilities and one thing and another, I didn't get there until 1979, for five months. I discovered the home of my great-grandmother Peigi Macleod on the Isle of Lewis, and from that six weeks in the outer Hebrides The Silent Ones emerged. We crossed Scotland to visit Ogilvie country in Angus and found it was also Simpson country, judging by the number of Simpsons in the Kirriemuir telephone books. During a month in Oban we did all the exploring possible by ferry, train, and car. *Jennie About to Be* was another flower of that spring and summer in Scotland.

I have notebooks of material for a book from our 1986 visit. This was when we visited Culloden for the first time. And while Dot stayed in the car up on the road, talking with the driver, I went down to Castle Urquhart, the only person in the ruins, and stared at Loch Ness, hoping passionately that I'd see IT. I believe Nessie is there, though she'd have to be a descendant of the one the early Christian monks saw, and that argues for more than one creature. Perhaps my next heroine will get a good look and a better picture, so she can prove she was neither drunk nor hallucinating at the time.

I was always grateful that I had such a beautiful place waiting for me at home whenever I left that other most beautiful country I love next after Maine.

Rowing across the harbor this September morning at low tide, in thick fog, with only bird voices to break the stillness, we were hailed by the harbormaster, who asked if that was us —*that* being the sudden boom of a foghorn on a vessel between Gay's Island and Caldwell. The harbormaster is Roland Stimpson, the skinny kid with the beanie who rowed us over to the island the first time. He and Barbara live almost across from our wharf, which makes for some companionable hollering when the wind is right. Barbara has traps out, and fishes a few off our wharf. Roland is just as quick and willing to help out now as when he was fifteen, and we have had to call upon him in some pretty drastic circumstances. Barbara is always ready to put the teakettle on to boil.

Among the Cushing grandchildren of the Pleasant Pointers who were here in 1944, only Roland and his cousin Dennis Young actually live at the harbor. Another cousin, Dennis Ames, runs the lobster business. But some things never change, and one of them is the ambience of this place, personified by these three men. When we moved in from Criehaven on that hot summer day in 1944, we felt like aliens as we entered the harbor between the unknown island and the foreign mainland. But only that once.

Never again.

ABOUT THE AUTHOR

Elisabeth Ogilvie grew up in Boston and Quincy but has lived in Maine since 1944. Thanks to her successful writing career, she has been able to live and work on Gay's Island for much of that time. After forty-four books, she says, she can still do some writing "for fun." In 1947 she won the New England Women's Press Association award for *Storm Tide. Woman's Day, Redbook,* and *Good Housekeeping* have all published Miss Ogilvie's work, and Readers Digest has produced a condensed version of *Jennie About to Be.*

Asked about hobbies, she replies, "I think my island home is my chief hobby—its shores and woods, its fields (which need constant attention to *keep* them fields), its wildlife, its complete ambience." Miss Ogilvie supports a number of humanitarian, environmental, and professional organizations and has been a member of Foster Parents Plan for forty years, sponsoring nine foster children. She still corresponds with her first, an Italian schoolteacher now close to fifty years old.

Travel takes her to Scotland ("the place I love best next to Maine"), and her favorite method of travel is via the *QEII,* "which means a lot of saving between trips." But the short trip across Pleasant Point Harbor, in a little outboard-powered boat, is the crossing that brings Elisabeth Ogilvie *home*—to Gay's Island, Muscongus Bay, Maine.